Advance Praise for

A Time for Choices

Michael Toms is one of the cutting edge thinkers and
media gurus for our generation. Anything he writes or
speaks is worth ingesting, including this book.
— Harvey Wasserman, author, *The Last Energy War:
The Battle over Utility Deregulation*

Restores my faith in the possibilities for reforming US politics
and democracy. These creative, wise commentaries on Bush's
global "War" on terrorism and evil can re-ignite public debate
suppressed since 9/11. New Dimension's diverse voices
challenge mainstream media to cover a broader range
of US views — our best path to shaping a better future
for all the human family on our small planet.
— Hazel Henderson, author, *Beyond Globalization*
and *Building a Win-Win World*

This is the damndest collection of American voices —
gentle-spoken and radical, humanist and spiritual, smart
about the facts and yet hopeful, wise about the future.
Not what you get on the evening news,
but a prophetic tonic for these troubled times.
— William Greider, *The Nation magazine,* author, *One World,
Ready or Not: The Manic Logic of Global Capitalism*

A
Time ★
for
Choices

For Nancy + Phil ~
Life, Liberty and
Justice for everyone,

Peace is a process)

3/17/03

A Time for Choices

DEEP DIALOGUES FOR DEEP DEMOCRACY

Michael Toms

Foreword by Kevin Danaher

NEW SOCIETY PUBLISHERS

Cataloguing in Publication Data:
A catalog record for this publication is available from the National Library of Canada.

Cover design by Diane McIntosh. Cover Image www.corbis.com

Printed in Canada by Transcontinental Printing.

Paperback ISBN: 0-86571-474-6

Inquiries regarding requests to reprint all or part of *A Time for Choices* should be addressed to New Society Publishers at the address below.

A Time for Choices is copublished with the New Dimensions Foundation, PO Box 569, Ukiah, CA 95482.

To order directly from the publishers, please add $4.50 shipping to the price of the first copy, and $1.00 for each additional copy (plus GST in Canada). Send check or money order to:

New Society Publishers
P.O. Box 189, Gabriola Island, BC V0R 1X0, Canada
1-800-567-6772

New Society Publishers' mission is to publish books that contribute in fundamental ways to building an ecologically sustainable and just society, and to do so with the least possible impact on the environment, in a manner that models this vision. We are committed to doing this not just through education, but through action. We are acting on our commitment to the world's remaining ancient forests by phasing out our paper supply from ancient forests worldwide. This book is one step towards ending global deforestation and climate change. It is printed on acid-free paper that is **100% old growth forest-free (100% post-consumer recycled)**, processed chlorine free, and printed with vegetable based, low VOC inks. For further information, or to browse our full list of books and purchase securely, visit our website at: www.newsociety.com

NEW SOCIETY PUBLISHERS   www.newsociety.com

Dedication

To all those innocent civilians who lost their lives in the
events of September 11, 2001, and to those who have lost
their lives since then, as a direct result of those events

Sail, sail thy best, ship of Democracy,
Of value is thy freight, 'tis not the Present only,
The Past is also stored in thee,
Thou holdest not the venture of thyself alone,
not of the Western continent alone,
Earth's resume entire floats on thy keel O ship,
is steadied by thy spars,
With thee Time voyages in trust,
the antecedent nations sink or swim with thee.

— Walt Whitman,
"Thou Mother with Thy Equal Brood," 1872

Table of Contents

Preface x

Acknowledgments xi

Foreword by Kevin Danaher, *The Global Paradigm Shift* xii

Introduction 1

CHAPTER 1 — REFLECTIONS ON 9-11 5

    Terry Tempest Williams, *Wild Mercy* 6

    Harlan Cleveland, *The American Spirit* 10

    Marianne Williamson, *Holistic Politics* 12

    Sharif Abdullah, *Touching the Spirit* 14

    Robert Fuller, *The Roots of the Problem Hold the Solution* 16

    Bishop Thomas Gumbleton, *Values, Ethics, and Morals* 20

CHAPTER 2 — WHAT IS DEMOCRACY? 27

    Kevin Danaher, *Breaking the Paradigm* 28

    Lynn Twist, *Living in the Conversation* 34

    Francis Boyle, *Civil Liberties at Risk* 39

    Michael Toms, *What Democracy Is Not* 44

CHAPTER 3 — THE MEDIA IS THE MESSAGE 47

    Paul Hawken, *Saving the World* 48

    Norman Solomon, *The Orwellian Zone* 52

    Robert Jensen, *Hope Goes a Long Way* 56

    Beau Grosscup, *Probing the Paradoxes* 60

    Anita Roddick, *Outrage as Energizer* 64

    Anna Cody, *How We See and Are Seen* 66

CHAPTER 4 — GIVING PEACE A VOICE 69

    Howard Zinn, *Through the Lens of History* 70

    Mark Hertsgaard, *Seeing America Clearly* 74

    Father G. Simon Harak, S.J., *Grief, Prayer, and Peace* 80

    Susan Griffin, *Thinking with Different Eyes* 86

CHAPTER 5 — THE SEARCH FOR SECURITY 93

   Terry Tempest Williams, *Restoring the Dialogue* 94

   Jane Hirshfield, *Holding the Heart Space* 98

   William McDonough, *On the Edge* 103

   Oriah Mountain Dreamer, *Hope in the Ordinary* 108

CHAPTER 6 — THE PEOPLE: THE 4TH BRANCH OF GOVERNMENT 111

   Matt Rothschild, *Beyond Patriotism* 112

   Noam Chomsky, *Challenging the System* 119

   Jeff Gates, *From Corporate Capitalism to Populist Capitalism* 122

   Amy Goodman, *Manufacturing Consent for Peace* 131

   Jacob Needleman, *The Inner Meaning of America* 136

CHAPTER 7 — GOING DEEPER: THE SPIRITUAL DIMENSION 139

   Joanna Macy, *The Great Turning* 140

   David La Chapelle, *Listening and Belonging* 144

   Rabbi Michael Lerner, *Looking Evil in the Eye* 148

   Dawna Markova, *Soul Rising* 154

   Thomas Moore, *New Ways of Being* 156

   Sogyal Rinpoche, *Prayer and Practice* 159

   Andrew Harvey, *The Power of Spirit* 162

CHAPTER 8 — MANY VOICES / MANY VIEWS 171

   John Mohawk, *The Lessons of History* 172

   As'ad AbuKhalil, *Taking Responsibility* 178

   Tahmeena Faryal, *Women and Afghanistan* 182

   Carlos Mota, *The North American Way* 187

   Ronald Takaki, *Multicultural America* 191

CHAPTER 9 — VISIONS OF THE FUTURE 193

   Vicki Robin, *The Power of Circle Technology* 194

   Jean Houston, *A Passion for Peace* 196

   David Whyte, *The Dangerous Truth* 199

   Clayborne Carson, *Martin Luther King Jr. Speaks* 205

   Epilogue 210

   About the Contributors 213

Preface

MICHAEL TOMS COMPILED these materials in his capacity as executive producer and host of the award-winning and widely acclaimed internationally syndicated public radio series, "New Dimensions." Between September 15, 2001, and March 17, 2002, he selected and interviewed more than one hundred individuals from a wide diversity of professions and perspectives. The book represents the essence of what he gathered in a quest to uncover responses to the events of September 11, 2001, to encourage dialogue and to present voices and views not being heard in the American mass media — the essential purpose of the New Dimensions World Broadcasting Network.

The original interviews in this book as well as others were produced for the radio series, "A Time for Choices" and are available via streaming audio at www.newdimensions.org.

Acknowledgments

EACH DAY OF MY LIFE I give thanks for the work I am able to do. It is such a grace and gift to dialogue with individuals who are actively contributing towards changing the world for the better. I am continually inspired by their stories and, through the media of radio, the Internet, and print, I am able to share them with listeners and readers.

I want to acknowledge with gratitude the people you'll meet in the following pages: ordinary individuals doing extraordinary things. They are included in this collection because of their outward expression in the world, which reflects their inner commitment to creating a better world, one that works for everyone.

Especially I want to thank Bec Kageyama, my executive assistant, for all of her unflagging support; Christina Fleming, assistant producer, who arranged most of these dialogues and was present for nearly all of them as well, listening on her headphones; and transcriber Jan Allegretti who gracefully met every deadline. I reserve special thanks for my life partner, Justine, who has always been there for me and is my best critic and editor.

I particularly want to express my appreciation to Chris and Judith Plant of New Society Publishers, both of whom have been wonderful to work with and have supported the concept of this book from the beginning.

Michael Toms
Ukiah, California
June 2002

Foreword
The Global Paradigm Shift

Kevin Danaher

OUR HISTORICAL EPOCH is being buffeted by three major crises. The first is a social crisis of growing inequality that is subjecting hundreds of millions of people to suffering that is both horrendous and unnecessary. The richest 20 percent of the world's population account for 86 percent of global resource consumption. The poorest 80 percent of the world's people, on the other hand, account for only 14 percent of global resource consumption.

This extreme and growing inequality results in poor children dying from preventable causes at a rate of one every few seconds. The amount of money it would take to eliminate this suffering is a mere fraction of what the world's political leaders spend each year on military hardware ($800 billion). Future generations will wonder how we could have wasted so much wealth on the mechanization of violence while so many went hungry.

The second crisis is the breakdown of natural systems. Just about every major biological system is in rapid decline or outright collapse. Topsoil is being destroyed by chemical-intensive and machine-intensive agriculture. Forests are being clear-cut by companies that view a 1,000-year-old redwood tree not as a gift of the creator but as $300,000 worth of lumber. Thousands of plant and animal species are being exterminated through habitat destruction and the introduction of invasive species via increasingly deregulated world trade. The ozone layer that shields us and our crops from harmful levels of ultraviolet light is being eroded. Groundwater is being polluted and wasted at rates greater than nature can replace. Glaciers are melting much faster than the historical average. The polar icecaps are melting. Sea levels are rising due to global warming, expanding the volume of the oceans. Some twenty-five million people (more than the world's refugee population) have been driven from their home communities by the spread of environmental destruction. Extreme weather is causing huge losses to people and property. And scientists are raising the possibility that these various trends could start influencing each other in a negative synergy that could speed up environmental damage much more quickly than originally thought possible.

These two crises are, in turn, producing a third crisis: the spiritual/moral crisis of so many of us knowing that the global dominance of money values is crushing the environment and human rights, yet lacking the courage to take action to change it. We often hear people express this cult of powerlessness with phrases such as "You can't fight city hall" or "I'm only one person, what can I do?" — as if anyone is more than one person. These are expressions of people who want to do the right thing but have been taught to feel powerless. This cult of powerlessness is especially rampant in the more affluent parts of the world such as the United States. Lamenting global poverty and environmental destruction yet taking no action to address these issues is very similar to the hypocritical minister who serves on the anti-pornography commission: he gets to look at it all and enjoy it, yet he can also appear moral by denouncing it.

The thinkers presented in this book point a way out of this dilemma. They are pioneers in a global values revolution: a paradigm shift of historic proportions. For the past 500 years our world has been increasingly dominated by a paradigm of money values/violence/God-is-on-my-side. The new paradigm springing up from the grass roots around the world — and articulated in these pages — can be characterized as life values/nonviolence/God-does-not-take-sides-in-intra-species-conflicts.

Under money values — enforced by large corporations and governmental institutions such as the World Bank and the World Trade Organization — a fish swimming has no value until you kill it and sell it in a market. All of nature and human creativity is measured in terms of what it will sell for as a commodity in the marketplace.

The profit-driven global institutions are creating a web of international law (the first global constitution) that subordinates life to commerce instead of subordinating commerce to life. But ask anyone the question "Which is sacred, life or commerce?" and you will see that most people understand that we should subordinate the money cycle to the life cycle, not the other way around.

It is now clear to a growing number of people that money values will be replaced by life values. This is inevitable, not just because nature always bats last, but because the collapsing environment will become harder to ignore and growing popular protest will force political leaders to move away from the destructive dominance of money values. We will firmly decide which version of the Golden Rule we will follow as a species: "Treat others as you would have them treat you" or "He who has the gold makes the rules."

Humanity is leaving its adolescence and entering adulthood. We are beginning to realize that we cannot treat people and nature as commodities. We are waking up to the fact that we are capable of conscious evolution. The contrast between the world-that-is and the world-that-could-be gets starker every day.

The old regime of money values grows more violent and illegitimate, while the global justice movement grows stronger and more firmly committed to non-violence.

This is the first stage of the first truly global revolution. Previous revolutions have been national revolutions aimed at seizing state power in the capital city. This revolution is transnational and it is a values revolution, focused on shifting from money values to life values.

The ideas you are about to read provide a reliable map of the global values revolution pointed to by Dr. Martin Luther King Jr. when he said: "A true revolution of values will soon cause us to question the fairness and justice of many of our past and present policies ... True compassion is more than flinging a coin to a beggar; it understands that an edifice which produces beggars needs restructuring."

Introduction

YOUR LIFE HAS CHANGED FOREVER. My life has changed forever. The world is different now, just as we are different. September 11, 2001, affected everyone, everywhere. More than three thousand innocent human beings died on that tragic day, thousands at the World Trade Center, nearly two hundred at the Pentagon, and still others in a farm field in Pennsylvania. People from eighty nations died in New York City. Clearly, this attack was not only an American event, but also a world event. And the whole world has experienced the aftermath of what happened on that grievous day.

On the night of September 12, 2001, I was watching ABC television as Peter Jennings handed off to Ted Koppel. There was a moment of reflection that provided a glimmer of light through the mass of darkness being presented by the major media. Jennings spoke of his own service in the Middle East and reminded Koppel of his service in Vietnam and Africa. Jennings mentioned how they both had been exposed to the depth of hatred and anger that some peoples and societies hold towards America and Americans because of the United States Government's foreign policy. As he was talking, I remembered the CIA's role in the death of Patrice Lamumba in the Congo, its role in the assassination of Chile's Salvador Allende, the Iran-Contra arms-for-money deal, our support of dictators like Trujillo, the Shah of Iran, Pinochet, and Batista. Our hands are bloody. My hands are bloody because I am an American.

I was born in Washington, DC, and raised in northern Virginia, the country of Thomas Jefferson, George Washington, Patrick Henry, James Madison, James Monroe, and others who helped to ground me in the original vision of this nation. It is this original vision of "life, liberty, and the pursuit of happiness," the Bill of Rights, freedom and justice for all, education for every citizen and so much more that is our salvation. It was a dream in 1776 — a vision of a government that had never been attempted previously, not even in Greece, the "cradle of democracy." At this unique time, however, the colonists, including such figures as Benjamin Franklin, John Adams, and Thomas Jefferson, had come in contact with the Iroquois Confederacy and borrowed much from this Native American government.

Although imperfect in its various manifestations at the time and since, the United States of America is based upon a spiritual vision of the highest order.

Through some mysterious grace there was assembled a community of men and women who came together and were able to envision the future in a way that had never been seen before. They were human just like us, with frailties, with hopes and fears just like us. And yet, they were able to accomplish something never done before, in the midst of enormous challenges, in a crisis situation, through holding to a vision from the deepest levels of their souls. They were willing to face death for their beliefs.

I believe that we can take sustenance from the Declaration of Independence, a spiritual document, and the Bill of Rights, as they were originally drafted and approved after intense deliberations. It is also my belief that we, as a nation, have strayed far from our original founding vision, both in spirit and action. It is true, as President George W. Bush has stated, that "freedom and democracy are under attack," but not just by external forces. Freedom and democracy are also under attack from within. We must search our own hearts and minds because the common ground we all share is that at the deepest level we want spiritual freedom and liberation. Thomas Jefferson wrote of this freedom in the Declaration of Independence.

This is a time for deep reflection, a time for me to look in the mirror and see how I may be contributing to what is unfolding around us. It is a time for humanity, compassion, forgiveness, and love. We have suffered a horrendous tragedy with an enormous loss of life. The waves of this disaster will continue into the future, and their effects are unimaginable. I struggle to get my mind around it, but I can't do it. All I can do is go deep within myself and seek the sustenance of my spiritual depths. We are at a crossroads; I am at a crossroads; you are at a crossroads. We are in the midst of an age-old story, that of the forces of light versus the forces of darkness. Will we choose the path of fear, anger, and revenge, or will we choose the path of nonviolence and love?

It is amazing to me that the U.S. Congress appropriated $40 billion less than 72 hours after the tragedy occurred, without much reflection or measured deliberations about an appropriate response. This from a group not known for fast action. It is stunning to me that this decision was taken with only one dissenting vote. A lone voice, that of Congresswoman Barbara Lee from Oakland, a California Democrat who voted against the War Powers Act, said, "I don't think we should take any action that should cause any more loss of life …Violence begets violence, and we don't want that to happen. That kills people." Congress, again, virtually without dissent or dialogue, also passed the so-called Patriot Act, which seriously infringes on civil liberties and, among other things, allows U.S. state-sponsored assassinations.

I see the innocent civilians who lost their lives on September 11 as a sacrifice. *Sacrifice* is a noble word. It means to "make sacred." The deaths of more innocent civilians do not honor the sacrifice that these people have made. Do not misunderstand me: I support justice being meted out to the criminals who perpetrated this horrific event. The bombing of Afghanistan, however, was not justice. It was vengeance rooted in anger. We now know that more innocent civilians have died in Afghanistan during the bombing than perished on September 11. The "war on terrorism" against an unseen and unidentified enemy will simply provoke retaliation. If violence really brought peace and security, we would have peace in the Middle East — but we have all witnessed the violence there for the past fifty years, and it keeps continuing.

The bombing of Afghanistan began with the goal of getting Osama bin Laden (whose whereabouts remains unknown at this writing), then quietly segued into getting the Taliban, then Al Qaeda, and now our government has carried its goals to the "axis of evil": Iran, Iraq, and North Korea as well as other nations.

As Gandhi and Dr. Martin Luther King Jr. reminded us before, violence begets violence; it is never the answer. When Timothy McVeigh was found guilty in an American court of law of blowing up the Oklahoma City Federal Office Building, he was eventually executed for his crime. We didn't execute his family, or his friends, or his community. That was justice within the American system. The "war on terrorism" is *not* justice. Despite our government's attempts to propagandize this war with the assistance of the major mass media, we are killing innocent civilians. How are they different from the innocents killed in the World Trade Center and the Pentagon?

I am an American patriot. I love this country. I love this planet. As such, I have a responsibility as a citizen living in a democracy to speak out and question the decisions that are being made on my behalf by this government using my tax dollars. The American Revolution arose from dissent and the desire to escape the tyranny of King George and the British Empire at that time. The Declaration of Independence, the Constitution, and the Bill of Rights are all about the sovereign voice of the people in a democracy. The Constitution begins with the words, "We the People of the United States ..." The people are the sovereign voice in America. The government works for us, not the other way around. We have a right to question and challenge the decisions of our government leaders. Indeed, it is our responsibility to do so.

The heart and soul of democracy are dialogue and dissent. The latter emerges from the former. My work and the work of the New Dimensions Broadcasting Network is about expanding the field of possibilities, realizing that as the horizon expands, the opportunities grow. *A Time for Choices* is about this field of possibilities and has emerged through dialogue. It may raise more questions than it provides answers, but that's okay. Indeed, that's the whole point.

As President Jimmy Carter recently wrote, "The problems may seem insurmountable, but they are not. We have the tools; we have brilliant dedicated people to find answers. All we need is a sense of sharing and the will to change. The will can grow from understanding. Once we understand, we can care, and once we care, we can change."

REFLECTIONS ON 9-11

THESE DIALOGUES WERE recorded within days of the events of September 11 and speak to the initial response of deep grief and surprise while containing eminently credible insights — prior to the bombing of Afghanistan on October 7, 2001. The only exception to this timing is the conversation with Bishop Thomas Gumbleton, which was recorded on October 9, two days after the bombing began. At the beginning, I had no idea that what I was doing would continue beyond the few interviews I had initially planned. I was simply following my heart's pull to speak with others about what was unfolding. As it has transpired, I have continued for six months and am still, at this writing, conducting interviews about this new era. At the outset, I had no notion of putting together a book. It simply became the obvious thing to do as the process continued.

What's important to know is that the grieving process has not ended. It continues for all of us, whether we know it consciously or not. When we observed the six-month anniversary of 9-11, it was clear, despite media voices to the contrary, that millions were still mourning what happened on that fateful day. Ground Zero is hallowed ground. History will remember this time as a great turning for America and the world. The 21st century has now begun in earnest.

Wild Mercy

Photo by Artuto Patten

Terry Tempest Williams has been a friend for more than ten years. She is one of the most lucid and heartful voices on the planet at this time, speaking and writing about how we can preserve the ecology of the Earth and save ourselves and future generations in the bargain. A naturalist, poet, and writer, she lives in the Red Rock country of southern Utah. I spoke with her just after she had spent a week marooned in Washington, D.C., as a result of 9-11.

TERRY: There was a group of photographers and writers celebrating this new exhibit at the Corcoran Gallery of Art, ironically called "In Response to Place" and sponsored by the Nature Conservancy. At that time there must have been six or seven photographers and myself sitting around a table signing books and getting ready for a press conference that was to begin at 10:00 a.m. These are photographers — powerful visionaries through their cameras — who normally don't cast their gaze toward wild and raw places. We were talking about the enduring grace of landscape when we heard, like the rest of America and the world, that the Twin Towers had been struck. We stopped. We couldn't believe it. We were paralyzed by the thought. We didn't have the particular images before us, only in our minds.

Moments later a security guard came in and said, "You need to evacuate. The Pentagon's been struck and we have reason to believe the White House is next. Run!"

Again, we were paralyzed. We finally stood up. I remember holding on to Richard Misrach's hand as we moved through the museum and ran out onto the street. You could see people running across the lawn of the White House, people exiting the Executive Office Building. I remember looking up to the sky thinking, "What's happening?" And you could see this dark plume rising from the direction of the Pentagon.

The next thing I remember is being crammed into this cab with six or seven of us and the cab driver turning around very calmly, saying, "And just where would you like to go?"

In that moment I think we all realized that there was no place to go. We're here — now. And the American landscape has changed — forever.

MICHAEL: *As you've reflected on those events since September 11, what do you see now? What reflections do you have? What wisdom have you gleaned for yourself?*

I think we're still in the process of sorting this through. I think it's going to take a long, long time for us to realize how this has entered our bloodstream. The most helpful thing for me was reading this small fascinating piece called "Seismic Shift," in *The New York Times,* the Friday following the attacks. To me, it was both a metaphor and the reality of what we've experienced since September 11, what we'll continue to experience in the uncertainty of the days to come as we stand in the center of change.

Basically, what the piece said is that this event registered in the earth, as seen through the lens of the Columbia University Lamont-Doherty Earth Observatory, in the Palisades in New York. They were saying that seismic activity on September 11 was registered. And they went on to say that at 8:46 a.m. there was the first seismic register, eighteen minutes later another, followed by a third, this one a bit stronger, more sustained. At 9:59, another. And twenty-nine minutes after that, the final pulse registered in the earth.

One of the scientists at the observatory said, "An earthquake is something that emerges from the earth and into a building. But this event, unprecedented by my eyes, began with a building and the subsequent effect upon the earth."

"Seismic Shift." Even a shift in consciousness — that's the image I keep holding onto. There was no place, not even in the earth, where this didn't register. And I guess the question I keep wrapping myself around is, "Who has the strength to see this wave of destruction as a wave of renewal?"

We hear certain voices, select voices, rise up out of the din from the mass media — which basically appear to be oriented towards some kind of military response, whatever that turns out to be — but yet, rising through the din, I think of Barbara Lee, the Oakland Democrat who was the single "No" vote on the War Powers Act. And then there are the cries coming out against those lone voices like hers — accusing, calling them unpatriotic, saying, "You're not with the program here. What's the matter with you?"

Terry, you're someone who, over many years, has been one of those lone voices around the ecology challenge, and you have suffered these kinds of arrows. What do you have to say about this at this time?

I was so grateful for Representative Barbara Lee. I felt that in the midst of this "manic patriotism" we did have one voice that registered dissent, that urged us to slow down until we had time to reflect, that urged us not to sign over all of our powers to one human being, primarily George W. Bush.

It was interesting, when I was wandering the streets of Washington, D.C., there was a woman from Costa Rica who, almost as a mantra, just kept saying over and over and over again, "*La paz de la gente es la paz de la Madre Tierra.*" The peace of the people is the peace of Mother Earth. I think we have never needed that more.

I was also thinking about Neruda and his *Book of Questions* — again, it's the questions that give me comfort. When he says, "*Que es los nombres a los numeros a los innocentes innumerable?*" Who assigns names and numbers to the innumerable innocent? I just keep thinking that we have forgotten the option of restraint — that it's no longer the survival of the fittest, but the survival of compassion. And I do think it's going to require strength and courage and a gathering together of those of us who define patriotism in another way — not just simply as the waving of flags, but also as standing our ground in the places we love and as continuing to honor the earth and wild places. When I hear, for example, Senator Murkowski from Alaska saying, on the very day of the attacks, "It's no longer under discussion whether or not we will drill in the Arctic. We will drill in the name of national security," I want to say: "This is still a democracy. And we still are a people of conversation and dialogue. Nothing can take the place of this kind of bedrock democracy — bad policy is bad policy."

Mayor Giuliani has been pretty much acclaimed as a hero — and in many ways he is one — as a result of some of the actions he took as mayor of New York in the aftermath of September 11. At the same time, I heard him say, "The price of freedom is obedience and order." A remark like that is a little scary to me.

It was interesting. I was flying out to a gathering in Jackson Hole, Wyoming. When a cab came to pick me up at my hotel to take me to Dulles Airport, it was 4:00 in the morning, and Washington, D.C., was a total police state: F16's flying low, the swat team dressed in black on top of the White House, I.D. checks around every corner. It was really unnerving to one's soul, to say the least. We were all experiencing both terror and this terrible grief.

Anyway, finally this cab arrives. It was 4:00 in the morning, and I'm thinking, "I've got to get home to the West."

A gentleman opens the door of the cab; he walks around, his head bowed. It's dark. He looks up, and he says, "I am from Afghanistan. Perhaps you would feel safer in a different cab."

I just burst into tears. And he burst into tears. We just held each other. And, you know, in that forty-five-minute drive to Dulles his mother called twice, so fearful, begging him not to be in his cab. He said, "I have to feed my children." He had been in Afghanistan in 1979. They had left as political refugees. I mean, the stories — they're still floating through my bloodstream.

But, what you were saying about blind obedience … We had this gathering in Jackson Hole, Wyoming, and there was a Danish woman there named Inge Kurtz. She's an amazing woman. She harbored hundreds of Jews in her home because she felt it was the right thing to do. We asked her, as one of our elders, "Inge, what do you have to share with us? We've never been here before in this country?"

She said, "What I would say is this: Beware of mob mentality." You know, beware of this blind obedience in the name of patriotism that ultimately takes our lives. And she said, "That's what I fear most, and it can take over in seconds." Then she said, "Hold to your instincts, hold onto your liberty, and just continue to stay in that place of reflection and resolve."

I thought that was really interesting from someone in her eighties who has been in her own war and made courageous decisions.

I would like to close our conversation with one paragraph from my book *Red: Passion and Patience in the Desert* called "Wild Mercy":

"The eyes of the future are looking back at us, and they are praying for us to see beyond our own time. They are kneeling with hands clasped that we might act with restraint, that we might leave room for the life that is destined to come. To protect what is wild is to protect what is gentle. Perhaps the uncertainty we fear is the pause between our own heartbeats, the silent space that says, 'We live only by grace.' Wild mercy is in our hands."

HARLAN CLEVELAND

The American Spirit

Harlan Cleveland *is one of the wisdom elders on the planet with a lifetime of experience in government, publishing, education, and diplomacy: he is the recipient of the prestigious U.S. Medal of Freedom. I first met him at the Fetzer Institute in Kalamazoo, Michigan, where we were attending a gathering of social innovators. My initial impression of Harlan as I listened to him speak in the midst of the circle of participants was that everything he uttered was profound wisdom. This definitely got my attention. After spending more time with him over the ensuing years at similar gatherings, he agreed to make himself available for a number of tapings, which have been completed and are being edited into a public radio series. He was one of the first persons I thought of to speak with about 9-11. As a former U.S. Ambassador to NATO, former Assistant Secretary of State, the founding Dean of the University of Minnesota's Hubert H. Humphrey Institute of Public Affairs, and President Emeritus of the World Academy of Art and Science, he represents a remarkable breadth and depth of experience.*

HARLAN: The terrorist attacks in New York and Washington were obviously enormous as human tragedy, and historic as a turn of events. I've been struck by the fact that most of the journalists are focusing on what well-known leaders around the world, and especially in the U.S., are saying about what happens next. I think the main thing to watch is how the American people are likely to react and what they tell their leaders to do about it. As I tried to explain in an article I wrote for non-Americans shortly after the disaster, that really is how it works in the United States of America. That is, on important policy issues, the people seem to get there first, and their leaders sooner or later follow.

I think the attacks shocked us and changed us. Nothing like this had happened since the Japanese attack on Pearl Harbor in December 1941. That attack instantly unified the American people, but most Americans now living don't remember it except as something in a history book. But ever since then, ever since the end of the war at least, we felt that we had a firm grip on Franklin Roosevelt's first freedom: freedom from fear. I'm not sure that any American less than half a century old could have imagined such a puncture in that freedom as we saw on television and in living color last Tuesday. But now we are, once again, instantly unified — not about what to do, but in our reaction that something needs doing. That's fine … and that's to walk around frightened about our future.

But the question is, "What do we do, and who's the "we" that should be doing it?" The first instinct, at least of some leaders, seems to be to lash out at the most obvious symbols of terrorism — to do so in a hurry, at whatever expense to our own democracy, and on our own. It's what you might call a self-isolating action. My guess is that the instinctive wisdom of the people will prevail over this itch of the instant-response hotheads. I also expect that the case for acting internationally in an interdependent world will trump the urge to express our unilateral impatience. Already, the U.N. Security Council and the European Union are getting active, and NATO is activating Article V ("An attack on one is an attack on all.") for the first time since the NATO treaty was signed in 1949. And under the impressively calm and clearheaded leadership of our African-American Secretary of State, Collin Powell, the U.S. has started a worldwide effort to build a coalition against all forms of terrorism. I think this will be, at best, the beginning of a long-term "coalition of the willing," as I call it. It won't be satisfied to decapitate a few obvious villains.

That gets us to the job of writing and enforcing new rules for peaceful change and civilized behavior in the 21st century. Like most things worth doing, this isn't going to be done in a hurry. It won't be done without casualties. It won't be done at bargain prices. For a start, it will doubtless cost a lot more than we were planning to spend on what we used to call "defense," and what really now turns out to be defense. This may require changing some suddenly premature Republican ideas about cutting taxes, but it will also change some Democratic ambitions about social spending that can be postponed.

But I think we, the American people, are heir to one tradition that's a feature of our history that strangely isn't expressed in any of the lyrics of our patriotic songs: the proposition that ours is a nation that rises to the occasion. We've done it before, and we'll do it again.

Marianne Williamson

Holistic Politics

Photo by Albane Navizet

In 1997 Marianne Williamson authored The Healing of America, *a book in which she predicted that "within the next ten years, America will experience a renaissance or a catastrophe. Something is going to happen to take us back to who we are." Beyond any of our wildest imaginings, that catastrophe has occurred. It remains to be seen if the renaissance will occur— it's still possible. Having interviewed Marianne several times over the years, I recall her fervor about the renewal of America coming from within each of us. In her book, she wrote that "the era of passive citizenship is over" and called for a birth of "holistic politics." This birth takes place when a convergence occurs of traditional political activists who increasingly look to spiritual wisdom for inspiration while spiritual contemplatives are increasingly eager to extend their service to the world into political realms.*

MARIANNE: The modern Western mind always thinks first about what to do. But there are times when the issue of what to do is not nearly as important as who to become. It's kind of like when you're diagnosed with a life-challenging illness — let's say, you've been told you have cancer. Most of us want to say, "Okay, give me chemo, give me radiation, operate on me, just get it out!"

But, sometimes in medicine and in politics it's not that simple. If you have a tumor, maybe it's a spider tumor and it's wrapped around healthy organs. You'd be told, "If we chemo too much, if we radiate too much, if we zap you there, we will also destroy the healthy organs." And so, over the last few decades we came to understand that when it comes to medicine there's a holistic perspective that is a more powerful healing modality than the simply allopathic one. Yes, we use allopathic techniques, but there're dimensions of Mind and dimensions of Spirit that are important aspects of the most powerful healing modality.

The same is happening here. It's not as simple as just performing some military maneuver, and then it's all over. And it's not even as simple as, "We'll perform some military maneuver and do the traditional political things we do — and it's going to take a really long time." I think many of us recognize that there are dimensions of Mind and Spirit that have great, great powers for us to harness here. When we recognize that, we also realize that the greatest thing America can do right now is to use this as an opportunity for some deep soul-searching.

Going back to that image of the medical diagnosis, I always say that when someone's been diagnosed with a life-challenging illness, they drop a lot of their personal B.S. in the first five minutes. And I think that's happened to this country already. So much of the shallowness, the obsession with violence, the obsession with the meaningless that in so many ways characterizes contemporary American culture — it seems to have evaporated, and I hope not just temporarily. That's why when you hear on the news, "Well, let's everybody go back to normal now" — but we'll never go back to "normal." I hope we don't. Let's not!

Let's use this as an opportunity to admit that we've been changed and to allow that change to be a change that deepens us, that matures us. America will never be quite the brash, young, pugnacious teenager, the rebellious type that we were before. We've aged. We've matured. My girlfriend said to me last night, "We've got lines on our faces at last." I think that there is so much for us to think about. We're already hugging our kids a little tighter, we're treating our friends more tenderly, we're counting our blessings for real. And also, we're thinking about how much we really do love this country. It's not "unhip" this week to say that. Now we're thinking about what this country really means to us, this thing that was such a blessing on our ancestors. And it's increasing our absolute intention that we bequeath it as a blessing on our children.

I'm very involved with sacred circles, you know, and with the Global Renaissance Alliance and other organizations and people out there working on circles. Anyone can go to Marianne.com or RenaissanceAlliance.org or SpiritualActivism.org and find the template for sacred circles — for sitting in meditation and prayer and speaking from our deepest hearts. We have questions to ask. We have to ask ourselves why so many people hate us. We have to ask whether or not millions of people have some very valid resentments against us. And while there's nothing valid in what the terrorists are saying or doing, obviously I fear that some valid resentments and anger are directed toward us from certain places in the world and contribute to this energy and these attitudes of violence.

So I think it's time for us to be deeply sober, to really pray, and to really talk.

SHARIF ABDULLAH

Touching the Spirit

I have sat in circle with and interviewed Sharif Abdullah *a number of times. The most recent circle was on Armistice Day, in November 2001, to observe 9-11 along with thirty-five others from different parts of the world. We agreed to assemble for a day of contemplative dialogue at a monastic retreat center in the San Francisco Bay Area. Sharif had returned from six months in Sri Lanka working with Dr. A. T. Ariyariatne, founder of Sarvodaya, the world's largest nonviolent peace initiative. As I write this, he has returned to Sri Lanka from his home in Portland, Oregon. Sharif is a man with street smarts, having grown up in Camden, New Jersey, where he felt the despair of poverty and racism. He wanted to turn to violence to relieve the bleakness of his situation. Instead of waging urban war, this African-American actively worked to integrate his own inner violence with his spiritual path. Sharif, who practiced Islam for many years, now blends all spiritual traditions into what he calls "the common faith." In my view, Sharif walks his talk more than most.*

SHARIF: The first thing I want to say is that I think the attacks in New York City and the attack in Washington, D.C., were atrocities. And I think we need to see what happened as more than an attack on America. We need to start thinking about this as an attack against humanity, a crime against humanity. The targeting of innocent civilians in that way was terrible.

Having said that, I think we need to respond! I'm not one of the people who're just saying, "Oh, well, we must have done something wrong to them, so we shouldn't respond." I think that we should respond. But our response has to be in line with our deepest values — the deepest values of our spirit and the deepest values of our country, a country that was supposedly founded on the values of freedom, of liberty, of democracy, of due process of law, and so forth. In order for us to pursue whoever committed this atrocity, in order for us to pursue whoever that may be, we need to start thinking about our spiritual values. If this is supposed to be a Christian nation, we need to go to the words of Christ and see what he said in times of trouble.

The thing that disturbs me the most is that we see images of a very angry and a very vengeful President, we see images of a very angry and very vengeful Congress. We need our policies, our affairs, run by people who are not angry and vengeful. I believe those people are out there. I believe that all of us are those leaders. We need to make sure our actions diffuse potential bombers, potential suicide bombers. If we can help people to get in touch with their spirit, a crime against humanity is impossible. But if people are not in touch with their spirit, and if we do things that drive them further from their spirit, then another crime against humanity is inevitable. Our choice is this: do we want to pursue a path of vengeance or do we want to pursue a path that actually leads us into a twenty-first century that all of us can live in? I believe those are our choices. And I actually believe that we will make the right choice.

MICHAEL: *What is sustaining you personally in the midst of dealing with this trauma, this tragedy?*

That's a good question because, as you may know, as a consequence of an article I wrote, I've been getting a number of threats and a number of very negative e-mails coming in, primarily because of my name. People are reacting to surfaces. They're not reacting to depths.

The thing that keeps me going in the face of threat and in the face of this very trying situation is my spiritual reality, my spiritual belief, my faith — my faith that the world really can work for all, that if I can change who I was in my past, then anybody can change. We can take a person who is willing to make a bomb right now, and we can change what's in their heart, and we can do that so forcefully that they become an instrument of peace, not an instrument of death and destruction.

I'm recalling — since you've recently returned from Sri Lanka — I'm recalling people like Sri Aurobindo and Vivekananda, radical revolutionaries who somehow turned into radical revolutionaries rooted in deeply spiritual values. They didn't change being radical revolutionaries; they were still committed to that purpose. It sounds to me like that's what you are speaking to.

Exactly. In my past, we had a bomb factory in Camden, New Jersey, in one of the organizations I belonged to. We were learning all sorts of recipes, how to make homemade Molotov cocktails — I still remember the recipe — and things like that because we thought there was going to be an urban war, and we were going to be at war. My goal in doing that was to create a world that would work!

I see now that my means were wrong, although my goal remains the same. If I could change, if I could change the nature of the person that I was, then a person who we're now calling a suicide bomber or terrorist can change. But the thing that changed me was not somebody putting me in jail for the rest of my life or bombing my village or all the other things that we're talking about doing as a consequence of this New York City atrocity. If we're trading atrocity for atrocity, we never get anywhere, or we get to a place we really don't want to be.

President Bush has said that Americans are willing to pay the price. I don't think Americans know what the price tag is. And I think that if we understood the kind of world we'd be creating by pursuing a policy of militarism — as opposed to a policy of actually diffusing the suicide bombers, diffusing the terrorists —we would be pursuing a radically different course.

ROBERT FULLER

The Roots of the Problem Hold the Solution

When I first encountered Robert Fuller, *he was directing a foundation that gave New Dimensions its first major grant to produce radio programming. I came to learn that he was already a listener to our broadcasts, which he had discovered upon relocating to the San Francisco Bay Area after serving as President of Oberlin College in Ohio. Since that time long ago and as a result of conducting numerous interviews with him over the span of years, I consider Bob to be one of those far-seeing visionaries, who always brings a new perspective based on careful analysis. Trained as a physicist, he pioneered the citizen diplomacy movement back in the late 1970s. I recall a New Dimensions program when Bob urged listeners to spend their vacation in the Soviet Union. Literally tens of thousands of Americans made their way there before the fall of the "Iron Curtain." In my view, he's always ahead of the curve.*

MICHAEL: *We're all in the middle of the trauma of this tragedy. All of us are experiencing it, each in our own way, and I wanted to ask you what your words of wisdom are. What do you have to say about this world-changing event?*

ROBERT: I force myself to think about this act of terrorism in the context of the other ones that we're all familiar with: the schoolyard shootings at Columbine, the Federal Building in Oklahoma. And now this one at the World Trade Center and the Pentagon. I've been fascinated by the very different reactions people have. It seems to me we go through three stages: First, we want to stop the immediate perpetrators. This takes the form of grounding flights, having a police sniper shoot someone who's berserk if you can, etc. The first impulse is to stop the immediate perpetration.

Then we turn our thoughts to defensive measures against recurrences. We set up screenings at airports and schools, and we try to identify the like-minded and incapacitate them.

Finally, we begin to look for root causes so that we can respond more effectively, and even prevent more people from becoming like-minded. We look for ever deeper causes, especially if the first two things — stopping the perpetrators and defending ourselves against recurrences — don't work.

Where people differ, really, is in whether they put their emphasis on the first or the second or the third of these responses. Some people really just want to get to the status quo ante, and they're content to identify the perpetrators and defend against recurrences, but they're not very interested in root causes. Other people go straight to the root causes and look beyond the immediate acts of terrorism. Actually, we need all these things to make ourselves safer.

But I think it's the role of the people you speak to, Michael, to focus especially on root causes. And there, too, it divides up. Some people will mention the Israeli-Palestinian impasse as a root cause, and surely a lot of the recruits that the terrorists attract are drawn because they are upset about the ongoing injustice in the Middle East. If the parties settled that conflict, that would remove some of the cause. Another deeper cause, perhaps, is the gap between the modernists and the fundamentalists or between the individualists and the religious authoritarians. Another gap that fuels this kind of thing is the gap between the rich and the poor in general, the indignities that the "somebodies" of the world inflict on the "nobodies" of the world. These indignities are pretty close to an ultimate cause. I focus on those indignities, whatever form they take, and see them as causing indignation, which erupts occasionally as terrorism.

So the root cause I focus on is our own conscious or — very often — unconscious treatment of other people in ways that offend their dignity so they become indignant. This gets to the question of why we're hated. We're vulnerable as Americans because we do rank number one geo-politically in the world.

For better and for worse, we are the top military-economic power, and power like that always makes you vulnerable to misusing it. I think the indignity that we engender in the world comes from our occasional misuse of that power.

So in the end, I want to take many of the steps that people are proposing: stopping the perpetrators and defending against recurrences. But I also want to look for, and eliminate, the root causes, which will stop the pipeline from being continually refilled with soldiers ready to engage in terrorism. And that's going to take a searching self-examination of the behavior of our nation state.

Tell me about when you went to Afghanistan?

Actually, the Russians took me in. They were, in 1998, very close to leaving, and they wanted to prove to a bunch of Americans that they were actually getting out. So they took a delegation of us in. Leading the group was Yevgeny Primakov, who later became Prime Minister of Russia; with him was a group of people that probably included Soviet KGB agents, for all I know. There were about a dozen Americans — some of the Americans were probably CIA agents. But I was just a citizen diplomat. The Soviets took us around, and tried to convince us that they were actually getting out. It was clear that they meant to, and sure enough they did.

I remember thinking, "Boy, that's a mistake we don't ever want to make." I mean, the Afghans had already dealt a terrible blow to the British Empire in the nineteenth century. And now, in the late twentieth century, they had actually defeated the Soviet Empire. I couldn't think of a place that would be greater folly to fight in than Afghanistan, if we were to make the mistake of getting into a land war with the Afghan people. Their government may or may not really be colluding with bin Laden. At this point, we haven't seen the proof that bin Laden himself is behind all this, although it does seem probable that he is, as one of several. But I learned there that you don't want to get in a war with the Afghans themselves. It's their main business. They have practiced war over the centuries, and they're extremely good at fighting on their home ground. It would be insane to get involved in a ground war there against the Afghan people the way the Soviets did.

You bring to mind the tales of Rudyard Kipling, and the way the British dealt with the land of Afghanistan, Uzbekistan, Kazakhstan, all of that area. And, yes, these people have been fighters all their lives, over the centuries.

Right. And when they didn't have some external power to fight against, they've fought each other, just to stay in practice!

Also, I think it's interesting to note that currently seventy percent of the Afghan people are women and children because many of the men have died.

And those people are just suffering unbelievably — the women are suffering partly because the Taliban treat them so badly, as we all know, and partly because of a drought that's causing a famine there. I would love to see a plan in which, if we go into the country, we go in with help, massive aid for the people. If we have to search out bin Laden — if that's the intention of our government — well, they'd better find a very antiseptic way to go about it, or it's going to backfire.

Meanwhile, you know, that's just number two on my list of measures you have to take. I mean, sure, if you know somebody's out to murder you, you'd want to try to intercept that impulse in him. But we really need to look for the reasons bin Laden is able to recruit so many willing soldiers into his army. The answers range from the ongoing problem in the Middle East to the fundamental indignities that bullying behavior engenders in the world.

I was interested in how, when Pearl Harbor happened, all the efforts that many people were making towards civil rights and overcoming American racism were put on hold for five to ten years, and we closed ranks to defeat an enemy who was even more racist than we were. Germany, at that time, was actually conducting a major genocide against a certain race, the Jews. Well, we, together with our allies, beat Germany. Our African-American population joined in that effort and helped with the war. It wasn't until the fifties that civil rights came to the fore again, and by the mid-sixties a lot had happened to blunt racism.

I think it's going to be similar here. I think we've got to overcome the rankism of these arrogant terrorists. By *rankism* I mean the abuse of power as vested in rank. We may not be willing to look at our own rankism right now. But once we have dealt with theirs, ours is going to come right to the top of the agenda. We will need to examine our own behavior in the world as the geo-political number one and to see where it is that we are pulling rank on people and pushing them around. I hope it's a parallel to World War II and that the issue of rankism is set aside temporarily; but then I hope it comes back and some real progress is made on closing some of the somebody-nobody gaps, the rich-poor gaps, the dignity-indignity gaps in the world, which are manifestations of the rankism that lies at the root of terrorist behavior.

Even if we get the culprits in this instance, there are many more waiting to express themselves over what can be usefully seen as a "recognition disorder" in the world. Recognition is the meat and potatoes of identity — it's identity food. And the lack of recognition, or any infringement on human dignity, breeds indignation. We must protect our antagonists' dignity, as we compete with them. We don't just give in, we compete, we have every right to compete, but we have to protect the dignity of our competitors at all times, at every step. It should be more like a foot race where, sure, you could lose, but you don't feel your dignity has been insulted if you lose. You were just up against a faster runner. No problem. But if he cheated or tripped you or pulled rank in some way, before the race or during it or afterwards, then understandably your dignity is insulted.

Issues of rank are still taboo, like issues of race and gender used to be. But I think we're about to take a real close look at rank. Learning to distinguish between rank and rankism could make the world a safer place.

BISHOP THOMAS GUMBLETON

Values, Ethics, and Morals

There are one billion Roman Catholics on the planet, who at least nominally owe their allegiance to the Pope who has long advocated peace and nonviolence. Another billion people call themselves Christian. Both Catholics and non-Catholic Christians see Jesus and his life as their original source, just as members of Islam see Mohammed as their founder. Jesus is revered as the greatest teacher of nonviolence, and both Gandhi and Martin Luther King Jr. often referred to him as their teacher in the arena of nonviolence. From my early childhood I have heard the United States of America, my country, being referred to as a "Christian" nation. Jesus preached, "Love your neighbor" and "Turn the other cheek" and "Love your enemies." The U.S. Government has not been behaving as if it represents a "Christian" nation. It's as if religion and spirituality are shunted off to a corner on Sundays and are not included in the warp and woof of business and political life. I'm not speaking about eliminating the constitutional separation of religion and state. I'm referring to human values, ethics, and morality, which come from Christian denominations of all types, whether they be evangelical, Catholic, Mormon, Seventh Day Adventist, Quaker, Presbyterian, or any of the myriad others. Bishop Gumbleton is the Founding President of Pax Christi; he has received the University of Notre Dame Peacemaker Award and serves as the Auxiliary Bishop of Detroit.

MICHAEL: *Bishop Gumbleton, we've entered a new time, literally a new world since the events of September 11, 2001. I'm wondering, in your position as a bishop in a large, metropolitan area in the United States, what reflections, thoughts, insights you have at this time, particularly in reference to the Pope's call for "peaceful negotiation and dialogue" in the current crisis?*

BISHOP GUMBLETON: I agree with you, first of all, that we have entered a new era. That means for me, however, that we can't use the same old solutions that we've tried to use before to solve the problems that confront us. In a new era, it seems to me we have to look for different ways to resolve what is going on in the world right now. For us as a nation simply to respond in the military fashion, as we have to every other threat in the past, I think is an extreme mistake because it simply will not resolve the kind of a problem that we face. In a sense, we seem to be totally dismissing the possibility that the people who are doing this to us are not simply fanatics or madmen or people who are irrational, but that they have a goal in mind. And we seem not to be able to discover what that is, or to even care about what that is. It's my strong conviction that unless we get down to the roots of the problem, we're not going to resolve it. I think there's evidence for that in the fact that our own national leaders are telling us that, even if we destroy Osama bin Laden, we still have to be prepared for future terrorist attacks. And they're warning us that the next attacks could be even worse than the current one. There could be germ attacks or chemical warfare attacks or even a nuclear attack. And so, to try to resolve a problem the way we are, with the full expectation that it's not going to be resolved, that in fact it's only going to bring about a response that will be even worse than what we've already experienced, seems to me to be very shortsighted and very unsatisfactory, obviously. It just won't do what we want to accomplish.

Before the Gulf War, Pope John Paul II pleaded with President Bush Sr. and President Hussein not to go to war, but instead to enter into authentic and sincere negotiations. We refused to do that then and we went to war anyway. After the war, in March of '91, Pope John Paul wrote an encyclical letter, a teaching letter, in which at one point he said, "War, never again." He said, "I said this before the Persian Gulf War and I repeat it: War, never again." Because, he says, war only brings turmoil into the lives of those who do the killing, and it brings tremendous suffering, especially to civilians.

But the most important thing, he said, is that when you go to war you simply leave behind a trail of hatred and resentment to make it all the more difficult to resolve the very problems that provoked the war. So what he was pleading for was that we would get down to the root problems: try to find out where the antagonism is, why there is this antagonism, and then try to do something about that. That's what I feel we have to do in this instance.

There are reasons why people hate us enough that they would bring about a terrorist attack such as they've done. I'm not saying in any way that the people who were killed deserved to be killed. No, they did not deserve that. No civilian, no person, in fact, deserves to be killed, in my judgment. We need to find another way to resolve our problems. They did not deserve to be killed. It was not justified what anyone did to the people in the World Trade towers and the Pentagon. However, again, why would somebody hate us enough to do that kind of a terrorist action? That's what we have to look at. And when you begin to consider what's been going on in the world, you discover there are many reasons why people would hate us and resent us. It isn't just because of our freedom, as President Bush suggested, or just because of our wealth. It's because they have seen how the United States has interfered in many places in the world and has, in fact, brought about what could clearly be called terrorist action.

I'm thinking of places like Central America, where as far back as 1954 we intervened in the country of Guatemala. We overthrew a government. This is easily documented. It was the CIA that brought it about on behalf of the United Fruit Company, and we put another government in place. For four decades the people of Guatemala suffered tyranny and oppression and torture and killing — up to 200,000 people died. I visited places in Guatemala where the military, with our support, our money, guns that we had provided for them, training we had provided for them, carried out a scorched-earth policy — killing all the people in villages, or driving them away and simply destroying all their villages, the crops, everything. This happened for four decades.

Now, there's bound to be anger and hatred that can begin to build up among people who experience that kind of evil. And it's gone on in Nicaragua and, as I already mentioned, in Guatemala. It also happened in El Salvador, where for twelve years we supplied arms — against the wishes of the majority of the people of that country. Archbishop Romero pleaded with President Carter just five weeks before Romero himself was shot. Before he was shot, he pleaded with President Carter, "Don't send any arms down here. They're only killing the poor." And yet we continued to send them and Oscar Romero himself was shot five weeks later.

That's the kind of thing that's been going on in the world, and certainly it's true in the Middle East where we have intervened. We brought about the overthrow of the Mossadegh government in 1953, that far back, and put in the Shah, a tyrant who oppressed his own people. We supported him up until 1979 when there was an uprising of the people with anger, hatred, and resentment towards the United States because they saw us behind the tyranny that was oppressing them. We intervened in Iraq and helped to put the Vass party in power in the late 1960s. And we supported that power. Secretary Rumsfeld spoke about how Iraq has used chemical weapons against its own people, but he never mentioned the fact that those chemical weapons were used when Iraq was one of our favorite countries and we supported what they were doing. We even provided the chemical weapons that they used. We were arming Iraq for years, and then we turned against them and now we're waging war against them, devastating their country — and we've continued to do that since the embargo. Some people are bound to be extremely upset with what we have been doing.

We need to look at our actions as a nation, as a people. We have to look and see what we have been doing, and then begin to repair some of that evil. If we were willing to do that, then I am confident that other nations in the world, other people, would not look upon us with anger and resentment but would rather look upon us with favor and look to us for the kind of things that we can do if we choose — that is, help to raise the living standards for people in other parts of the world. We can share some of our technology, share all the good things that we have instead of simply using other nations for our own benefit, which we have done so much in the past. That's what I believe we have to do.

Bishop Gumbleton, when President George W. Bush announced the bombing of Afghanistan, one of the things he said in coming to the decision for launching the bombing was that he did so "after a great deal of prayer." Can you give me some insight into the question, "Who are we praying to and what gods are we talking about here?"

It disturbs me greatly that the President would say that and do that. Before he gave the speech to the Congress, I know he gathered together about thirty religious leaders with him for about a half hour and prayed. There were two Roman Catholic cardinals in that group. Now, he had already made his decision. He was ready to go on national television and announce to the American people what he was doing. So, yes, he prayed before he did that but to me that's not the kind of prayer that we need in a situation like this. We need not to pray that God will do what we want, but rather to pray in a way that we begin to listen to what God might be saying to us in these circumstances, saying to us through some of the prophets from the Old Testament, saying to us through Jesus, and leading us into a different way. But if you don't go to prayer in a listening mode and try to discover what God wants, if you only go to prayer to somehow ask for support for what you've already decided to do, to me that's not authentic prayer. We have to go to prayer very humbly so that we are very open, very vulnerable, very much ready to listen. If we pray that way I think it's certainly possible that God can show us a different way to bring about a peaceful solution to the crisis. But when you go to prayer when you've already made up your mind what you're going to do, then I don't think it's authentic prayer. You're simply asking God to do what you have decided, to help you do what you have decided. In other words, you're saying you want God to be on your side, instead of saying, "I have to be where God is, on the side of God." And that might not be where you would decide to go otherwise. So I think that's not the kind of prayer that helps us very much.

Bishop Gumbleton, I think that the concept of a "just war" emerged from the Christian tradition and was applied to the Second World War, then was applied in Korea and Vietnam. And I'm thinking of World War II where, again going back to the praying to God, the U.S. called itself a Christian nation and was praying to God for victory and success, while Germany, also a Christian nation, likewise was praying to God for success. Again, it's a question of which God are we praying to. But the real question is the concept of a "just war". Is that concept still viable?

Well, yes, very definitely, it is a continuing teaching within the Christian tradition. But again, back to that prayer business, what you said simply illustrates what I was saying. Both sides are saying, "We want God on our side," instead of saying, "Let's find out where God is really leading us." Both sides misinterpret what prayer really means.

But as far as just one theology is concerned, that's not the original tradition that Christians were asked to follow. In the Gospels Jesus rejected violence for any reason whatsoever. The first Christians, for three hundred years, rejected the use of violence. When a member of the military was baptized, he gave up his military career because a Christian was not expected to wage war — in fact, he was expected *not* to wage war. It was only in the late fourth century that the "just war" theology developed under Saint Augustine, with an attempt on Augustine's part to try to prevent war from happening, but then, if it did happen in spite of your efforts to prevent it, to insist that war had to be waged under very limited conditions, under very strict criteria. And so with Augustine — and later on as that theology continued to be developed by Thomas Aquinas and Suarez and other theologians, down to the modern times — the theology always starts with the presumption against war, that you may not go to war unless you can be sure the conditions are present that would justify overriding the presumption against war.

So that theology, if it were interpreted correctly, would be almost impossible to use to justify any war, especially modern warfare. Look at what's happened in the past century, the twentieth century. You discover that modern warfare has been an escalating kind of warfare that brought about the death of more and more civilians. In every war during the twentieth century, the percentage of civilians killed increased.

And now in the twenty-first century as well.

Well, it's going to be the case, sure. And civilian immunity is one of the main criteria that you must maintain. If you can't maintain civilian immunity then you're not meeting the criteria for a just war. Also proportionality: You have to be sure the good you will achieve is not going to be surpassed by the evil that you do when you go to war, because it's understood that when you go to war you're doing something evil. The only way you can justify it is that a greater good is going to come from it, but if the evil you do surpasses that, well then, there's no way to justify the war.

But you know, it was almost prophetic what Pope John XXIII said — in fact, it was prophetic, not just "almost." I really would say it was prophetic. Back in 1963 John XXIII and the Bishop of Rome wrote an encyclical entitled "Peace on Earth." He was writing not too long after the end of World War II, so he was very much aware of what had happened during that war, and especially towards the end of it. He understood that we were in a new era, the atomic era. And he said, "In the atomic era it is irrational any longer to think of war as an apt means to vindicate violated rights." So, in a way, he was wiping out the "just war" theology because he said that we were in a whole new period of history. Like Einstein said, everything has changed now except our thinking. John XXIII was saying that our thinking has to change — that it is "irrational ... to think of war as an apt means to vindicate violated rights" — because we're in this period where war almost inevitably is not going to be contained in a way that could ever make it justified, and we risk the very existence of the planet when we go to war these days.

As I mentioned earlier, our own leaders are telling us that the next action against us — in retaliation for the attack we just carried out while people on the other side would think that we attacked them in retaliation for their attack against us and so on and so on — could well be germ warfare, a warfare of uncontrollable dimensions, or it could be nuclear warfare. It's irrational for us to embark on a course that could have that kind of outcome. So I think John XXIII was absolutely right. We have to eliminate war as the means of resolving our problems. It just simply can't be done any more.

Bishop Gumbleton, I really appreciate your candor and your remarks. Just one final question: Bringing it back to the microcosm and the individual, what do you suggest individuals do to sustain themselves in these times?

Well, the most important thing, I think, is for people to band together in an international movement — and the beginnings of such a movement are present in the world already — to come together with other people who are ready to reject war, to rid the world of nuclear weapons. There's a huge movement for the abolition of nuclear weapons. Do that. Rid the world of other weapons of mass destruction as well. Then really function as a global family, in a world that's globalized as far as communications, transportation, and also the economy are concerned. We live in a global economy now. We also have to live in a world that acts in accordance with international law, we have one globalized system of law that all nations are expected to abide by, and we have international courts to uphold that law. We have to do for the international community what we have done for ourselves and what others have done for themselves as nations. If we can bring about civilization within a nation — that is, civilization under law certainly — we can certainly do the same thing on an international basis. But we have to have a willingness to be part of that international family, not to try to be the superpower. That's where the United States has to really back down. We can't just be *the* superpower. We have to be part of a community of nations in a very authentic way. I believe every person should be working for this with all the energy we can bring to it.

WHAT IS DEMOCRACY?

THE ROOTS OF THE WORD *democracy* are Greek: *demos*, meaning "the people," and *kratos*, meaning "rule" — "the people rule." In America today, can we truly say the people rule, when in the 2000 election, despite the popular vote in favor of the other candidate (Gore), a president was selected by the Supreme Court, usurping the constitutional authority of the Congressional or legislative branch of the government to settle presidential election disputes? Speaking of Congress, we have the best one money can buy, because of the obscene amounts of campaign dollars necessary to run for political office. These dollars come mostly from corporations, for example Enron. The current U.S. Energy policy was determined by the Bush leadership in consultation with various energy companies and others to the exclusion of environmentalists and conservationists, even though 80% of the American people want to do whatever is necessary to preserve the environment, i.e. water, air, the ozone layer, etc. We might ask ourselves the question, "Where do the people rule in a government beholden to moneyed interests?"

KEVIN DANAHER

Breaking the Paradigm

NAFTA (North American Free Trade Agreement) and GATT (General Agreement on Tariffs and Trade) were passed by Congress in 1993 and 1994 respectively. There was at that time considerable evidence indicating that these corporate globalization initiatives would do more harm than good with respect to jobs, wages, and the ecology and that they would, in fact, infringe on democracy itself.

It was also clear that a distinct connection existed between globalization, "free market" capitalism exported as democracy's gift to the developing world, and the deteriorating ecosphere. Because of New Dimensions' longtime interest in ecology, I became more engaged in exploring what globalization was about. This quest led me to the work of Kevin Danaher and Global Exchange. Kevin is an activist in the best sense of the term, and his articulation of the issues and challenges we face on the planet gives us a wider view of the effects of globalization.

KEVIN: I think we have to look at this as a values question. There is a paradigm shift going on, on a planetary basis. For the past five hundred years the paradigms that have dominated the world have been money values, violence, and "God is on my side." There is now an alternative paradigm out there that is not about money values but about life values: human rights and the environment, nonviolence, and "God doesn't take sides."

And that's what we're involved in here. So Bush and bin Laden are really coming from the same old paradigm: money values, oil, millionaires, the justification of violence, and "God is on my side." You can see it as far back as five hundred years ago, in the colonial explosion that sent Columbus to the Americas to initiate genocide against the Native Americans. It led to that whole process of slavery and colonization and massive extraction and redistribution of wealth, such that today the richest twenty percent of the world's people account for eighty-six percent of global resource consumption. Now, as a result, the poorest eighty percent of the world's people get only fourteen percent of global resource consumption.

There were three forces that pushed that global, violent redistribution of wealth. First, the money values drove the initiation of global capitalism: Columbus was coming for gold and silver. The second force was violence: mounting cannons on sailing ships was the particular innovation that allowed the Europeans to conquer the world. And third was the notion that "God is on our side," the thinking that "we have God's 800-number." Columbus' own diaries reflect his belief that by killing the Indians he was bringing them to Christ.

And now we're in a struggle in which the far right of the three major monotheisms — Christianity, Judaism, and Islam — the far right of each of those paternalistic monotheisms is fighting with each other. And we're put in the middle. You know, it's like, "You must choose!" No, wait a minute. I'd rather not choose between one right-wing, paternalistic monotheism and another, where each one believes in money and violence and "God is on my side." I'd rather get out of that into a totally different paradigm, a paradigm that won't take us to hell but instead will take us to a utopia. *Utopia* is a good word. If the strategy of violence worked, Israel would be the safest place in the world right now. We'd have peace on a planetary level. But it doesn't work. Violence begets violence. As Martin Luther King said, you cannot drive out darkness with darkness. Only light can do that. You don't fight hate with hate, you fight it with love. You don't fight fire with fire, you fight it with water. These are basic truths that are known throughout all cultures. If you want to be treated right, you treat other people right — the Golden Rule. The people in power have changed that Golden Rule from "Treat others as you would have them treat you" to "He who has the gold makes the rules." And that's our choice. Which Golden Rule are we going to follow?

So I think we're at a crossroads, historically. I think September 11 was a sort of paradigm-busting event, in that it forces people to ask questions that, before, they were allowed to hide from. If we do our job right as educators, we will say, "Wait a minute. Are we going to be more secure? Are we going to be safer or are we going to be less secure? Is this a possible solution? Do we want to go out and kill individual mosquitoes with a sledgehammer? Or do we want to dry up the swamp of injustice and inequality from which the mosquitoes breed?" So there are big questions out there now before the public, and we need to get people to keep asking those questions and to talk to as many different kinds of people as possible. America is, after all, the most diverse country in the world. Unfortunately, our media are dominated by corporate money interests. Still, we have the most diverse population in the world, and if we get a clean, respectful conversation going we can work our way out of this. But the foreign policy we need to lead us into the future is not going to come from the corporate elites who control our government. It's got to come from the people. And that's the greatest source of strength for our society, after all.

MICHAEL: *It's interesting, synchronistic, that today is October 12, Columbus Day. We still celebrate the day Columbus supposedly discovered America. It brings to mind again that we have lost something like 3,000 individual human beings in the tragic events of 9-11. These people gave their lives — I like the word sacrifice: to "make sacred." It just seems to me that we cannot, in response, commit acts that will result in civilian casualties, under any circumstances.*

I had a lot of friends who served in Vietnam and came back and were very angry. They weren't angry because of their sacrifice. They were angry because their sacrifice was not honored. And I think if we want to honor the people who were sacrificed on September 11, we need, as you say, make them sacred. How do you make something sacred? You don't go in the direction of money and violence. You go in the direction of spirituality and love and kindness and generosity. So if we're going to try to rectify the problem of us being victimized and we do it by victimizing other innocent people — that's the same as if you were walking down the street and a dog came up barking at you, and you got down on all fours and started to bark back at the dog. You don't do that. You rise to a higher level of consciousness. So the challenge here is the same as it is in a one-to-one confrontation: if you slap me in the face, my immediate tendency is to slap you back. But a lot of great spiritual leaders said, "No, you turn the other cheek." When Jesus said it, I don't think he was saying it like some passive wimp. I think he was saying it sort of like Robert de Niro or Al Pacino would say, "Hey, that was a pretty good shot. Why don't you give me a whack here on the other one?" In other words, do you think you're going to get somewhere by using violence, by hitting people? No. It's not going to get you what you want.

So we have two ways to frame the September 11 events. One is to get down and bark back at the dog and do violence. The other is to say, wait a minute, instead of framing it as war, which elevates these guys to the status of warriors — which I would rather not do because I think they're criminals — let's frame it as criminal justice. That approach leads us away from a nationalist, isolationist attitude based on the notion that "we Americans have been hurt." After all, lots of people have suffered from terrorism. If we define it as a crime against humanity, it takes us in the direction of linking up with all the people around the world who have been victims of terrorism — and there are many of them — and puts us in a position to work toward activating the international criminal court (ICC). That court has already been ratified by more than 60 nations, so it is coming into existence. The process of establishing the ICC was begun in the mid 90s to deal with this particular kind of problem, a transnational act of violence against innocent civilians. It would give us a way to establish the kinds of principles that now are the mainstays of American jurisprudence — innocent until proven guilty; truth, the whole truth and nothing but the truth — and establish those sound principles on an international basis.

Up until now, the U.S. government has been the main government blocking the establishment of an international criminal court because they don't want Henry Kissinger and the like having to testify at some point about the crimes of our own government. If we move toward establishing that court, yes, there will be some current or former public servants who might be embarrassed or who might even be brought up on charges. But they are our public servants. They are our employees. We, the citizens, are the fourth branch of government and are supposed to rule over the other three branches of government. And God help us if we cannot criticize and rectify the bad policies of the public servants who are supposed to be working for us. We're not supposed to be sheep just following what they tell us to do. We elect them. We pay their salaries. We are "the boss." The public airwaves are the commons. It's public property. The corporations that currently utilize the public airwaves to sell our minds to the corporate advertisers are the tenants. We are the landlords of the public airways, and they don't even pay us rent.

So we need to do a very deep questioning and review of the way in which our system of governance has been taken over by narrow corporate, moneyed interests — I mean transnational, corporate interests. If the major export of the Middle East were broccoli instead of oil, none of this would be happening. At the time that the U.S. government made a deal with the House of Saud — Saudi Arabia is the only country named after a family — back in the thirties, General Motors and other transport corporations linked to automobiles were buying up several dozen U.S. metropolitan light rail vehicle systems — surface trains. Los Angeles had the largest light rail vehicle system in the world at the time. Those were systematically destroyed and replaced with cars and buses running on petroleum-driven internal combustion engines.

We're now recognizing that we cannot continue to get our energy from fossil fuels. That is a cul-de-sac. And enough people are now moving in a renewable direction, saying, "Wait a minute. We need to imitate nature, not dominate nature. We need to be friends with people around the world, not just think we can bully them around and take their resources away." So I think there's a profound paradigm shift going on. Our job as educators is to make people aware of that larger paradigm shift.

During this time, with the events that are taking place, what has been personally sustaining you?

Well, I'll tell you, it's not easy because, like everybody else, I grew up in New York. I have a lot of friends and relatives and people who have been directly affected by the events. I have people very close to me who are just sick. They're physically ill because of this. And so, the first thing is the shock. That's what terror does. It shocks you into immobility. Then, at a certain point, you have to sort of slap yourself and say, "Wait a minute. What's needed here?" In any emergency your immediate instinct is to panic. But then you have to override that and say, "Wait a minute. This is not the time for panic. This, of all times, is a time for very calm, clear thinking about what we need to do."

But look at what happened. Our government bombed a country that had already been bombed into the Stone Age. There was hardly anything left to bomb. There were millions of refugees. If we had really wanted to help feed them we would have dropped millions and millions of meals, not just 34,000 meals. With this course of action, our government went right into a trap. What's needed in unexpected situations is to respond with something unexpected. The Bush administration could have taken the criminal justice route: go and get a coalition of nations to bring in the perpetrators through police action, put them on trial in an international court, do massive relief to the refugees — not just air drops of meals, but massive relief, massive education of women in particular. You want to undermine a regime that is based on male dominance and this sort of fascistic minority version of Islam? Those are the ways to do it, not with bombs. With bombs you're creating a recruitment mechanism for their cause. They're going to take the photographs of the innocent victims and circulate those around the world. And then when the government in Pakistan or the government in Indonesia or the government in Saudi Arabia gets destabilized, then what are we going to do? Are we going to send troops in there, too, to prop up those governments?

I wrote a letter to *The Wall Street Journal* saying that the big corporations need to understand that they are the most vulnerable element of U.S. society. We're vulnerable here at home, but U.S. corporations abroad — the Nike factories in Indonesia, businesses with operations in other countries — are extremely vulnerable to these kinds of people. When I raise delicate questions like this in the mass media, I get two kinds of responses. I get the call-ins and the hate mail that says, "Are you an American? You're an idiot. You're not a patriot." I get this kind of thing from guys who couldn't find Afghanistan on a map. But then on the other side, where the glass is half full, are the women, the Arab Americans, the African-Americans. I did a two-hour show the other night that reached three hundred African-American stations. I was the only guest. Every single call was critical of U.S. Government policy, from people who actually read and pay attention, from Vietnam veterans who fought in the war and came home to be spit upon. And they were all saying a similar thing: We have a responsibility as citizens of the most powerful country in the world. We have a responsibility to be knowledgeable about U.S. foreign policy and its impact around the world.

You bring up an issue that's important. We're getting thousands of responses from all over the country and all over the world, actually, because people are hearing us in Australia and other places. And by and large they're 99.9% against what the U.S. government is doing.

You know what this is like? This is like when the O. J. Simpson verdict came out and we saw the polls that said seventy-five percent of African-Americans approved, seventy-five percent of whites were opposed. What I said to the white people, then, who were all angry about the injustice of him being let off, was, "Hold that feeling. Hold that feeling of injustice. Embrace it. Get used to feeling what it feels like. Now you know what African-Americans feel like most of the time." So now, when we feel the injustice of being victimized, are we going to learn from it and use it to step forward to a different kind of posture? Or are we going to just continue with the same policies of the past, as if nothing has really changed? I think it's instructive to look at the opportunism of Robert Zoellick, the U.S. trade representative who went to Congress and said that the President needs fast-track authority to negotiate trade deals.

That was exactly what he was saying prior to September 11, but now he's wrapping it in the flag, in the security issue, and in the honor of the dead people. This guy gives opportunism a bad name. The people who wanted bigger military budgets and bigger CIA budgets — in other words, bigger budgets for the very institutions that got us into this mess in the first place — they jump on the graves before the people's bodies are recovered from the rubble. Couldn't we please just have a pause in all the opportunism until the bodies are recovered, and then implement policy? No, no, no. Immediately we've got to go bomb people. We've got to answer the blood lust. And that's the road to hell.

Living in the Conversation

Working with the late R. Buckminster "Bucky" Fuller in a series of weekend seminars that New Dimensions sponsored in California provided my first introduction to the intention and commitment to excellence of Lynne Twist. She was the manager of logistics for two of these events in San Francisco, and her work was so good that people attending didn't notice the logistics because things went so smoothly. Since then I have come to know Lynne more personally as an intervie-wee, funding consultant, personal cheerleader, and friend. As the president of the Turning Tide Coalition, she is fostering a worldwide movement for a thriving, equitable, and sustainable way of life on Earth. Her extraordinary work on behalf of The Hunger Project for over 20 years was responsible for raising $100 million to alleviate starvation on the planet. Lynne is one of those women who are leading the way for the world's social transformation and for the emergence of women in cultures throughout the world.

MICHAEL: *What reflections, insights, thoughts do you have about the new world that we all have entered since the events of September 11, 2001?*

LYNNE: Well, there are many ways to talk about that. In one way, we haven't entered a new world. We've really been shaken into seeing the world that was already there. One way of explaining what has happened is that the veil has been lifted, particularly for the people who live in the United States, regarding the world that we're living in and the impact that we're having, both positive and negative. Another way of describing the new world we're in is that we have been shaken on a human level — all six billion of us — in a way that was so shocking and so traumatic that all of us have gone, I believe, to a kind of ground zero of our own. And that is the ground zero of one's life: Who am I? What are my priorities? What are my core values? What is my future? Where do I stand? And what am I living for? Those are two ways of talking about the new world. The first way — where we're beginning to wake up in our part of the world to the harsh reality of the world that we're living in and our distorted view of it and our distorted relationship with it — is, I think, a critical passage for people who live in and benefit from the macroeconomic system. That's not necessarily only the people in the United States. It's people everywhere who are part of the consumer culture, the voracious culture that will do anything to consume and accumulate more — which is a runaway, unsustainable mode of living that I think we've all been worried about for a long, long time.

It's as if we knew something horrible was eventually going to happen. But now that it has, it's a shock, even though at some level of our being we expected it. But the way it happened and the intense horror of it and the unbelievable cruelty of it are all part of the shock. And I think that is also, unfortunately, what it needed to be to shake us out of our trance. The other way of speaking about it is to talk about the incredible experience of having anything that you thought was stable no longer be stable. For me, and I think for many people, it's like an earthquake. I've been in many earthquakes because I live in California, as do you. When they're happening, your whole experience of the ground is transformed because suddenly it isn't there for you. But earthquakes usually only last for a few seconds. The events of September 11 and those that followed are like an earthquake that won't stop — the shaking, the tremor won't stop. It's as though there's a vibration under the human family now that is starting to vibrate, and the vibration is getting greater and more unsettling every single day.

So for me, the distortions are starting to reveal themselves: our distorted perception of Islam, Muslim people, and even the whole Arab world; our distorted relationship with our role in the world as a culture, the American culture in particular; our distorted relationship with both our generosity and our efforts to be a nation that promotes, establishes, and ensures freedom for ourselves and for others. All of that has been shaken, and I think we're all questioning it. I think this is ultimately very, very healthy. When those structures fell — those huge, unbelievably towering World Trade Center structures — what crumbled with those structures was a whole set of false beliefs. Those beliefs have crumbled so that now we have to look at whether or not we want to rebuild them: beliefs about world trade, beliefs about capitalism, beliefs about the commercial economy, beliefs about the testimony to the free market, beliefs about the greatness of our national pride. And to have the World Trade Center and the military industrial complex be the targets of attacks — the attacks being made with our own planes, the perpetrators who ended up flying the planes into those buildings trained by our own flight instructors, using our own technology to really do something violent and destructive to us — all of that makes it even more powerful. It's something that no one could have predicted, nor is it something we can have much chance of preventing in the future. It's like our technology, our way of living, our way of perceiving the world has turned in on us in a way that has almost broken our hearts and kicked us in the stomach. At the same time, I see the horror of our response. Gandhi said, "An eye for an eye will make the whole world blind." I think many people are horrified, myself included, by the violent, irrational, and poorly thought-through response we're making as a nation.

I'm also horrified by my inability to have my voice heard by my own leaders. I think it's become apparent, particularly during the last presidential election, that our government doesn't hear our voice any more. They govern by the results of polls, not by the voice of the people. I don't consider the results of any poll — even if I participated in it — to be my voice. I think Americans need to wake up and communicate directly with their elected officials, and not count on the polls to let us know what our opinion is. Polls are artificially constructed sets of questions that can draw almost any response. But when you really speak your own mind to the people who represent you — your senator, congressperson, President, your Secretary of Defense, the people who wield such enormous power — it needs to be done forcefully, not in response to strategically designed questions, but more out of the heart and soul of who you are. I'm urging people to communicate with their government.

I'm also urging people to listen for the greatness of our leaders. I didn't vote for George Bush, I don't think he was elected fairly, I almost never agree with him and, personally, I don't really have an affinity for him — I just don't really like him. However, he's the President of my country. I know that pain and trauma and passage through brutal challenges have made me greater each time I've had to go through those kinds of transitions in my life. Everyone will grow from this horror, including our President. Every morning when I wake up I think about him, and I think about being the man who has the authority and the responsibility for the world's remaining superpower — the only superpower in the world, a country so rich, so powerful that it became blind. I think of what it's like to be the leader of that country — a country that became blind and has now been driven to a place where we must re-see, re-vision, or re-look at who we are, respect the world we're living in, which is another way of saying "re-see" the world we're living in. I think about the awesome responsibility our President holds for that activity and that deep and profound thinking, and the unbelievable pressure on him to act, and to act quickly, to take decisive action. Those two states are extremely difficult to face. We have those kinds of situations in our personal life from time to time, but never on the magnitude of what he faces every morning when he awakes.

The train is rolling and it's left the station, and President Bush has said some things that I think he probably would look back at now and want to change. But I want to listen for the magnificence of this man, the greatness of this man. I've learned through some of the e-mails that I've received, as we all have during this time, that Abraham Lincoln was not a popular nor even a very good President at the beginning of his presidency. And it was the confrontation with slavery and the immense horror of having to face civil war that turned him into a great man.

So I pray for George Bush. I don't just listen to what he says, but I listen for wisdom, in a way that hopefully will pull from him the magnificence that lives in any and every human being, that can be brought forth in this man and the people surrounding him during this time. I haven't seen it yet, or even glimpses of it. But he is the guy in the job. And criticizing him and putting him down is cheap compared to what he needs from us now. I don't give him my unequivocal support. I'm a resister, and I have a lot to say about what's happening in our country. But I'm listening for the possibility that he could become great, that he could access a pool of wisdom. And I think that if we don't have that space for him, if we shut down that space for him, then he can't access that. So I think this is a critical time to really rethink our relationship with our leaders.

And then I would say that the whole event of September 11 has accelerated a process that I believe is taking place in the world. I often quote Tom Hurley, who works with the Chaordic Alliance and used to work with the Institute of Noetic Sciences, who coined this phrase, as far as I know. I think it's time to "hospice the death of the old structures that are already on their way out." Anything unsustainable, as Elizabet Sahtouris says. "If it's unsustainable, it is doomed. It can't last." That's what *unsustainable* means. So we don't need to be angry and beat on the unsustainable practices and institutions of our time — they are dying. They are dying their natural deaths. What we need to do is hospice that death and accelerate it.

At the same time we need to midwife the birth of the new ways of being. Amidst the horror of this global turmoil we can, in fact, do that. The turmoil, the war on terrorism, is, to me, a deep abomination and a completely, profoundly serious error in judgment. I am horrified by the bombing and reacting and trying to hunt down people who I believe should be tried in an international court as criminals rather than be elevated to the status of people with whom we're at war. I believe they should be dealt with as people who performed crimes against humanity, not as people who attacked America. However, this turmoil that we're in can itself be the environment in which we can rise above the madness and generate a world worthy of the 21st century and the future of all life.

We are on a totally unsustainable track in so many areas of life, and this war on terrorism is totally unsustainable. It's another product of unsustainable thinking. And it will not last. We've been told it will go on for a very long time, but it can't succeed, and it can't go on. I think we need to be looking at — deeply, inside of our souls — what it is we stand for and what kind of world is the real scenario that will be born out of this horror. We need to begin to build that scenario and have conversations that generate it.

I believe that we don't really live in the world. We live in the conversation we have about the world. And we have absolute power over that. We can't change the fact that planes crashed into the World Trade Center. We can't change the fact that the Pentagon was partially destroyed. We can't change the fact that those things happened and that thousands of people died. We also can't change the fact that the sanctions on Iraq have probably killed between 220,000 and 500,000 children, and that's our doing. We can't change the fact that our policies vis-à-vis Saudi Arabia have propped up a government of unbelievable repression. But we can change the conversation we have about the world in which we live because that's really where we live, in the conversation we have about the world. And over that we have absolute, omnipotent power. We have levers and dials to generate the conversation for sanity, for inquiry into what it is that we're not doing that we need to be doing now as a people, as a nation. We have enormous power to shape the conversation, and in my view, conversation is more powerful than bombs, and it's more powerful than money. Because when it comes right down to it, we live in the conversation we generate about this world, and we have enormous power there.

I particularly think that women have a huge and very important role to play right now. Women are organized like never before. Women have a voice that has a volume, a clarity, and a listening like never before. During the Gulf War, the Internet was not a commercial success yet, so women really couldn't organize themselves and speak powerfully to stop the madness of war in the way that they can now over the Internet. Now we can. The Beijing Women's Conference took place. It was one of the most powerful conferences I've ever attended in my life, one of the biggest and most important conferences in the history of the world. Beijing Plus Five took place, with women and men. And yet, I'm particularly committed to having women really use the enormous power of our voices to stop this madness and to involve ourselves in the dialogue and inquiry about how to move forward through this incredible turmoil in such a way that we stop the violence and the punitive, reactive nature of our leadership and examine in silence and reverence where it is that the United States has taken action and why. We need to look at how that has at some level caused the horror, not only of the World Trade Center actions, but also of our response to it. We have a lot of soul-searching to do, and I think it's time to do it.

Just one more thing. I think our hearts have been broken. Everybody has had a time in their life when their heart was broken — it was either on Valentine's Day when you were six years old and you didn't get the valentine you wanted or in high school when you broke up with a beloved girlfriend or boyfriend, or you were jilted by a lover somewhere along the way. We've all had our hearts broken and we know how painful that is and, at the same time, how powerful it is as we follow our life's path. I believe America's heart has been broken, and it's painful but it's beautiful. Love is flowing. We can feel the pain and the beauty of our own heart. We can drop from the cerebral, strategic, military, commercial way of thinking into the heartful, forgiving, compassionate, inquiring way of seeing the world. That's what I myself am doing, and I know millions of other people are doing that, too.

I suggest that the conversation I'm talking about be generated straight from the heart — not something mushy or wimpy, but the kind of conversation from the heart that has the deep rigor of true compassion, forgiveness, and courage. Courage comes from the heart, and we need to exhibit a kind of courage never called for before, at least not that I can remember in my lifetime. The whole world is in one conversation. We have the opportunity to shape that conversation and, in so doing, to shape history.

FRANCIS BOYLE

Civil Liberties at Risk

Francis Boyle *first came to my attention within days of 9-11, when I read his statement that the "United States is under an absolute obligation to resolve this dispute with Afghanistan in a peaceful manner as required by U.N. Charter 2(3) and Article 33 ... Accordingly, this dispute must be resolved by invoking the 1971 Montreal Sabotage Convention and the 1997 U.N. International Convention for the Suppression of Terrorist Bombings. Furthermore, the United States should offer to submit this entire dispute with Afghanistan to the International Court of Justice in The Hague (the so-called World Court)."*

As a professor of International Law at the University of Illinois College of Law, a licensed attorney for 25 years, and someone who has done considerable criminal defense work, he is eminently qualified to speak to the challenges all of us as Americans face in these perilous times. The following dialogue is timeless in that the situation has progressively worsened since we spoke with each other.

MICHAEL: *Can you speak to President Bush's executive order for military tribunals?*

FRANCIS BOYLE: Yes. First, we must consider this executive order within the context of what is a wholesale assault on the United States Constitution and the civil rights and civil liberties of the American people since September 11. This assault has been undertaken by the Bush administration and Attorney General Ashcroft, as well as White House Counsel Gonzalez and the Federalist Society lawyers that populate the Bush administration. I won't go through all of those here, but this seems to be the culmination of the process. It's hard to imagine anything more dangerous or serious than this breathtaking executive order. It is an outright violation of the due process of law and of protections of the United States Constitution itself as well as of international treaties to which the United States government is a party. It is a usurpation and violation of the powers that Congress has under the terms of the Constitution, and an attempt to abrogate the Writ of Habeas Corpus, which is completely unconstitutional — Habeas Corpus is one of our most important constitutional rights, going all the way back to the Magna Carta. It would take me an entire law review article to go through all the problems with this executive order.

Attorney General Ashcroft cited the use of military tribunals after the assassination of Abraham Lincoln, just as the Civil War was ending. He also cited the use of military tribunals in the American Revolution. What about those citings? Do they have any validity?

Well, we could sit here and debate those precedents, which I am happy to do. However, the standards have changed since the Second World War — certainly the standards of international law have changed. Here in the United States we have the International Covenant on Civil and Political Rights that the United States Government has been a party to since 1992, which clearly would prohibit many of these draconian sanctions being imposed on aliens. We also have the International Covenant on the Elimination of All Forms of Racial Discrimination. It's clear this is a form of racial profiling, racial persecution against Arabs and Muslims, people from that ethnic and religious background. We are also parties to the Third Geneva Convention of 1949 that is directly on point with regard to dealing with prisoners of war. In addition, we are parties to the Fourth Geneva Convention of 1949 that protects civilians in times of war. The executive order, by attempting to base itself on World War II and Civil War precedents, simply ignores these treaties that are the supreme law of the land under Article VI of the United States Constitution.

Both Rumsfeld and Cheney as well as Bush have been quoted as saying that the war criminals of the Taliban and Al Qaeda are not entitled to U.S. constitutional rights because they're war criminals. Does that compare with what the American government did with the war criminals after World War II, the Nazi war criminals at the Nuremberg trials? What is the difference?

First, it is very important to distinguish between aliens here in the United States and those abroad. For the most part, the United States Constitution really does not protect foreigners abroad. But, putting aside the question of aliens here in the United States who are also subjected to this executive order from President Bush, those abroad — the Taliban fighters, the Al Qaeda fighters — are certainly subject to either the Third or the Fourth Geneva Convention of 1949. As you know, Ashcroft has called them "war criminals," and he is the Attorney General. Well, then, by means of doing that he is, implicitly at least, taking the position — and I certainly would take that position as well — that they are combatants within the meaning of the Third Geneva Convention of 1949 and are therefore subject to the full scope of protections under the Third Geneva Convention. This would permit prosecution of individuals for war crimes. However, there are very extensive protections within the Third Geneva Convention for prosecuting prisoners of war for the commission of war crimes, protections that would simply prevent kangaroo court proceedings — or so-called drumhead proceedings — and summary executions being inflicted upon them.

The danger comes now. The problem is this: In the public articulation of this executive order, we have basically said to the Taliban fighters and the Al Qaeda fighters, "We will not treat you in accordance with the Third Geneva Convention of 1949 and all the requirements." All that does now is open up United States armed forces to reprisals. Certainly, there is an international armed conflict between the United States and Afghanistan that has triggered the four Geneva Conventions of 1949 and the Hague Regulations, the Customary Law of the Laws of War. United States armed forces who fight in Afghanistan are all protected by the Third Geneva Convention of 1949. They have all the protections set forth as prisoners of war. But if we are taking the position that we are not going to afford similar protections to the Taliban fighters and the Al Qaeda fighters, all that then does is open up our own armed forces to reprisals whereby if any of them fall into the hands of the Taliban or Al Qaeda fighters, wherever they may be, they can say, "Well, your president has said he is not going to give us prisoner-of-war treatment, so we are not going to give you prisoner-of-war treatment." This is extremely dangerous. It exposes our own armed forces to similar types of drumhead trials and summary executions. I don't believe that the White House Federalist Society lawyers who drafted this really thought this thing through at all, and what the terrible implications might be for United States armed forces whose lives are at risk in Afghanistan. This is a shameless public relations ploy by the White House that could cost the lives of American men and women in Afghanistan today.

I want to take you back to Nuremberg. Why did we hold the Nuremberg trials as we did, and why would we not want to have a public trial as we bring some of these people to justice? Why would we want to hold secretive military tribunals instead of doing something like Nuremberg?

That's a very good question. Stalin and Churchill wanted to take out the top Nazi leaders and execute them. The only difference of opinion they had was in the numbers that they wanted to see executed. But President Roosevelt took the position that to do so would reduce us to the level of our adversaries, the Nazis. Roosevelt's position was that it was in the American tradition that there be a trial, that the trial be open and public and fair, that rules of procedure be followed, and a variety of other matters that I will not discuss here. And, indeed, there were some acquittals at Nuremberg. Not everyone was hanged. It's very hard to say that the Taliban and Al Qaeda are worse than Goering, who was indeed tried at Nuremberg, let alone Ribbentrop and many of the others. But this is the stance basically being taken by this Bush executive order. I think it's completely blowing these people out of proportion.

Again, I take it as a propagandistic move, a public relations ploy here in the United States. But, again, the problem is that it will severely erode the civil rights and civil liberties of people here in the United States as well. *The New York Times* has already reported that the Department of Justice is now in the process of transferring some of these 1200 detained aliens to the custody of the Pentagon for processing under this executive order. That affects all of us living here in the United States. And if you read the executive order, it is very clear that they, too, could be subjected to this kangaroo court proceeding. There's no other word for it. I myself have, in the past decade, formally participated in and argued in three United States military court-martial proceedings: one in the Marine Corps and two in the Army. I can tell you that out of the three, one was a complete and total railroad or kangaroo court proceeding, call it what you want. The conviction was later overturned on appeal by the Army Review Board, although that was reversed by the Court of Military Appeals. Right here, of course, on this executive order, you can be sentenced to death, and there is no appellate tribunal. So this is a fraud. This is extremely dangerous — you could have these people being run before these tribunals and sentenced to death and summarily executed. It's very dangerous and, again, these people are here in the United States. Those abroad, of course, that's a different issue.

I just want to be clear that I understand what you're saying. Are you saying that, because of this, it's conceivable that this same rule or the rules under this new military tribunal could also apply to someone holding a Green Card in the United States? Is that right?

Yes, any alien. That is correct. Any alien at all. They made that quite clear in the executive order. That is correct. They are not applying it yet to United States citizens. You know, we have no idea what they're going to do from this point on. But any alien here in the United States, any foreigner, non-U.S. citizen — sure. And as you know, the Department of Justice under Ashcroft issued circulars to all United States attorneys to direct the FBI to go out and interview 5000 Arabs and Muslims from the Middle East who are foreigners. Any one of them could be picked up and detained. Yesterday's *Wall Street Journal* [November 15, 2001] announced that Ashcroft has instituted indefinite detention for aliens. Those regulations just came out. So we now have 1200 or so already detained; there could be another 5000. And any one of these people could be subjected to kangaroo court proceedings pursuant to President Bush's executive order. As I said, I know from personal experience that certainly one out of the three military court-martial proceedings that I participated in and argued in, on behalf of members of the United States armed forces who acted as a matter of principle — and I did appear pro bono — one out of three was a total kangaroo court proceeding. And that was subject to all the protections in the Uniform Code of Military Justice and the Manual for Courts-Martial, which does not apply here. And it was still a kangaroo court proceeding! And that was one out of three. I would not say the other two were kangaroo court proceedings but, based on my experience, military justice is to justice as military music to music.

Here is another point I'd like to clarify. You've mentioned the Third and Fourth Geneva Conventions — both of those conventions took place in '49. Were there later Geneva Conventions?

Yes, there is the Geneva Protocol I of 1977 and the Geneva Protocol II of 1977 as well. They have some additional rules. But the basic treatment for combatants is set forth in the Third Geneva Convention of 1949. That, as I said, protects United States armed forces now in hostilities in Afghanistan, unless of course we're now saying we are not going to give similar protection to Al Qaeda and Taliban fighters. That opens the door for reprisals against our own armed forces.

One more question: What can people do to express their opinions about what's happening?

Well, let me say this. I'm a political independent — I'm neither a Democrat nor a Republican. I've worked with people of good faith and good will of all political parties in this country. I think that given this executive order, which simply is astounding, and given this massive assault that we have seen being undertaken against civil rights and civil liberties here in the United States, there is one alternative that people, both conservatives — who, by the way, fought off the Ashcroft police state bill in the House (it was not the liberal Democrats, it was conservative Republicans) — and Libertarians and those liberals who are concerned, can consider. That alternative is to start a national campaign to impeach President Bush for high crimes and misdemeanors, for violating the Constitution of the United States of America. I think that under the current circumstances it's one of the very few options we really have at this point. I think this executive order goes beyond the pale, and it shows you the mentality of people like Ashcroft, Gonzalez, Bush, Cheney, and the rest of them. So if you want to do something now, that would be a proactive approach to trying to stop this rapid movement towards a police state. Clearly, it's only a matter of time before the awesome powers of the FBI and the CIA — powers given to them in the Ashcroft police state bill — are turned against the American people. And I think that under those circumstances, impeachment is really the only alternative we have.

MICHAEL TOMS

What Democracy Is Not

The following was written two weeks after 9-11 and continues to be relevant because media polls are rampant. Clearly, the U.S. Congress has been reluctant to challenge the Bush leadership because of his "numbers", meaning that many polls keep reporting that the great majority of Americans are in favor of his actions. The funny thing about media polls is that they rarely report what questions were asked, when they were asked, or how they were asked. Most often, polls are based upon yes or no questions, an either-or dichotomy. Having other choices is not an option.

When I was growing up in Virginia, there was a "poll tax," which was required to be paid in order to be able to vote. In effect, it was a repressive, anti-democratic measure to inhibit poor people, African-Americans and others, from actually voting. Thankfully, some years later it was eradicated as an unconstitutional infringement on a basic American freedom. Now we face a new and insidious version of the "poll tax." On Tuesday, September 25, 2001, the front page of *The New York Times* displayed the headline, "Poll Finds Support for War and Fear on Economy." According to a survey of 1,216 adults, presumably across America, eight in ten say, "They will forfeit some of their personal freedoms to make the country safer;" seven out of ten consider themselves "very patriotic," and 92% think that "America should take military action." The article goes on to say, "The margin of sampling error is plus or minus three percentage points."

This media creation, much like Dr. Frankenstein's monster, is as dangerous to our freedoms as the "poll tax" because it, too, is a fundamental attack on democracy as envisioned by the Declaration of Independence, the Constitution, and the Bill of Rights. Each of us is an individual. Each of us is an original. Each of us has his or her life experience, perceptions, biases, hopes, fears, memories, and so much more. Media polls are literally a tax on our freedom to think, to arrive at a decision through our own unique process. Polls lump us into groups, audiences, markets, consumers, clicks, etc. Polls are always variable and are a product of the questions, the context, the moment in time, and they result in someone making judgments about what "we" think. I was not a part of this poll. Were you part of this poll? This poll does not speak for me. Does it speak for you? I am struck by the phrase "very patriotic" which, according to this poll, seven out of ten people consider themselves to be, and yet I don't agree with much of what this poll presumes to state on my behalf.

The Oxford Dictionary defines a *patriot* as someone "whose ruling passion is the love of country." Certainly one of my ruling passions (we all have many) is love of my country. The Latin origin of the word *patriotism* is *pater*, meaning "father." If we go beyond the Latin root back to its Greek origins, the word means "love of our ancestors and ancestral roots." Returning to the poll — three out of ten citizens do not consider themselves "very patriotic." What does this mean? Who is asking the questions and why are they asking them? How are they asking them? The reality is that each of us has his or her own perception of what patriotism means. I have mine; you have yours. Polls kill dialogue. They destroy democratic action. Yet this is a time for dialogue. This is a time for coming together in community, for deep listening and for deep questioning. There are no quick answers. I urge you *not* to allow polls to influence your thinking, imagination, or creative process. There are other ways of perceiving and responding to the challenges we face at this time.

THE MEDIA IS THE MESSAGE

THE MEDIA PERMEATE our lives. The times we live in have become known as the Information Age. Yet what information are we consuming and what information is available to us? More mass media are controlled by fewer monolithic corporations than ever before. The choices proliferate, and yet there's little of substance to see or hear. In the midst of abundance, we are starving for substance. I want to acknowledge C-Span and that TV network's around-the-clock coverage of the deliberations of Congress as a point of light in the media darkness. They are the exception that proves the rule. The media power brokers say they're giving the people what they want, and the numbers support their claim. However, most people consuming media don't know they have choices. The news has become infotainment. For example, I now seek out Australian Broadcasting News online and the BBC online or via shortwave radio.

The average television viewer watches eight hours a day. The average radio listener listens three and a half hours a day. This enormous media onslaught is driven by a quest for numbers on the part of the media megaliths to support advertising and profits. This system, in turn, has been given free rein through deregulation — and in the end, the people and/or consumers lose. Olympic levels of distraction, yes, but there is an insidious structure in place which stifles creativity and precludes meaningful dialogue and debate — the core of democracy. Nowhere has this become more apparent than in the post-9-11 era. The almost total absence of significant dialogue in the media has been nothing short of appalling. This lack of a real public conversation has been augmented by the suppression of dissent through the government leadership's labeling of critics as antipatriotic and un-American. However, this nation's first principles are rooted in dialogue and dissent. Long may they flourish.

Paul Hawken

Saving the World

In the course of my work over the years, I have encountered Paul Hawken at various stages of his journey. From his early book about the Findhorn Community in Scotland to his most recent, Natural Capitalism, written with Amory and Hunter Lovins, I have observed that Paul lets no moss grow under his feet. A committed environmentalist and author, he was propelled by the success of his books The Next Economy, Growing a Business, and The Ecology of Commerce into the growing circle of those advocating business reform and sustainability. He is not afraid to speak out for what he believes and is being heard at some of the highest levels of business and government.

PAUL: What is noticeable is that in the language of war, which is what we're hearing, there is a confliction of language. It takes distinctions and differences that we are accustomed to making and then smooshes them together. In other words, the world becomes simple, overly simple. Emotions become simpler, and fears become straightjacketed. We all have fear, but now the fears are channeled by the media. I think a lot of people in the progressive movement felt somewhat obliterated, not just simply by the event — I think every person felt that — but obliterated in the sense that a right-wing agenda has taken over the political and media landscapes, almost without question or comment.

What the social and environmental justice movements are about is quite the opposite. They're actually about creating new distinctions and expanding differentiation and diversity. Their function in the world is to help us see things more clearly by enabling us to appreciate differences. A sustainable world is about expanding the possibilities for all people. But the language of war — even if you don't actually go to war — does quite the opposite. It compresses sensibilities and gives people a false sense that there is only one choice: conflict. Anything else, it says, would be a capitulation, would make us insecure or defenseless or vulnerable.

MICHAEL: *One of the things that appears to be happening in the media is that there's a great emphasis on patriotism. How would you define patriotism?*

America stands for patriots who question their government. It's interesting that we have become what we fear, much like in the Confucian warning. America was founded by people who questioned authority. America was founded because of corporate abuse. America was founded because people didn't want a small group of people having power over a large group of people. It's ironic that a patriot is now defined as someone who doesn't question the concentration of power in the hands of a small group of people. And it's not just that a small group of people has the power, but that it actually has the power to define the nature of the conflict, the very meaning of it.

Patriotism to me is the courage to call into question conventional wisdom. That has always been what America has stood for. Of course, it is not what America has stood for internationally or in its interventions overseas.

In some ways I think the democracy that was envisioned in 1776 really still survives in some ways in small local communities. That's where democracy really lives. How can we expand that to the national dialogue? In some ways there's almost an isolation that occurs within the beltway of Washington, D.C., as though there's Washington, D.C., and then there's the rest of the nation. What do you see?

Well, of course that democracy was idealized. Democracy in the 1770s was white male landowners getting together and talking about the village and the region. We have, throughout our history, continuously expanded the definition of democracy, step by step by step, and not always with the approval of the majority. That was true with the civil rights movement, the women's movement, etc. So we have to remember that the democracy that we idealize is a recent phenomenon. It's not that old a tradition in America. Thus, it's easy to lose. Actually, we almost have the 1770s democracy back, which is to say that we have rich, white men — there are some people of color, but really, basically rich white men — deciding the future and destiny of this country.

I don't believe you restore democracy in the way that we imagine it, the way we were taught in our civics courses in junior high school, until you separate money and government, until you separate business and government, until government actually is responsive to people and business is responsive to stakeholders ¾ which is the way it should be. Business and government can then have a conversation, a dialogue, but a conversation that is not tainted, influenced, or expressed by money. As long as that pecuniary expression is there, you have an oligarchy, which is what we live in. It's a plutocratic oligarchy, a government run and paid for by big business. Until the American people find that their best interests are not served that way, we're going to continue to have such a governing structure. I don't know what kind of events, awakenings, or situations will call forth the recognition that, in fact, we have a government that works for a very small number of people and that a very large number of people pay the price. The rest of the world sees that. That's what's so interesting. The rest of the world sees that very clearly. It's very hard for Americans to see it within their borders.

How does that come about?

The media. We don't have diverse media. We have a medium of television, radio, and so forth. But we haven't got media in a plural sense. We do in the sense that there are different types of media. But when we think of media, we think of many voices, many modalities of expression, so that we can have a balanced view. We just don't have that any more. We have Rupert Murdoch, we have AOL Time Warner ... It was Ted Turner who said not so long ago that there are going to be two media companies in the world when this is all over and that he wants to be part of one of them. I don't think he was saying that approvingly or disapprovingly; I think he was just talking matter-of-factly. And he is part of one of them.

One of the things I've noticed is that the Internet has become almost like an antidote to the major mass media. I've noticed on the Internet, and maybe the circle that revolves around it, that literally hundreds and hundreds of voices appear with very different views than we're seeing in the major media. It's almost like going back, as we've been talking about, to the 1770s, to the Committees of Correspondence, which were groups of people in villages and towns across the colonies that met and then passed on what they found to other villages and towns. That process catalyzed the American Revolution. It's almost as though that's happening now on the Internet. So there is that kind of other voice out there, albeit on the Internet and I think it shows what can happen.

You're quite right, the Arundhati Roy pieces that were published in The Guardian were submitted to the major media in this country — The New York Times, The New Yorker, and so forth — and they were turned down. These are brilliant pieces and they were turned down for conflicting reasons. Some said there was too much content, others said there wasn't enough. It's just ridiculous. Here she is, really one of the clearest voices in the world today, speaking about the resistance to globalization and corporatization, and we don't hear her in this country.

At the same time, there are also a lot of conservative or right-wing list serves out there; there are racist list serves, too. There are list serves that are fomenting harassment of people of color from South Asia. So the Internet is not an unalloyed good. Since September 11, I have been deluged with extraordinary articles and links, which I read, save, and file. It has made me at once better informed and aware, too, of how ignorant I have been of Islam, of the situation in the Middle East, its history, the historical agreement with Ibn Saud, etc. Basically we are the major supporters of the only country in the world that's named after a family. And we wonder why the natives are restless. We are oblivious about what our support has done to people, about the suffering it has caused, the polarization of income, the violation of cultures that we are constantly feeding through our dependence on oil.

What is sustaining you personally in this new time that we've all entered?

The wildness ...the outdoors ... whether it's in the woods or on the water. I live on the water. Every year the coots, pintails, goldeneyes, and Cinnamon Teals come back right around this time. There's one coot, and it comes back to my boat every year. It's been doing it for at least five years. It will pretty much eat not quite out of your hand, but almost. And it came back yesterday. You really can't distinguish it from the others, except that it comes kind of wiggling its tail through the water to my float, and it looks up, as if to defy impermanence. I'm not big on feeding food to wild animals, and I didn't start out feeding this one. But the person who began feeding it left the area, and so it comes back every year.

Wildness lets one better see the insanity, the small-mindedness of the positions and views that informed both the attack on America — the World Trade Center and the Pentagon —and the worldviews that precipitated it. And as helpful as the Internet is, I also think too much information can be toxic. You can get so absorbed by it that you lose a sense of balance, a sense of self, a sense of relationship, a sense that life is going to continue on this planet, one way or the other. From that point of view, looking over the mountains and hills to an urban environment, you realize how far we have wandered from who we are. You don't know who you are unless you know where you are, and you don't know where you are unless you can identify the plants and the grasses and the soils and the rocks around you.

Such as in the watershed in which you live?

Exactly. For me, it's just about walking into wildness and trying to let some of that stuff drop away. It's about regaining a view that provides you with a kind of a hope, a real hope, a hope that has feet and legs, a hope that can walk, can stand up — a practical, grounded hope.

Just like you were saying, there's a window of opportunity here. I went to a university eight or nine days after the attack, and I spoke to the faculty first. Then I gave a public presentation. At the faculty Q & A, I was asked if what I said had changed since September 11?

At first, it didn't change what I said. But it certainly changed me, who was saying it.

It used to be that people would kid me — actually, mostly my kids. They'd say, "Dad, you're just trying to save the world. Get a life!"

And I thought they had a point.

But after September 11, I think trying to save the world is exactly what every person has to do.

I think we all came here to planet Earth to do that.

Yes, and it's a good thing. It's real clear now what to do for the rest of our lives. And that's a blessing.

NORMAN SOLOMON

The Orwellian Zone

"I try, therefore I am," has become the modern-day American axiom. Many have come to believe that acquisition and ownership will guarantee a better place on the societal ladder, and this belief has become tightly woven into the fabric of our national consciousness. Shortly after 9-11, we saw the President of the United States using the media to encourage Americans to go back to shopping, "to return to normal." In a profound way, the media, which is supposed to inform us about these things, often helps to put us to sleep and to distract us from what's important and relevant. Television programming has reached the level of a national joke. Numerous studies continue to point to the connection between television programming and violence in society as well as to its clear attempt to foster rampant consumerism. Not hard to imagine, considering that that's what commercial sponsors want us to do: buy more. Conglomerates dominate the mass media, and the news

media with their addiction to ratings have evolved into infotainment. At the same time, a few lights flicker brightly here and there, like New Dimensions Radio, Democracy Now, *CommonDreams.org, David Barsamian's* Alternative Radio, *David Freudberg's* Humankind *public radio series,* Counterspin *and* FAIR, *Mark Sommer's* Mainstream Media Project, *and* The Institute for Public Accuracy. *Its founder,* Norman Solomon, *whose syndicated column and books I discovered long before meeting him, is one of those pointriding journalists willing to joust with the media megalith, dedicated to pulling back the curtain to reveal the truth of the Wizards of Media Oz — which he does consistently throughout his writings.*

NORMAN: One of the aspects I've found really striking is the kind of mirroring that takes place once the killing is under way. President Bush said early on in this crisis, in mid-September, that this is a battle between good and evil. Increasingly, it seems that the energy which is so destructive is bouncing back and forth between the adversaries, so that the Taliban and the U.S. are both saying not only that the other is terrorist but also that the entire goodness is on our side and the entire evil is on the other side. It may be a human characteristic to do that, but when that is the mode of media communication, then it shuts down people's capacities to look at the complexity of history. This helps to define the limits of public discourse. So one of the challenges is for people at the grass-roots level to discard this good-versus-evil rhetoric and to look at how we all could live constructively on the planet together.

MICHAEL: *How do you see that from the standpoint of what's happening with the major mass media now? How do you see the reportage on this war?*

Well, in the months since September 11 there's been a real split in the coverage. There's been — within the limits of what the medium is, whether it's radio or TV or print or whatever — some very empathetic coverage of the humanistic aspects of the stories: the coverage of the suffering, particularly in lower Manhattan, and the very human elements. But at the same time, when the major media have looked at the actual policy issues and at what should be done and the history and the roots of how we got into this very horrible situation, there's been a real shutdown. We've entered, perhaps more than ever before in U.S. mass media, a kind of Orwellian zone. It's a kind of history-free zone or, to change the imagery, kind of a free-fire zone for propaganda. Something has locked in that says we're at war, which was the initial response from the U.S. government on September 11 and has been ever since. That seems to have created this enormous momentum in the mass media such that, since we're at war, as journalists we have to serve the government in its war aims.

So there's no receptivity to understanding how the cycle of violence has gotten us where we are. There's been very little openness to talking about how the
U.S. government's actions have been integral to the cycle of violence. It's an
enactment of Gandhi's statement that's been used by many activists in recent
weeks: "An eye for an eye makes the whole world blind." In a sense the U.S.
news media, by getting into that mode, has blinded itself and is a force for blind-
ing us. As a result, it becomes very difficult for us to truly understand this
rhetorical question that is being tossed about, "Why do they hate us?"

If we go back to the previous time that the U.S. engaged in military retaliation because of terrorism, which was in 1998 after the two U.S. embassies
were bombed in Africa, we find that the U.S. media just won't go there and
won't look at it. There are passing references to the 1998 U.S. cruise missile
attack on the pharmaceutical plant in Sudan. But just as a case in point, if we
really were to look at the facts we could understand how reliance on military
response has actually fed into the cycle of violence. When we're in that cycle,
what goes around does come around. In that instance the U.S. destroyed a
plant that was creating at least half of the total pharmaceutical drugs for the
very impoverished country of Sudan. The best estimates we have are that perhaps ten thousand people in Sudan have died as a result, because of a lack of
access to basic, lifesaving drugs produced by that plant. When Sudan went to
the United Nations for an inquiry, the U.S. government blocked the U.N. from
investigating the exact human toll of that attack on Sudan. This is an example.
What took place is a historical, human reality. It's also a metaphor for how we
as a society tend to wink at the murderous actions done with our tax dollars, in
our names.

If there's any silver lining to the horrific events of September 11 and their
aftermath, it's about people's vocal and palpable yearning for peace being
expressed through vigils in the United States every day around the country. It's
about a growing awareness among many people that this is a destructive course,
an awareness that if we truly revere life we don't make war, but we creatively find
ways to protect and affirm life.

*That's well said. In today's news we're hearing about major alerts. President Bush
has stated that more terrorist attacks are likely to happen in the future. Anthrax
scares, military law in cities and airports, increased surveillance everywhere, but is
that making anyone more secure?*

I think this is a fundamental question. What's wrong with this picture? We have
been told that the U.S. and Britain bombed Afghanistan to safeguard and
increase our security here at home, but as soon as the U.S. and British attacks
on Afghanistan began on Sunday, October 7, the FBI issued a heightened alert

warning that the probability of a terrorist attack on the United States had just spiked upward. It's a basic contradiction. When I try to figure out what risks are involved — whether it's boosting the cycle of violence that would include the likelihood of more terrorist attacks in the U.S. or destabilizing the Pakistani government, which has twenty or thirty nuclear weapons in its arsenal, or the possibility that this would add to violence and murders on a large scale in various countries that would then spin into further cycles of violence — I don't see how, in any way, the war in Afghanistan is worth the risks. Any purported benefits seem vastly overshadowed in human terms by the logical consequences. To me, all of that is a message that says we need the peace movement to become stronger and stronger. It's really our only hope.

We're hearing a lot about patriotism, and it's being bandied about as something that means waving the flag, America moving forward, defending democracy, and defending freedom. What is your view and definition of patriotism?

The deeper aspects of patriotism, I feel, involve a love of country as a home for people with whom we share space, with whom we share a mixture of heritage and experiences and multidimensional cultural experiences and possibilities. The authentic forms of love of country, it seems to me, are most deep and life-affirming if they are part of love of the planet, and love of life, and sharing together as people and, for that matter, the whole ecological reality of the planet. I'm afraid that in contrast to those aspects of patriotism, which are very real for many people, there is this overlay that uses the flag to justify any and all decisions made by the top officials of the U.S. government.

In the weeks following September 11, we've experienced, I think, a kind of massive propaganda, a bait-and-switch operation, where many people put out the flag in mid-September and late September, exactly as an expression of grief, of human solidarity, and of love of country. Then in early October, as the U.S. launched missile and bomber attacks on Afghanistan, the bait-and-switch process went into its completion phase. Those same American flags were then utilized by news media in the imagery, and in the popular kind of a context, to affix Old Glory onto this military blitz on Afghanistan — the dropping of bombs, the launching of missiles.

I saw an MSNBC news report in early October 2001, which showed footage of U.S. equipment and planes on an aircraft carrier, and they had an American flag waving in the background. Then there was footage of some warheads sitting on the deck, and the letters NYPD had been scrawled on the warheads. The message was intended to telescope the experience of the last few weeks — the pride in the firefighters and the police who risked and in some cases lost their lives going into the World Trade Center, all that emotion and human connection was being grafted and overlaid onto the weapons that were going to be used to take innocent lives that certainly are just as precious as those that were lost on September 11.

What can individuals do at this time? What are your thoughts and recommendations?

I feel that people communicating with each other, outside of and beyond the major mainstream media, is absolutely crucial. Whether it's through the New Dimensions website (www.newdimensions.org) or any number of other websites — like www.zmag.org or www.accuracy.org, the website of the organization I'm part of, the Institute for Public Accuracy, or others — it's crucial to share information and then use the information in our own communities to organize vigils, peace rallies, and educational events and outreach. It's important to go out into the community, not in an argumentative way but in a very assertive way, and to create dialogue, to petition and rally to call for peace, and to manifest in ways that can be heard and understood by the entire public, in ways that can create grass-roots pressure for peace on elected officials in this country.

Robert Jensen

Hope Goes a Long Way

Robert Jensen *is a man of hope who speaks from a grounded place, recognizing that difficult challenges confront us, but not unwilling to face them. He is radical in the truest sense of the term — he is "of the root; far reaching, thorough; going to the root." We need people like Robert Jensen if we are to see a renewal of this nation's democratic vision. In his words, "Real hope — the belief in the authentic underpinnings of hope — is radical. The belief that people are not evil and stupid, not consigned merely to live out pre-determined roles in illegitimate structures of authority, is radical. The willingness to act publicly on that hope and belief is radical." Here, he speaks to the times.*

ROBERT: Like most Americans, those of us who have done antiwar activism or have been critical of American foreign policy are sort of shocked. It's been like getting the wind knocked out of you. It took us a long time just to breathe again. But by the end of that first day, by the end of September 11, it was quite clear that the Bush administration and, in fact, the Democrats in Congress were ready to wage war, and not just any kind of war. Already, from the beginning, the hints were that this would be a different kind of war. They were talking about massive military retaliation against an enemy that was not clearly drawn. By the next week when President Bush gave his speech, it was clear we were talking about an unlimited war against endless enemies. In doing so, in some sense I think the Bush administration took away our time to grieve the tragedy we all had to live with, took away the time in which we could have made sense of it. It forced those of us with an antiwar background to mobilize, to take action to try and head off what is going to be a disaster of unprecedented proportions if the Bush administration goes forward with the kind of plans they've been talking about. There's already dissension within the administration, and it may be that those plans will be headed off.

It's so important for citizens to become active and to make their voices heard. We've often been accused of being insensitive or of acting in bad taste when bringing up these kinds of questions, but I don't think that's the case at all. I think, in fact, that it does no good to the people who have died if the United States goes off from this tragedy and creates a kind of apocalyptic scenario in the world that is only going to end in more death, more destruction, without, in the end, making the United States any more secure. I will not feel more secure when I wake up in the morning and I find out there is a massive military reaction by the United States.

So for all of those reasons, those of us with an antiwar background have been mobilizing. What's so hopeful is that there are people joining us who have never been involved in organized politics before, and especially never involved in left or progressive or antiwar politics. There are a lot of people who just have a feeling in their gut that the way these people in Washington are talking is very dangerous. We're having attendance at organizational meetings and teach-ins that is three, four times what we would have ever had in the past. It may be that a lot of the motivation that's bringing people to these meetings, that's bringing people to teach-ins, is this sort of visceral understanding that there's something very dangerous about what they're planning in the White House and in the Pentagon and in the State Department now. I really do hope that, whether as a result of our efforts or of sanity coming down upon the White House in some other form, it turns out that we're wrong, that those plans never get put into action. But I think one of the ways we can make sure they never come to be realized is to become politically active.

There's something very strange going on in this country right now. We live in a democracy, and the fundamental concept in a democracy is that the people are sovereign and the leaders do our bidding. What that means, if it means anything, is that people have to have a role in formulating policy. They have to have a role in speaking about those policies. But a very scary thing is happening now: if you object to the President's policies, you are now being called anti-American or a traitor or unpatriotic. But something is just turned on its head there. In fact, to be a citizen in a democracy means to take responsibility for evaluating the policies that our leaders put forward. So when people say you are un-American because you are not rallying around the President, my response is that I would never want to rally around a President. I don't think that's the appropriate way to proceed in a democracy. One makes an evaluation of what policies are important and sensible and sane, and then one pursues support for those policies. If that puts me in conflict with the President, well then, so be it. That is the nature of a democracy. The fact that we are in a time of great crisis and tragedy and people are still trying to cope emotionally does not mean we should give up our rights as citizens to dissent. In fact, it's at a time of great crisis that dissent is most important because so many people are feeling so much pain.

It's difficult, in the middle of that much pain, to see and to evaluate. And yet, that's what we need to do as a people, to come together, not just to unify and grieve, which is very important, but to come together to evaluate and debate. It's at this time that this kind of debate is more necessary than ever. I really hope that the people in Washington and the people in the media will back off from this talk of patriotism being defined only as support for the President's policies, and start to understand that we do live in a nation in which we are all morally responsible for coming to terms with those policies and making our own judgments and trying to make our voices heard.

MICHAEL: *That's very clear. You have mentioned democracy and the democratic vision that created this country, going back to the 1770s. Clearly our founders were very concerned about individual citizen participation. It seems that this is a time when we really need to return to that vision. What do you think?*

Well, I think we should be honest about the founders. They wanted citizen participation for certain kinds of citizens. They were not interested in widespread citizen participation. One of the great fears of the founders was that the masses would in fact take this opportunity to participate too much.

But still, within their own circles there was this animating vision of participation and of sovereignty of the people. I think you're right on that count. It is a tradition we can draw upon: we can realize that even in times of war it's not only necessary to have that kind of participation, but it's more important than ever. It's more essential because there's so much on the line, especially when you're in a nation that has the most extensive destructive capacity that's ever existed on the planet. What better time is there to weigh in as a citizen when so much is on the line? There's an enormous amount at stake, not only for the people around the world who may be the victims if, in fact, the United States does go off on very aggressive and very belligerent military action, but here at home we have a self-interest in this as well. We're not going to make the world safe with that kind of military action. If we're going to achieve real security for the people of the United States, we're going to have to start talking about international cooperation in the law enforcement efforts to bring terrorism to justice, not about military action taken unilaterally to destroy, with the hope that somehow we'll get the terrorists. I doubt this is a very effective plan.

What is personally sustaining you in this time?

Well, of course in the end what sustains one is hope. And hope is sometimes all we have to lean on. But beyond that, of course, what sustains me is the personal relationships, the political relationships with people whom I trust, the knowledge that in this crisis time we can come together. I've been working politically here in Austin, Texas, where I live, with a very small group of people for about three or four years, and I thank the heavens that they were here when we mobilized because these were people I could trust, just as they could trust me. There was no question about commitment, there was no question about whether we would engage ourselves in this.

When certain troubles came down on my head at my employment, when the president of my university publicly condemned me for having what he called very foolish ideas, in a sense it didn't matter. The most powerful man on my campus could say whatever he wanted, because I had a community of people — a small community, I will admit, but a very loyal community — that I could lean on for the support that I needed. And I think they know they can lean on me.

So at two in the morning when you've just finished your last meeting and writing your last analysis, and you go home and you're exhausted and you're scared because you don't know whether the world is going to have a happy ending here, that's where the strength comes from. It's from people. But that's true of all our lives, in any context. That's what makes living make sense — the people we connect to.

BEAU GROSSCUP

Probing the Paradoxes

Seeing through the contradictions and going beyond the media conditioning, Beau Grosscup *focuses on the political rhetoric and the Orwellian unspeak. Being selective about the media we consume, reading between the lines, and opening our hearts while we feed our minds will enable us to act more in balance. It's not a matter of being cynical but rather of seeing the reality for what it is, of staying the course with hope and joy. The paradox here is that so many of history's great human accomplishments actually began as "hopeless causes."*

BEAU: It's been one month now since the September 11 events, and the initial response of mourning, of compassion — and obviously we must include the call for revenge — has passed for the most part. Hopefully we're beginning to ask the question, "Why?" instead of just focusing on the question, "Whom?" When we do that on the issue of terrorism, we have to realize that these events don't happen in a political vacuum. That's uncomfortable for Americans who have been encouraged to think of terrorism in very polarized and black-and-white terms — that is to say, it's a deed done by others and not by us, it comes from foreigners and foreign cultures, it's not something that we engage in. We've been encouraged to believe that when the United States uses power abroad, we do so in a benevolent and righteous fashion for righteous and humanitarian reasons. In that context, the question, "Why?" is going to lead to a plethora of information and discussion and deep debate, as it should, including debate about the United States and its role in the world.

What we have to understand is that if we accept the notion that these events don't happen in a political vacuum, we have to focus on questions like, "What has been our role in the world? How do others view us and our actions abroad? Does that have anything to do with these events?" That's going to be very hard for Americans, particularly those from the patriotic community, which is different from the jingoistic community that holds an "America, right or wrong"

60

perspective. American patriots have a right and a responsibility to make up their own minds about what is in their country's interest. It's going to be a difficult discussion because the world has watched as the United States has, for one thing, invoked sanctions on Iraq for ten years now, which has killed hundreds of thousands of civilians, half of them children. For another, the United States purposely dropped bombs on civilian targets in Serbia and Kosovo. Again, most Americans understand that terrorism has something to do with violence or the threat of violence against civilians. That's why we're so distressed by what happened on September 11, because from our vantage point those were innocent, civilian Americans.

But the world has watched us do these kinds of things. It has also watched the United States' contradictory stance on terrorism with regard to people like Osama bin Laden and Iraq's leader Saddam Hussein. Both of these men have carried out terrorist acts on our behalf, using the instrument of terrorism in the 1980's with our encouragement. Then in the 1990s and beyond, they're being chastised for using those same instruments. The world watches those contradictions.

It also watches the American leaders since Jimmy Carter attempt to take the high moral ground on the issue of terrorism. The world sees that contradiction and obviously, as well as unfortunately, there are people around the world who act on those contradictions and say, "Well, what's good for the goose is good for the gander." As uncomfortable as those conclusions or those decisions or those facts are for the American populace, it's important that we break through our polarized image of terrorism and understand that in many ways the enemy is us. That is to say, we do use the instrument of terrorism as well, and people all around the world realize it. That doesn't mean the United States deserved what happened, but it does help us to understand the context in which these events occur.

MICHAEL: *What about the bombing in Afghanistan and the killing of innocent civilians?*

Well, again, this is what the world is watching, just as they watched the missiles go into Khartoum, just as they watched the missiles go into Afghanistan in 1998, when civilians were killed. They're saying, "Why are you engaged in a war on terrorism by using the instrument of terror yourself?" They're also — particularly the more moderate and understanding and supportive members of the world communities, whether they be nationalist or religious or economic-social —obviously abhorred by that reaction. It does seem to be a reaction driven by revenge. It does seem to be a reaction driven by a contradiction that says we're engaged in a war on terrorism and yet we're going to use the instrument of terrorism on our behalf when we deem appropriate. And, by the way, we'll find rationalities for using it.

Whenever civilian casualties are brought up on TV, the military spokesmen say that that's a result of the Taliban putting civilians in the way of the military targets. Of course there's going to be "collateral damage," but that's not our fault. That's not our responsibility, that's the responsibility of the Taliban. So there's going to be debate going on but, again, the world is watching and they may not accept those kinds of rationalizations.

You mention watching the media. How do you feel about what the U.S. media are reporting and how they're presenting what's going on?

I think the reporting of the major media is a product of the fact that the military has shut them off from the central information that they require in order to be critics. Even if they wanted to be critics of American policy, they haven't been allowed. The military learned a lesson from Vietnam, and that is that you can't allow independent reporting of U.S. foreign policy, particularly in times of war. So in part I understand why they've gotten such limited information. At the same time I abhor the "rah-rah" jingoistic attitude of many of the commentators, who find ways to justify and rationalize U.S. policy and who ignore the question of how other people are looking at us, of what they are thinking, and of what impact that has in terms of those people seeking revenge against the United States for these acts.

That's a good point. I think that for the five days following September 11, the lid was on with regard to civilian reporting of what they're calling "collateral damage," that is, the deaths of civilians. But really, you can't control that. You can only control it for a few days because reports come in from other media elsewhere in the world.

Yes. But remember that the Bush administration has made it very clear: "You're either with us or you're against us" in the war against terrorism. Having polarized the situation and divided the world in that very stark black-and-white fashion, they are able to say to these people who are critical, these other media sources who are obviously bringing this information to the fore, "Hey, you are sympathizing with the terrorists." That attitude is going to be a very hard to break through.

What about civil liberties? In airports we now have martial law; in New York City there is, essentially, martial law. How do you feel about that?

That has been a problem for me for a long time. The fact is that we live in a liberal democratic society in which there's always going to be this tension between individual rights and the need for public safety. What's driving these kinds of actions is the notion that there is a security fix to terrorism. Here again, we're having to listen to people who are being called "terrorist experts" and "national security advisors," who argue that there is a security fix to terrorism. The American public needs to try to break through that. There are so many instances of tight security — for example, at the Olympics in Atlanta — where, despite all the security, there was an act of terrorism. We should learn something from that. We should also be aware of the fact that there are people who are willing and eager to change the fundamental nature of our society, and we need to publicly work against that with public sentiments, with public plans, with arguments for the maintenance of individual liberties. And we need to make those arguments to our political leadership.

So give me some insight as to how one could do something about that. Is it writing to your congressman? Is it going out on the street and holding a poster? What do you suggest?

The first thing I suggest is that we have got to individually and collectively challenge this incomplete image of terrorism that we have been encouraged to accept. As citizens of this country we need to apply the same analytic framework we use when we look at the issues concerning the United States. We're a pluralistic society; there are different interpretations of what's going on, and we're proud of all those things and need to engage in debate. We need to apply that to the issue of terrorism, particularly terrorism abroad, because when we do that it breaks through the image of a monolithic enemy, whether it be Islam or whether it be the Palestinians, the Arab mind, whatever it might be. It breaks through that notion so we can begin to understand that the more moderate members of those communities are on our side in terms of this search for the answers to terrorism and the search for justice and equality. But we've got to do that. We've got to break through that imagery on an individual basis and explore the complex nature of terrorism, even if it means exploring and beginning to come to terms with our participation in that dastardly deed.

So in this time, what is personally sustaining you as you experience the grief and trauma of these events?

Really, it's a commitment to patriotism — a commitment to the notion that I as an individual citizen have a right and a responsibility to judge these events with an open eye, without a reflex action. And it's the understanding that the American public, given a chance, given an opportunity, will do the same. If we'll do that, then we'll make ourselves a better society. We'll also be able to deal with the contradictory nature of U.S. policy abroad, and the way that people respond to that contradictory policy. That's what sustains me.

Anita Roddick, OBE

Outrage as Energizer

The rise of the vigilante consumer challenging the corporate culture and of the concerned citizen exercising the domestic right of dissent, has led to a worldwide movement opposing globalization. Anita Roddick, founder of The Body Shop, has, with the refreshing candor and directness typical of her, often spoken about poverty, crime, hunger, low wages, environmental deterioration, and other problems associated with globalization, while at the same time offering practical solutions and ways that individuals can make a difference and create a world that works for all. Her media savvy is legendary. She's someone who has used the media well to communicate her values. Outraged by the fallout from oil exploration and its infrastructure in Nigeria, she was, together with other NGOs, part of a campaign on behalf of Ogoni tribespeople that resulted in the giant oil multinational Shell issuing a revised operating charter which committed the company to human rights and sustainable development. She is a spiritual warrior in the world.

ANITA: The major insight is that there will be no more isolationism, that everybody has to work together. There won't be any "This doesn't touch me, this doesn't affect me." This new fear, this terror, is so different, has never been part of our scenario. We should have to rethink the enormous amount of money we spend on military budgets because when nineteen men with makeshift knives can cause this much mayhem, it doesn't make sense any more. I think there will be a search for a real understanding of anything that may cause this type of terrorism, and we should look for it under every stone. Is it economic injustice? Is it the rich against the poor? What are we doing that is fueling this type of thinking? We should really look at the role that religious fundamentalism is playing, and understand it, and see how it's affecting our lives. But mostly, what we need now is a revolution in kindness.

MICHAEL: *Say more about this " revolution in kindness." What do you mean by that?*

I mean that we have to look at any proximate solution to help the weak and the frail. We have to extend this enormous wealth that we have, this economic wealth we have in a few countries, and be measured by how generous we are. I think we have to stop this xenophobia. We have to rethink some of our institutions. What are we teaching young people in American business schools? Are they just developing the same status quo, this belief that maximizing profits, that accumulation of wealth is all that matters? Maybe what is needed now is a real change in education that embraces not a religious education, but a spiritual education. The Gandhian philosophy would be to focus on how you look after, how you're in service to the weak and frail. If we put any amount of our energy into helping the weak and the frail, with all the creative solutions that we have, we can see at least a light at the end of the tunnel.

What is personally sustaining you in this new time?

Outrage! It's the sense that I cannot *not* do something. I can't just sit and think that this doesn't affect me. We're at the beginning of this new millennium, and we're still at each other's throats, we'll still acting in heinous ways. I can't spend time thinking and articulating. I've got to spend my entire time looking for solutions — whether it's supporting economic initiatives in Peru or whatever. For me, the biggest catastrophe out there is poverty, so I've got to work toward finding any solutions that would offer a light at the end of the tunnel of poverty, and also toward finding any solutions regarding loneliness. In England we have enormous loneliness — bipolar depression that comes out of loneliness. Anything that any one of us can do to shave away loneliness is, I think, a way to help us see a light at the end of the tunnel.

ANNA CODY

How We See and Are Seen

The Center for Economic and Social Rights (CESR) was established in 1993 to promote social justice through human rights. CESR works with social scientists and local partners in affected communities to document rights violations, to advocate for changes in policies that impoverish and exploit people, and to mobilize grass-roots pressure for social change.

Anna Cody, an Australian who lives in the United States, but has spent time in other countries as well, is a program coordinator for CESR. Because of her organization's interest in what is happening to civilians in Afghanistan, I was led to speak with her.

MICHAEL: *Do you have any suggestions as to what individuals can do to express themselves about the war on terrorism?*

ANNA: Well, I'd suggest that you contact your congressperson and express your concern for how civilians are being affected in Afghanistan. I think one of the most worrying parts of this is that here in the United States we were all appalled at the effects on civilians when the World Trade Center were attacked. What's happening in Afghanistan is that it's civilians who are paying the price for having Osama bin Laden in their country. That's just not fair. It's not right. And it shouldn't be happening.

In this time, what's been personally sustaining you since the events of 9-11?

I'm Catholic, so I would say certainly faith, on some level, a belief in a god of surprises, a belief that unexpected things can happen. I keep hoping that unexpected things will happen in a good and positive way. I believe very strongly that military attacks are not the right response. And so it is very important to make my voice heard. When I was in high school learning about the Second World War, I thought there was no way our societies would ever do such a stupid thing again. I'm shocked and appalled that we continue to have wars and expect to be able to change things in that way.

Are you hopeful?

I'm hopeful about some things. But whether or not there'll be a change, whether or not large numbers of people will die in Afghanistan — I'm very concerned about that. Probably the area that gives me the most hope is the Middle East and the possible peace process between Palestinians and Israel. That would be the area that I would feel most hopeful about, politically.

Another area of hope is the discussion about Islam, and perhaps some greater understanding of the differences, the diversity, the complexity of any religion, including Islam. That might be another thing that comes out of this.

Have you always been in the United States?

No. I'm Australian. I have lived in the United States, and I've also lived in Central America for some time.

As someone who was born in Australia, who now lives in the United States, who has spent time in other countries, what do you feel about how the world views the United States? It seems in some ways that we in the United States are very much insulated from the rest of the world. What do you think?

I think that may have been part of the big shock and the horror of what happened on September 11 and afterward. I think there are real problems within the United States. People outside the United States generally don't have a clear picture of what it's like — the different voices, the voices of dissent, the community organizing, the alternative media. None of that gets any coverage outside of the United States. So what people outside of this country see is a very limited view of the United States. It focuses on wealth. It doesn't look at the poverty that exists within these borders, and the human rights abuses within this country.

And I think that people within the United States are generally not encouraged to look closely at the rest of the world because this is such a powerful nation, because it's so big, because it's such a large economy. For whatever reasons, they don't look outside, don't start to put themselves in other people's shoes. In a place like Australia, which has eighteen million people, we're constantly looking outside. We're constantly getting sources of information from all around the world. So we have an idea of how we're seen, as Australians, whereas I think Americans haven't had to think about how they are seen from the outside.

Perhaps this whole experience will encourage that.

GIVING PEACE A VOICE

JOHN LENNON'S SONGS "Give Peace a Chance" and "Imagine" still ring in my ears thirty odd years later. Holding the possibility of peace in the world begins within us. Even though no one predicted the fall of the Berlin Wall, it occurred because some people imagined it. The late Indian philosopher sage J. Krishnamurti always spoke of the conflict within having to be addressed in order for peace to be possible. My interpretation of his message is that peace is the absence of conflict both within and without. The external world in many ways mirrors what is inside of us. Through psychological projection we see ourselves in the mirror of the external world. The Swiss psychoanalyst Carl Jung first spoke of projection and the human psyche in terms of light and dark (shadow) sides. Are we courageous enough to seek the terrorist inside us? The shadow or dark side will transform itself when the light of awareness shines through. Just as other nations have a collective light and dark side, so does America. Well known for its generosity and its freedoms on the light side, it too possesses this shadow, for example the destruction of the Native American culture, the suppression of Black Americans, the patriarchal dominance of its political life, the support of dictatorship regimes throughout the world. The time is upon us all to own our shadow and to do the difficult work necessary to manifest peace in all our actions daily, holding the possibility that peace will emerge in the world around us — one day at a time.

HOWARD ZINN

Through the Lens of History

A renowned historian who has authored numerous books including his epic masterpiece A People's History of the United States *and his autobiography* You Can't Be Neutral on a Moving Train, *Howard Zinn was one of Alice Walker's mentors at Spelman College, where he served as professor.*

Following 9-11, he said, "The images on television horrified and sickened me. Then our political leaders came on television, and I was horrified and sickened again. They spoke of retaliation, of vengeance, of punishment. I thought: they have learned nothing, absolutely nothing, from the history of the 20th century, from a hundred years of retaliation, vengeance, war, a hundred years of terrorism and counter-terrorism, of violence met with violence in an unending cycle of stupidity." I asked Professor Zinn about the new time we have entered since 9-11.

HOWARD: The new time we have entered since 9-11 is a time when for the first time Americans realize that, as powerful as we are, as rich as we are, as much weaponry as we have, we are terribly vulnerable. We used to think it was a matter of nuclear missiles and traditional war. No. Terrorism is different: it makes the most powerful nations vulnerable to small numbers of people who are ingenious and can use technology in their own ways. It's a very new situation for people in the United States; I think it's an opportunity to rethink the position of this country in the world.

MICHAEL: *You've written a book about war,* Howard Zinn on War. *What can we learn from history in this new time we've entered?*

I think one of the things we might learn, especially from the history of the last fifty years, is that violence and military build-up and the technological development of weaponry have all reached the point where we cannot any longer think of war as a viable solution for whatever problems there are in the world, including terrorism, simply because war inevitably involves the indiscriminate killing of large numbers of people. War is a kind of terrorism, and very often its consequences are even greater than the consequences we faced in New York on September 11.

This may force us to rethink the whole question of whether violence, war, or military solutions can really solve the problems we have, because since World War II that's what we've been doing. World War II, unfortunately, put war in a good light — that is, we got accustomed to the idea that there's such a thing as a good war. People fought World War II as a good war, a just war. I say this is unfortunate because we held on to the romantic glow, the moral glow surrounding World War II, and used it to cover every war since, wars which didn't have any of the semblance of morality that World War II had. Those other wars could not by any stretch be considered good wars. As a result, we've engaged in war after war, thinking that they would solve our problems. Of course, they never did. The Korean War didn't, the Vietnam War didn't, the Panamanian War didn't, the Gulf War didn't. They only multiplied the problems that existed. We have to reconsider the whole question of war and begin to think about something we have not been willing to think about, and that is humanitarian solutions, non-military solutions for the problems we face in the world.

With all these different wars we've been dealing with, questions about the "war on terrorism" come up. It's been presented as a long-term war, and we don't even know who the enemy is. It may be the Taliban and Al Qaeda, but beyond that there are all sorts of unidentified people who are our enemy. What about that kind of a war?

That's why to call it a war is misleading the American public. A war has an identifiable enemy, and when you defeat that enemy the war is over. But this is not such a situation. We will defeat the Taliban, but the problem with terrorism will still be there. What the United States did in this case, what the Bush administration did with the support of the Democrats as a bi-partisan policy, was to attempt to handle a problem that was too complex for them to deal with. They simply picked on a place so that they could say, "This is the source. Afghanistan is the source." Even though most of the highjackers came from Saudi Arabia, they said, "Afghanistan is the source. The Taliban are the source, and so we'll concentrate our efforts there, we'll bomb Afghanistan. We'll destroy the Taliban."

And yet, we know that even if we destroyed the Taliban, even if we captured bin Laden, the possibilities for terrorism — the probabilities of terrorism — will still be very strong, simply because the grievances that are behind the terrorism are still there. They exist not just in Afghanistan, not in any one country, not just among a small number of terrorists. They exist among millions of people in the Middle East. But we don't want to face the fact that we have to deal with these very deep-rooted political and economic grievances. So we pick on a country and bomb it and hope that the public will be satisfied, but it certainly will not solve the problem of terrorism. It truly is a long-term problem, and it will remain long-term unless we begin immediately to address the underlying grievances, which have to do with American foreign policy.

Another outgrowth of the "war on terrorism" has been the establishment of military tribunals, the detention of aliens without giving them access to the normal system of justice that we have. What about the impact of these actions on civil liberties?

Unfortunately, those are issues that come up every time we are in a war or a near-war situation. This history goes back a long time. It goes back to the Alien and Sedition Acts of 1798 when we were in a Cold War situation with France. It goes back to the Civil War and to World War I. Anytime we are in a critical situation, a situation of war or near-war, it is very easy to persuade the public that you cannot have your ordinary freedoms. You cannot have freedom of speech. You cannot criticize the war effort. In World War I, two thousand people were prosecuted for speaking out against the war, and an atmosphere was created in which it became very difficult to criticize the war.

Not only that, the Supreme Court laid down the doctrine of a clear and present danger, saying that if there's a clear and present danger you can't have free speech. That makes sense on the face of it, except when you apply it as the Supreme Court did in World War I to a single guy handing out leaflets on the street, opposing the draft and the war. When you look at that and say, "Here's a clear and present danger to the country," you are misleading the public.

It's exactly in time of war, or near-war, that you need the most open discussion, the greatest freedom of speech, because lives are at stake: the government may be sending young people into war and there may be huge numbers of casualties. That should not be done without a full national discussion. We saw the effects of not having a discussion at the time of Vietnam when that incident took place in the Gulf of Tonkin. The government lied to the public about it. Congress immediately went to work drafting a resolution giving the President authority to do whatever he wanted in Southeast Asia, and soon we were at war. There was no public discussion. It took several years of such discussion before the public grew aware of what was going on in Vietnam and created a great movement against the war and brought it to a stop.

We need discussion on whether we are doing the right thing in Afghanistan. We need the public to know what we are doing to the people there. It needs to know that we are terrorizing the people of Afghanistan by driving hundreds of thousands of them from their homes. The public needs to know about that if it wants to make an informed decision about whether we are doing the right thing. If the government begins — as it is already beginning to do — to clamp down on our liberties and make people afraid that they will be detained or wiretapped or appear on some list, then it is suppressing the kind of democratic dialogue that we need to have in a time of crisis.

What is your view as a historian? If you were to fast-forward yourself to a time ten, twenty, fifty years from now, how would you write about this time as a historian?

I would write about this as a time when for the fifty years that followed World War II the United States had been the great superpower in the world. Finally, at the turn of the century something happened that caused the United States to reassess its role and to begin to think that perhaps having troops in countries all over the world — having naval vessels in every sea, intervening militarily in the Middle East and in Central America and in Southeast Asia —was a dangerous course to pursue. This great superpower that had been playing a negative role in the world began to realize that it had been using its wealth for military purposes when it should have been using it for humanitarian purposes.

I'd like somebody to be able to write, thirty years from now, that the people of the United States began to reassess their position and to think that maybe their country should no longer be a military superpower. That they began to think that maybe it should be a humanitarian superpower; that it should use its enormous wealth to help people in their own country and in other countries, with food and medicine. In other words, that they began to make very drastic changes so that the United States would not be looked upon with hostility in the world, but would be looked upon as a powerful but benign friend to people all over the world. I'd like to be able to report that thirty years from now.

Mark Hertsgaard

Seeing America Clearly

The first encounter I had with Mark Hertsgaard *was around his remarkable and groundbreaking book* Earth Odyssey, *which addressed the planetary ecological challenges from the perspective of the human species. Having interviewed him several times since then, I appreciate his capacity to think outside the box. He is now working on a book about how America is seen by those around the world and why America is the way it is. Clearly, most Americans have no concept of life beyond our borders. Prior to becoming President, George W. Bush had only traveled overseas three times, and he typifies the situation. It is time to remove the blinders, to open our eyes and ears to the way life unfolds in other countries, especially those in the southern hemisphere. Americans are consuming upwards of 40% of the world's resources while only making up 6% of the world's population. Mark Hetsgaard understands this global scene like few journalists I have met.*

MICHAEL: *Since the events of September 11, 2001, much has happened, including the bombing of Afghanistan and the "war on terrorism." What is your view of the aftermath of 9-11?*

MARK: People keep saying that September 11 has changed the world forever. I'm not sure that it's really changed the world. It has certainly changed how we look at the world, though. As much sadness as there has been, this could also be a useful thing, or at least something useful could come from it, if we learn to look a little bit more deeply.

I was traveling overseas when September 11 happened, researching a book about America and about why America fascinates and infuriates the rest of the world. What you're always struck by when you're overseas is how everyone else in the world pays attention to America, has ideas and opinions about America. This kind of interest, to put it mildly, is not reciprocated on the part of Americans. Before September 11, most Americans rarely, if ever, thought about the outside world. Now, unfortunately, we've learned the hard way that what other people think matters. With any luck, one of the lessons we'll take out of this is that we are not only not invulnerable but that we simply can't afford not to care about our fellow neighbors here on planet Earth.

From your perspective, why do you think most Americans don't have a perception of the rest of the world?

The rest of the world doesn't have any choice but to pay attention to America. Our economy is the world's largest and the most powerful, our media are in their face all the time. I remember talking to a guy in South Africa who said, "Look, I think we have an advantage, because we know all about you from your media and you don't know anything about us."

Why is that? Why is it that we don't pay attention? I think it's because people have felt that, hey, we're the richest, most powerful nation in history — we don't have to pay attention. The United States can do what it wants, when it wants, and if outsiders don't like it, too bad. Well, we've learned differently now, we've learned that what outsiders think can matter, and we have to pay more attention to that.

As a journalist and someone who's written several books and has been reporting on National Public Radio, how do you think the media has handled what occurred on 9/11?

The difference between what the American media does with this story and what the rest of the world does with it is very striking. To start off with the positive, I think that *The New York Times*, for example, has been quite good in covering the September 11 attacks as a local story. They've been comprehensive and thorough and insightful. But where I would fault the American media is in how they see — or don't see — the story in the larger context. Let me cite two very specific examples.

You'll remember when President Bush, on September 20th, gave his speech to the nation and the Congress about this. Speaking to other countries, he said that in the fight against terrorism, "You're either with us or you're against us." Now, that's exactly the kind of phrase that our friends and enemies overseas certainly notice. One of the things that people overseas always say about America is that it is self-righteous. The Americans think they have the answers to everything and the right to impose them on everyone else. And when Bush says that you're either for us or against us, it plays into that ugly American stereotype. On that day, *Le Monde* — the main paper in France, one of the main papers in the world — reported Mr. Bush's "You're for us or against us" three times on the front page. It was in the headline, it was in the subhead, and it was in the first paragraph of the story. You turn to *The International Herald Tribune*, the international paper put out by *The New York Times* and *The Washington Post*, and it also covered Bush's speech on the front page. But you didn't find that quote until the twentieth paragraph of the story, buried deep inside. That contrast gives you some sense of why Americans don't understand what happened on September 11 — because Americans don't understand their own foreign policy and how it looks to outsiders.

This leads me to the second example. It is very striking how little attention the American media have paid to the question of civilian casualties in Afghanistan. As of January 10, 2002, I have not seen one story that looks at the cumulative total of civilian casualties there. You do see the occasional story about, say, an errant U.S. bomb that has landed in the Red Cross compound or something. But you have to go overseas to come up with the figure — the last figure I've seen as of mid-January is about thirty-eight hundred civilian casualties in Afghanistan. That is more than the number of innocent civilians who died in America on September 11. That should give us pause, and yet it can't give us pause because it's not even appearing in the American media.

I think it's clear that even when the bombing first started and there were reports of civilian casualties coming from overseas media, it was almost like there was a blanket on the American media about that. And those reports were largely discounted by the Defense Department, which said that they were uncorroborated and that we were certainly doing the best we could to avoid any "collateral damage," as they called it. It was a long time before any reportage came out in the U.S. media about any kind of civilian casualties at all.

Part of the problem is the mindset in the American media, which was very well exemplified by the directive that the head of CNN, Walter Isaacson, laid down to his reporters. He told them, "You are not allowed to mention civilian casualties in Afghanistan unless in the same breath you also mention the casualties in America on September 11." That kind of mindset is what I think creates this lack of context and lack of attention to a very significant aspect of the story. It doesn't matter whether you're pro-war or antiwar — you need solid, accurate information in order to be able to make up your mind about this. Unfortunately, I think the American media have been much more interested in the Defense Department view of this war than in a broader, more democratic view of the war.

We have the executive decisions that have been made around this "war on terrorism," as it has been called. From my perspective, the legislature has just kind of rolled over and said to the executive branch, "Okay, whatever you want to do, let's do it." And then, as you pointed out, with the media blackout on information from beyond our borders, the whole thing appears to be on one track. There's no dialogue, no way of even talking about it. This is antithetical to democracy.

It is true that the Congress, and indeed I would say most of the political class in the United States, has fallen in behind the President and the Pentagon on this. It's worth noting that that's generally what happens in wartime, that there is rarely the kind of questioning that you're talking about during wartime. To start with, for example, the United States Congress has not passed a declaration of war.

Exactly. So are we really in wartime? I mean, is there a choice to say this is war? Or is this a criminal action? Clearly it's a criminal action. It's an action that obviously is terrible and awful and the perpetrators should be brought to justice. But do we do that by declaring war? Or do we do that by using the mechanisms that exist in the world community to bring people to justice?

Well, that's another contrast. In the European coverage in the weeks after September 11, you saw those kinds of options ventilated and argued about, attacked, criticized, and defended. There's no monolithic view in Europe. There were certainly newspaper and media outlets there that were gung-ho about the war. But others were saying, "Now wait a minute. Maybe it's better to proceed as in a criminal action, not as in a war.

My point is that we have not had that kind of a wide-open debate here in the United States. And yet, we like to think of ourselves as the proudest, oldest, strongest democracy in the world. Certainly the most profound decision any government can take is going to war. The founders of this country very consciously put that decision in the hands of the Congress to widen it out, so that not just the President, not just one man can decide to take the country into war. In this case, Congress could have made a declaration of war. They chose not to. But again, this is something that's hardly unprecedented. It was the same in most of the military actions that the United States has taken since World War II.

I recall the Tonkin Gulf Resolution that got us more mired in Vietnam in 1964, which then later turned out to be a total fabrication anyway.

That's true. The tapes of President Johnson's conversations have now come out showing that it was a fabrication. He regretted it after the fact, and not surprisingly, because it ended his Presidency.

It calls to mind the kind of momentum that gets created when a nation engages in war. With the kind of momentum that's going on now with the Defense Department, what's next? Who's next? Then there are those who would say,

"What do you mean, who's next?" Again, there's no dialogue, no discussion. It's almost as though the decision is made, we're out there, we've got to keep going.

I think this gets us back to our earlier point about September 11. In some ways I don't think it's the world that's changed so much as our view of the world. The silence of the media, the complicity of the rest of the governing class, the failure to have a declaration of war — we've seen all of these things in previous military conflicts that the United States has gotten involved in. My hope is that, while that's going on, at least some of our citizens will wake up after the terrible, unspeakable tragedy of September 11 and say, "Maybe we need to look a little bit more deeply. Maybe we need to ask some other questions here." I hope that will happen because what we've been doing so far is really not going to solve the problem.

I think it's a matter of remembering that the citizenry is the fourth branch of government, and recalling Lincoln's words, "Government of, by, and for the people." That's what we're supposed to be about. People need to speak.

Yes. And, as I say, September 11 in a way has illuminated how rarely we do speak and how our democracy, and I'm sorry to say this, in many ways is a democracy only in name. Big money now has so much control over the decisions in Washington. This book I'm working on, about how Americans are seen overseas, I began researching shortly after the debacle of the Presidential election of 2000 between Bush and Gore in Florida. I happened to be overseas at that time as well. In fact, I was in Cuba, of all places. People were just laughing at our election fiasco. I remember a taxi driver saying to me, "You know, you guys still haven't decided who your President is. Maybe next time we should send some election observers up to you and see if we can help you out." The United States is very happy to self-righteously preach to the rest of the world about how to run democracy, but we don't always live it at home. My hope is that September 11 will perhaps reawaken us to the first principles of this country, and to the fact that we've drifted far away from them.

Well, your story of the taxicab driver reminds me of interviewing Jimmy Carter in January 2001, right after what happened in Florida. Here's a former President who's been very much engaged in monitoring the elections in other countries since he left the Presidency. He made the statement in that interview that under the rules of monitoring elections they would not have allowed the election results in Florida. The election process just hadn't been set up the way it should have been. It was interesting that an ex-President was making that statement that the election would not meet the criteria that they are using in other countries.

Yes. The same criteria you'd apply in Liberia wouldn't have been met in Florida. I've heard Carter say that, and that, indeed, the Carter Center would not have even agreed in advance to go in and monitor those elections because there were so many structural problems.

There's a terrific book out now that explores that issue, called *Jews for Buchanan*. It's the best analysis I've seen of what actually happened in Florida. It's written by John Nichols, who's the Washington correspondent for *The Nation*. Of course, the title, *Jews for Buchanan*, is a joking reference to the way those ballots, the butterfly ballots, were so screwed up in Florida that many elderly, left, liberal Jews were recorded as having voted for Buchanan.

One of the useful things in the book is that they quote Mr. Buchanan directly saying, "I didn't win those votes and George Bush didn't win Florida." It's very clear that Al Gore should have won Florida. And Buchanan talks about the kind of pressure that major Republican leaders exerted on him the morning after the election when he, Buchanan, began to say these kinds of things. They told him to shut up.

Another useful thing in *Jews for Buchanan* is that it shows just how central race was to what happened in Florida, and that there was a systematic effort to suppress the black vote there.

If you were to look into the immediate future, what would you see?

I think the future is up for grabs. Much will depend on what happens with the economy. You'll remember that Mr. Bush's father had a ninety-one percent approval rating after the Persian Gulf War. Yet he went down in defeat not that many months later in his reelection bid against Bill Clinton because the economy fell apart. We'll see if that same thing happens here to young Mr. Bush. We do see that there are a lot of problems with the economy. The other question is whether or not he is going to expand this war to Iraq and other places. I would hope that doesn't happen.

But a lot will depend on the American public. If the public rises out of its stupor on this and becomes a little bit more active in the political sphere, I'll be much more optimistic about the future of our democracy.

FATHER G. SIMON HARAK, S.J.

Grief, Prayer, and Peace

 A priest with the West Side Jesuit Community in New York City and Adjunct Professor of Ethics at Fordham University, **Father Harak** *has been in the Mideast numerous times. A few months after 9-11, he said, "After September 11, we began to ask questions about our place in the world, including asking the question, 'Why?' But this was short-circuited. We were provided with the meaning, rather than taking time for serious reflection. We were given a name and a target that was supposed to provide the answers." Having attended a Jesuit college preparatory school, and appreciating Jesuits' abilities to ask thought-provoking questions, I was attracted to Father Harak's statement and spoke with him directly.*

MICHAEL: *What insights and what ideas do you have to share about your perspective on what has happened since September 11, 2001?*

FATHER HARAK: I think that we have to start by recognizing, still, our need to express our shock and our grief at what happened to us and to my city on September 11. One of the more significant things that's happened in the peace movement recently is that there was a march from Washington, D.C., where one of the highjacked planes struck the Pentagon, up to New York. That march was attended by many of the people who had lost relatives, friends, sons, daughters, fathers, mothers, husbands, wives in the attacks. The motto of that walk was "Our grief is not a cry for war." What's happened, I believe, is that this sense of grief, of being stunned, has been short-circuited and was detoured into this really wild and pointless attack on the people of Afghanistan. That leaves us still with our grief, still with our sorrow, still with our sense of shock and disbelief that we have to work through in order to come to a proper understanding of what's been going on.

There's also a peace group called Global Exchange that has taken several people who have lost relatives in the attacks here in the United States over to Afghanistan to meet people who have lost relatives to the American attacks in Afghanistan. The idea is, of course, to get together and to share their grief with one another, to share the sense of shock and sorrow and loss, and by so doing to increase the bonds between people. Of course, violence does the opposite of that. Bombing does the opposite. It separates and divides people, as did the violence of the attacks on September 11, as does the violence of our continued attack on Afghanistan and, of course, our eleven-year attacks on Iraq.

What we're trying to do in the peace movement — and I believe it's very significant — is to get people together on the heart level and the human interaction level, and to come to realize who the enemy is. It's not the United States. It's not Al Qaeda. It's not Afghanistan. It's not Islam. It's not Christianity. The enemy is the bombing. The enemy is the killing. Once we recognize that, then we can go about trying to construct a more just world.

What strikes me is that we call ourselves a Christian nation. As a Christian, as a Catholic priest, do you find that there is a contradiction between being Christian and going to war? Is there a just war?

Well, I'm one of those people who is pretty careful, or trying to be more careful, about following Jesus' command to love your enemies. In my understanding it's very hard to love your enemies and kill them at the same time. I'd be happy to listen to someone else describe how that might happen. But I have a feeling that if we were to undertake that kind of reasoning, "Okay, let's figure out how we can love people and kill them, too," then our marriages and our friendships and our brotherhoods and sisterhoods would all kind of disintegrate rather quickly because we claim to love these people and we don't kill them. How we can claim to love our enemies and kill them, too, is really completely beyond me. But I guess some people, some fairly intelligent minds, attempt that. I've even heard Jesuits, who are fairly intelligent, attempt to describe how you can love people and still kill them.

The pope, in his World Day of Peace statement, put out a very important distinction. Pope Paul VI has said that if you want peace, work for justice. Of course, that often turns up on the streets as "no justice, no peace." I don't know if they know they're quoting the pope in that. But Pope John Paul II has stated, "No peace without justice. No justice without forgiveness." The point he tries to make — and makes quite successfully — is that forgiveness is not the opposite of justice, that is, practicing forgiveness does not mean you must forego justice. The point is that forgiveness is the opposite of resentment and revenge. Forgiveness always has to be present, otherwise the call for justice spills over into some kind of revenge, or even into the kind of terrorist attacks that occurred or the attacks on Afghanistan that are occurring right now.

I personally believe that we need to do a lot more reflection, first of all, on what we mean when we say, "Love your enemies." We surely are distinct among the monotheistic religions in saying that. We are not distinct, I guess, in our failure to practice it, as a whole. But, of course, the idea of justice also has to come in, because we can't have peace without justice. I think we need to pay attention to people like Francis Boyle from the University of Illinois, who is an international lawyer. He says that there are twelve or thirteen different international instruments of laws, conventions, for the pursuit of the people who perpetrated this attack on the United States, and that that's the way we should have gone instead of bombing Afghanistan. Of course, the bombing will only create more positive attitudes toward terrorism because it itself is a form of terrorism.

So as a Christian, I'm for not killing. As someone who's following Jesus I say, no, I have to love my enemies. But out of that love and out of that forgiveness, I have to call them to account just like, for example, a mother would ask her child to take responsibility for his or her actions. In the same way, out of love we say, "Listen, you have to take responsibility for these things that you've done." We had Nazis, and we had hunters who've tracked down these guys for fifty years and who are still tracking them down. We can track down the people who were responsible for this and then bring them to trial. What I would say is, let's get the folks who lost people in the attacks on September 11 and bring them to trial. Have them bring their photos that we used to see so often here on the streets of New York City. Have them bring the photos and tell the stories of those loved ones who were taken from them by these terrorists and the planners. Then have the terrorists in prison for a great long time, to think about what they've done and how many lives they've disrupted.

But I also hope that in the course of that, there would be at least some Christians who would say, "You know, this was my father, this was my mother, my son, my daughter, my husband, my wife. But I'm still a Christian and I believe that my faith and my God call me to forgive you, even for this. So I do. I forgive you even for this." I believe that that would work on the heart of these people far more than all the condemnation in the world — that's the nature of forgiveness — until they themselves would come to that place where forgiveness has conquered everything and would see the wrong of what they've done, and their hearts would be converted, which is basically what we want. I don't want them dead. I want them converted to see the error of their ways and to return to the land of the living.

I can't see killing or violence as a Christian strategy, but I do see justice — laced with forgiveness, as the pope has said — as the paramount practice of those who wish peace.

You live in New York City. Were you there on September 11?

I was in Memphis on September 11. But I have many friends who told me that what was so scary was that you never knew what was going to happen next. They didn't know if there were cells of people in the city ready to start taking arms, to start shooting, if there were going to be more bombs, or whatever. It was a very scary time. Even now, people are pretty jumpy. I can sense it in myself, too, I suppose. As you get closer and closer to Ground Zero, people get funny. The area gets quieter and quieter. People talk less and less until finally you're at the site, where people don't speak at all.

So it's a time of great sorrow. And there's still a certain amount of apprehension and fear that continues here, all of which is part of the grieving process that we have to undertake and honor in this country, and especially in this city.

Speaking as someone from outside of New York City and speaking for others who watched what happened in New York, I find it interesting how people there responded. It was really a model for dealing with crisis and horrific challenges. It was done with a lot of compassion and love, which was very obvious. It came through. And yet somehow, it seems that our government didn't really respond in quite the same way.

Right. Again, what struck all of us in the city, and maybe across the country as well, was the incredible heroism of the police and the fire fighters, who went in there and, while everybody was running out, were running back in, trying to save people. Saving people, even at the cost of your own life — that was partly what I was trying to refer to earlier. If only we could think this way, as part of the "loving your enemy" thing, about the perpetrators, you know? If only we would go after them to save their lives. Certainly, anyone of our faiths will tell us that their eternal life is in jeopardy if they maintain this disposition of hatred and terror. This puts them in jeopardy.

But as our government set about trying to pursue justice, this was surely not what we were after. It seemed that the government thought that its only job was to provide security, and absolute security at that, as though such a thing were even possible — so that you would never, ever be in danger at any time. Once you start pursuing these false things, which is what our government seems to have done, then not only do you inflict this terrible threat and terror on the rest of the world — Who's going to be next? Maybe Yemen, or Iraq? — but you also begin to deprive people of their civil rights at home. We're beginning to see that here, as you know. We think about military tribunals, which have not yet been extended to citizens. But surely, there are twenty million non-citizens in the United States and they're subject to these so-called military tribunals. We have people who are being racially profiled, and people seem to be okay with that.

In southern California, and also in a place in Florida, they have twenty-four-hour-a-day cameras on the streets, so it's like a Big Brother type of thing. As you know from reading George Orwell, one of the tenets of the police state, of the *1984* state, is exactly this eternal war — everybody is always at war, and so we need security. Once we start down that kind of wrong path, not only does it again affect others terribly, but it eventually comes back and poisons us. That's what all the philosophers and theologians have told us. Even Plato once said, "It is better to suffer harm than to do it" — because to do it is to corrupt the self. That is, I fear, what we're doing here at home. We're losing the very thing that made us Americans in the first place: our civil liberties. Somehow we've gotten confused, thinking that the purpose of America is to provide security. It isn't. It's to provide freedom.

Are you hopeful about the future?

I have a kind of apocalyptic hope. It's an apocalyptic hope in that so far every empire has collapsed. I don't know what you studied in college, but I was studying Latin and Greek, and the glory that was Greece and the grandeur that was Rome. Every empire has made the same mistakes, has told itself the same stories, and has gone down the tubes in the same way. So in that sense I have a kind of apocalyptic hope that this can't continue, that this American empire will eventually collapse as all empires in the history of the world have collapsed. We're not immune to the forces of morality in history and in the universe, just because we're America and because we tell ourselves that we're one thing when in fact our actions display something else. My own feeling is that things are not going to get better for a long time, especially as these people keep talking about eternal wars. Wartime is never good for anybody, and yet this is what we're being promised.

But at least there's a great deal of hope in the small little mustard seed types of things that the peace movement is doing. And when you hear about people, again, who have lost folks in the attacks on September 11, and even other people, who are out to forgive, to make community despite attempts to rupture it, that gives me a certain amount of hope on a low level. But when I look at it cosmically, I have to get apocalyptic and say, well, we are going the way that every empire before us has gone, and none of them thought they were going to fall until it finally happened. Why should we be exempt? In that sense I have hope, in that this can't continue forever. We live in a moral universe, we're created by a moral God, and we can't continue to keep wreaking havoc on the world, its environment, and its people without collapsing.

The United States is an economic empire, which of course is backed up by the fact that we now spend more on our military than the next twelve nations combined. Isn't that right? Our military budget comes in at around ten thousand dollars a second, every second, every day, twenty-four hours a day, seven days a week, three hundred and sixty-five days a year, ten thousand dollars a second on the military, for killing people.

It's relentless. One of the things that happened at some point in the war on Afghanistan and the bombing was that they signed a contract with Lockheed for two hundred billion dollars for more F16 planes. And I thought to myself, two hundred billion dollars, I mean what two hundred billion dollars would buy in the way of life, liberty, and the pursuit of happiness for people around the world.

And education. And what was it, was it two billion dollars about twenty years ago, to eliminate smallpox from the face of the earth? That was it. Two billion dollars. And they're estimating that it would cost six or eight billion dollars to provide clean water for every child on the face of the earth, and education all the way through elementary school.

Someone once told me the difference between a million and a billion, because I don't have a head for those kinds of things. He was a mathematician, a Jesuit. He said that if we're talking here for a million seconds we'd be talking for eleven days. If we're talking for a billion seconds, we'd be talking for thirty years. So you'd have to spend a dollar a second for thirty years in order to spend a billion dollars. I mean, you just talk about ten billion dollars, that's three hundred years. You talk about a hundred billion dollars and, wait a minute, that's three thousand years. Two hundred million, that's six thousand ... wait a minute, that's like before the pyramids. And that's just one dimension of what we're spending on this war

This is our money, by the way.

Yes, exactly. It's our tax money. And then, you know, we're doing without schools, hospitals, job training skills, inner cities, buildings, the environment. They had to sacrifice something to spend over fifty percent of the discretionary budget on the military.

I think what we need is this: If the military wants more weapons, they need to do bake sales.

Yes. That was the old story. Remember? But, of course, they'd have to do a heck of a lot of bake sales to get even one of these guys, to buy cruise missiles that we launched over there at these hapless, poor shepherds in Afghanistan. You know, they pop out at a million dollars apiece — it's insane. But even apart from the morality of what we're doing to these brothers and sisters of ours, again, it's going to eventually come back and bite us. You can't do evil without it doing worse to you. Evil can't cast out evil. Violence can't cast out violence. Hatred can't cast out hatred. It doesn't work.

So not only is it a time for pausing and reflecting, I think it's also a time for prayer.

That's true. That's one of the chief things. In fact, without it you can't do what we're trying to do; you can't make peace without prayer. And I don't think the prayer has to be to a specific god. It's like in the Twelve Step programs: you don't have to believe in God. You just have to believe you're not it, just even that — acknowledging that there's somewhere, somehow, someone, some force, some power greater than you who's in charge, or at least in charge of trying to get things healthy. Then we can live. Once we think — and this is true even for the peace movement — once we think that we're it, that there is no other recourse except us, we're in trouble. So if prayer does nothing else but remind us that we're not it, then it's a good thing.

Susan Griffin

Thinking with Different Eyes

Photo by Simo Neri

Susan Griffin is a storyteller. Storytellers pass on the wisdom of the culture and have done so since time immemorial. Her Pulitzer Prize-nominated book A Chorus of Stones *is a collection of personal stories about the devastation and carnage wrought by war. But they are more than just stories of war. The human frailties and human courage that connect deeply and are molded by the pathways of violence and war are there as well. It is this power of perception and honesty that Susan Griffin brings to the table.*

SUSAN: I have a lot of trepidations, as I'm sure most people do. Of course, there are the trepidations about the terrorists themselves. I'm glad the Taliban were overthrown. I'm not happy that there was so much bombing, but I'm glad that the Taliban is no longer in power because of their violations of human rights. But the major leadership of Al Qaeda is still out there. And there are also many, many other terrorist groups. So that's frightening.

And then I'm trepidant about the violations of civil liberties that are going on within this country and the long-term implications of that. I'm also trepidatious about a commitment on the part of our government to wage what they're saying amounts to a long-term war — and they don't specify the length of time. What happens to a society when war is continually waged is that it becomes structured around war. It becomes a war-like society. In general, I think that the values of democracy are basically not the values of warfare, that they're antithetical to each other. The great irony in this fighting for our American way of life is that, if we commit ourselves to a kind of perpetual state of warfare, we're going to be the ones who undermine the American way of life more than anybody else.

MICHAEL: *It's interesting that you say that because I've been looking at the language of the Declaration of Independence recently, in particular the phrase "inalienable" or, as in the original Declaration, "unalienable" rights, which means the same as "inalienable" rights. When you look up the dictionary definition of inalienable, you find that it means "cannot be taken away." Then you look up the origins of the word* democracy *— it goes back to the Greek "democracia," meaning "power of the people." So, just as you've said, the values of democracy are not contained in war. Certainly, if by waging war you deprive people of life, liberty, and the pursuit of happiness, you're not acting in accordance with the Declaration of Independence that speaks to all humanity, not just to Americans.*

Yes. Absolutely. That's the other question we need to get to.

But first, if you have perpetual war you have a lot of people that have to be in the army, and the army has a set of rules that is not democratic. The whole hue and cry against having military tribunals is based on that. In a military tribunal, people do not have the rights that American citizens consider theirs under a democratic form of government. And you go on from there. Somebody who is a soldier is not living in a democracy. He's living under a temporary form of tyranny. And the more we militarize the whole society, the more the whole society's going to become a form of tyranny.

And then there's the question of what we're doing to other people. I think the more we bomb, the more we have a policy of bombing, the more the bombs fall on civilians, the more we're creating terrorists. Can we solve the problem of terrorism by only using the military? No, I don't think so. I think most people who know much about terrorism agree with that. A military solution is at best only partial, and at the same time it keeps creating more terrorists.

There was an article in *The New York Times* magazine. It was talking about Egypt, for instance, where a large part of the intelligentsia as well as a large part of the population has always been very favorable to the West. Now it's increasingly getting less popular to associate with or in any way favor the West, or even to adopt Western styles. And that's because of this bombing.

I think it's time that the world — the people, really, and the governments following suit — take a stand against attacking civilians. I think we need to get beyond left and right in this. We need to say that terrorism is terrible and recognize that in the past both the extreme left and the extreme right have been involved in terrorism, and we need to repudiate that. In the same stroke, we need to repudiate the attack on civilians that America has for decades militarily involved itself with by supposedly bombing military targets, but somehow civilians get involved. That's because the bombing simply isn't that accurate, and sometimes what's called a military target is mistakenly identified, and sometimes a military target is something like the telephone company or Pacific Gas and Electric, and that's right in the middle of a community. We need to take a stand, as citizens in every country, against targeting civilians, whether it's collateral damage or whether it's intentional damage, whether it's done by terrorists or whether it's done by governments. I think we should be moving towards that in our peace accords. The treaties about missiles and nuclear weapons should simply be part of that, and we as human beings, as civilians, have a right not to be targeted in warfare. That's a human right.

I think that there's been a general, collective consensus trance around the fact that when you're bombing from thirty-five thousand feet, it's acceptable to have what they call "collateral damage," that civilians will be hit and will be killed. Certainly the remarks of the current Secretary of Defense Donald Rumsfeld have done nothing to assuage that particular view.

Well, far from it. The whole term "collateral damage" — it's a euphemism. George Orwell wrote a wonderful essay on that in the thirties or forties. He talks about the Institute of Peace that really wages war. "Collateral damage" is a term used simply to hide the fact that civilians are being killed. I suppose that bin Laden could use it to refer to the civilians killed at the World Trade Center — although he didn't, horrifyingly enough. He actually came out and said that attacking American civilians and making us terrified was part of his aim. But a terrorist could actually say, "Well, we wanted to get the World Trade Center because it was a center of economic activity we find oppressive, and the people dying in it are collateral damage." That's a term that should just be erased from our vocabulary. There should be no such thing as collateral damage. It's damage. It's not collateral to the people who have been killed.

What is sustaining you personally during these times?

One of the things is that I'm part of a community. I live in Berkeley. Berkeley's often typified as a very far-out, outrageous place, but it really is just a tolerant place, and a very creative one at that. I see people here and, in fact, in communities across the United States making enormous changes in their lives and in their communities, changes of a spiritual nature, of a social nature, grueling changes. They're starting to get a better understanding of what life is about and are moving to a more compassionate position towards people in their own lives and within their communities. To me, this is very hopeful. It doesn't mean that terrible things aren't going on and that the major trends aren't terrible, but when you see that sort of shift internally among a significant group of people, you know that the world is going to make that shift eventually. This is perhaps the avant-garde of people making those sorts of changes, but I think it will happen. The question is, "Are we going to survive? Are we going to survive until that shift becomes more widespread and starts to have social and political consequences?"

I've seen major changes in my lifetime that I didn't expect. A funny kind of thing happens when there's a pivotal moment, it's like that moment when water boils, where suddenly it looks like a very dramatic change, but things have been happening for a long time. It's not even things that are organized politically, necessarily. But it's a deeper kind of soul movement among people, so that some of it even goes on unarticulated. But people know it. They recognize it.

I've seen a lot of those changes. I was born towards the end of the Second World War and was coming of age during the McCarthy period. I went to college in 1960, and that was when the McCarthy period began to end. Then there was the antiwar movement. For a long time Vietnam was not even a place that anybody knew. Nobody even knew we were having any sort of conflict there. And then this very large movement emerged. The Civil Rights movement was the same thing. I saw a huge movement grow out of a period in which segregation was being basically accepted throughout the country.

And the feminist movement — that was very significant to me. I was going through a period in my life when I was thinking I was one of just a handful of women who felt we didn't like the sort of traditional divisions of labor or the prejudice against women going out and doing what we wanted in the creative life and work life. Then suddenly there was an entire movement that changed things, I think, far more than young people understand now. For instance, women couldn't go to work wearing pants. Just a small detail like that gives you the extent of it. Salaries for women were really significantly lower. It's still a problem, but it's improved somewhat. Women sometimes couldn't even have their own credit cards, couldn't have loans in their names. These were really serious social problems that our society began to address.

So social change does happen. Perhaps we're seeing this moment now, when the polls are supposedly showing that people are ninety-five percent behind the war. I'm not sure that's really reflecting how people feel over the long run. These polls are not very subtle.

I was polled around the question of Barbara Lee's vote in Congress. The poll was being conducted by the University of California and the Contra Costa County newspapers. In the first place, the pollster gave me an inaccurate portrait of how Barbara Lee voted. He claimed that she voted against the war on terrorism, when in reality she voted against giving the President sweeping war powers. She voted for money for the "war on terrorism" and the rebuilding of New York, and the civil defense program within this country.

I knew how Barbara Lee voted, so I corrected the pollster. I said, "This is inaccurate. You shouldn't be calling people and telling them this."

He said, "Well, it's what's on my computer. It's what I have to say."

I was appalled.

But in that same poll I was asked, "Are you in favor of or against the way Bush is conducting the war on terrorism?"

Well, this was very early into the process, and the bombing had only just begun, and I thought Bush had done very good work in starting to build a coalition. So I said, "I can't respond to that question with a simple 'yes' or 'no'," because I was not in favor of the bombing nor of escalating the bombing as he said he wanted to do. But I think the coalition building has been very good. I'm very glad he approached Pakistan, and all of that's very good. And I think it's very good that he has been saying let's not carry this anger at terrorists against anybody simply because they are in the Islamic faith. I thought all of that was very good, but there was no way in the poll that that could be registered.

I think that, with all the flag-waving, we shouldn't have a knee-jerk reaction about this. That's very, very important for pacifists and people who are progressive, and I count myself among them. Bush's reaction is a knee-jerk reaction. I don't put it in the same category as Vietnam at this point. I mean, we were attacked, and I think it is a different circumstance and that has to be understood. But you're attacked, and then the knee-jerk reaction is to attack back. But we on the left, too, mustn't have a knee-jerk reaction. Some people are saying this is just like Vietnam, or like this, or like that. It's absolutely, as a matter of fact, a unique situation in history, where a major nation is attacked in a major way by an organization, one that isn't really part of a nation. We did respond by attacking Afghanistan, but the organization is spread all over the world, really. In fact, it was carried out from within our own borders.

So I think we need to be careful with our language. I, for one, feel compassion for the people who want to say, "Let's go get 'em." I don't agree with that. I think it is a very self-destructive position. It makes me frightened for myself

and for my family because the "let's go get 'em" attitude always creates a reaction, and the reaction will be more violence, and the violence will just escalate
and go on and on and on. It can bring us into nuclear warfare, and nobody wins
there. But I think we need to have compassion for that attitude, and understand
that it's not necessarily coming from jingoism or ultra-patriotism or anything
except the human desire to defend oneself. That's a feeling we all can sympathize
with: to have courage under fire and to want to stand up and fight for my life
and the lives of my children, and to feel compassion for all the people who died
in New York and in the Pentagon and who were in those airplanes, and to feel
outrage for those innocent people. I think it's important to understand that
those are good feelings. Those are commendable feelings. If we can move from
compassion and realize that, if you have those feelings of anger on behalf of people that you love or people who are part of your nation, people you identify with
who've been attacked, you can then begin to think also of how other people feel.
In other words, you're not wrong to feel that, nor are the other people who have
been attacked wrong to feel that. Then we can try to extend compassion to the
whole field.

That's the part of Gandhi that some of us forget: he moved always out of
compassion. He never preached hatred, or even the demonizing of the British
whose policies he was opposing. He made a distinction. Gandhi said he wasn't
opposing the British or the wealthy Indian class that was also oppressing people.
He was standing by the truth. I think that this is a challenge for all of us to do
some transformational work with our souls, but also to do some transformational work with our thinking.

THE SEARCH FOR SECURITY

As I TRAVEL THROUGH AIRPORTS and live in the post-9-11 world with its endless "war on terrorism," a $40 billion budget for "homeland security," and an emerging American police state, I don't feel any more secure than before September 11. How do you feel? More questions emerge. What is security and can we ever be truly safe and secure anywhere? Outward security is an illusion. We buy insurance, live in gated communities, use the most sophisticated security technologies, hire bodyguards, and make a host of other feeble attempts to feel secure — yet we don't ever know the future. Those 3000 human beings who died in the World Trade Center, the Pentagon, and on a Pennsylvania farm field awoke that fateful morning like on any other day, not really knowing what the future held but believing, like the rest of us, in the illusion of a future.

Nuclear weapons are not going to save us. More violence is not going to save us. Closing borders is not going to save us. Capitalism is not going to save us. We're the only ones who can save us.

Terry Tempest Williams

Restoring the Dialogue

Photo by Arturo Patten

Here we visit once again with Terry Tempest Williams *after she has been to Ground Zero in New York City. She spoke with me from her home in the Red Rock Desert of Southern Utah where, in the name of "national security," once again the government wants to allow oil drilling. Again, she goes deep and asks essential questions as well as responding heartfully to my queries.*

MICHAEL: *It's several months after 9-11. What do you see at this time, in this place, at this point?*

TERRY: I can tell you what I see today. Early this morning I saw a buck and a doe — two deer, mating. That was thrilling. I saw an ermine in the woodshed, still white from winter. And I saw a black widow that I thought was dead: I reached down with a piece of paper to take her outside, and she came back to life. Apparently she'd been in a state of dormancy. So I see the rhythms of the earth continuing. That's what I hope for our own species as well: that we'll be evolving, emerging with a renewed sense of place.

We live in the Red Rock Desert of southern Utah. Right now we have snow on the red rocks, with the red sand bleeding through. I was thinking, the other day, here it is in the middle of January and the meadowlarks are singing. I find that an incredibly restorative note.

I did go to Ground Zero, in December 2001, with my niece Diane, who had just turned twelve. I always take my nieces to New York City on their twelfth birthday, as a rite of passage, so they'll know that there's a larger world beyond Salt Lake City. Diane wanted to see Ground Zero. She had not seen the images on television — she was away at camp at the time, in the mountains of

Utah. I was deeply moved by what we saw at Ground Zero and, perhaps most importantly, by what we felt. There was a tremendous sense of quiet and unity, and the politics seemed to be burned away there. What we felt was literally a portal of souls. It was very, very powerful.

So it is hallowed ground.

It certainly felt that way to us. I heard something really interesting from Laura Simms, a friend of mine who is a storyteller living in Manhattan. She made the decision to spend the fall — the year, really — going into the public schools of New York City and telling stories to the children. She felt that it could be a form of healing for them. She carefully picked a repertoire of stories that she felt were full of hope and healing; they were all full of light. When she went into the schools and began telling them to the children, they said, "No. We don't want to hear those stories. Scare us. Tell us a scary story."

The teacher said, "No, no, don't. These children are in too much pain."

But Laura trusted the children's request. She proceeded, in this one school in particular, to tell the most frightening story she could think of. And the children absolutely loved it. It was as though they wanted to sit in the center of their fear and know that by the end of the story they would survive. I thought that was very, very instructive.

What about yourself? What do you feel you need to do in the coming year?

I feel it's a year to listen. I feel it's a year to be brave — to find that balance between action and contemplation. I was reading William Faulkner, some of the essays and speeches that he delivered in the South during the years of deep segregation. There was a passage where he said, "Never be afraid. Never be afraid to raise your voice for honesty and truth and compassion against injustice and lying and greed. You will change the earth." That's what is, I think, at the center of my heart. I want to be able to listen. I want to be able to be brave. I want to be able to act in ways that might make a difference, as small and as large as those may be.

When you went to Ground Zero, what did your twelve-year-old niece think? What was her perception?

It was interesting. You know, I think we always fear for our children. We want to protect them and create a context, so that they can be held in their own understanding. And yet I'm always struck by how they stand fully in their own truth, without our guidance.

There's a gallery in SoHo that has a special exhibit, a photographic exhibit called "Here Is New York: A Democracy of Photographs." After we had been to where the Twin Towers once stood, Diane and I went into the gallery, and here you see this array of images, by professional photographers, tourists, residents of New York, children — the whole gamut. They literally are being hung, taped, thumbtacked, clothespinned on wires across the ceiling, on the floor, the walls, everywhere. You look at these photographs and you ask yourself, "Which one speaks to me?" You can choose an image to take home for twenty-five dollars; this donation goes to the children's fund.

I said to Diane, after we had been to Ground Zero, "You may select an image that you can share with your family in Salt Lake."

There were remarkable images, everything from what looked like a nuclear winter to firemen holding each other, to flowers and offerings left at the site, to paper cranes, to a child sitting in the center of a peace rally holding a candle — everything. And without much hesitation, Diane picked the image of the second plane crashing into the World Trade Center. I was really startled by that because it really was the most graphic, the most horrific, the most terrifying of all the photographs in the exhibit.

I said, "Diane, why are you picking that image?"

And she said, "Because I don't want to forget."

When I listened to her tell her parents about the experience, I realized that the other thing Diane took back with her was the stories. She had been listening to the stories that people were telling at Ground Zero: a young woman there with her mother, telling her what it was like to escape; a fireman there with his son, talking about the friends he had lost. She had been just listening to the stories that people were telling, how they were talking to each other. I think that was very powerful for Diane. Again, to bear witness is so important.

The image I took home from the trip was one of Diane standing in front of a banner that said "Courage." And I think that's where we stand now: How do we choose to define courage?

That's a good question. As you were traveling around, going to Maine, New York, returning to Utah, how was it to travel? What did you see, feel, hear during your airport visits and when you were traveling on planes?

You know, looking back — I think when we're in the middle of our lives we don't see these things —actually looking back over the fall, what struck me was that the period between September 11 and October 7, the period before we had begun bombing Afghanistan, was like a grace period that I'd never experienced before. It was a time of contemplation and possibility. Are we large enough to do nothing? Do we have it in us to act with restraint and compassion? It was a time of consideration. It was a time of discussion. And it was a time of prayer. When we started bombing Afghanistan — I remember that Sunday, being in the Seattle watching President Bush on television informing all of us that the air strikes had begun — I felt like we had another shattering moment, another fissure, if you will, in the landscape of this country. After that, another shift. I felt like things went back to the atmosphere of fear rather than forward to an atmosphere of hope.

That's a good observation. It seems that because the decisions that our government is making on our behalf are based on security, they're based on fear. The idea is that we have to do this for national security. What surprises me is the reaction of most Americans who say, "Oh well, I'm willing to put up with this. I'm willing to do this. I'm willing to sacrifice certain civil liberties."

I go back to the Declaration of Independence and the phrase "inalienable rights." That's not just for Americans, it's for all people, all humans — we all have certain inalienable rights. "Inalienable rights" are rights nobody can take away. And yet some of these rights are being taken away without any kind of dialogue or response other than people saying, "Oh well, that's okay."

That's been the terrifying and disappointing thing. It feels like we were in a period of conversation, and now all of a sudden the conversation has stopped in the name of national security, as you say. I was fascinated by the fact that every time a discussion did come forward in this country, we were given a "high alert." I wanted to call him General Ashcroft rather than Attorney General Ashcroft — I thought that was a striking coincidence. Certainly on the environmental front, there is no discussion with the Bush administration. It's not "if" we'll drill in the Arctic but "when." Maybe I have a skewed point of view because I live in Utah, but it's really terrifying. Oil and gas exploration is going on right now outside Arches and Canyon Land National parks, with oil derricks standing inside Dead Horse State Park, one of the most scenic overlooks in North America — again, in the name of "national security." You have someone like Representative McGinnis out of Colorado asking every environmental organization to denounce ecoterrorism or become suspect. I loved the message that came out from the grass-roots organization Wild Law that said, "Congressman McGinnis, we'd love to denounce all ecoterrorists." They then proceeded to mention Exxon, Mobil Oil, Weyerhaeuser — all the corporations that have been terrorizing the environment. There are many forms of terrorism, and environmental degradation is one of them. But there doesn't seem to be much of an appetite for that kind of dialogue right now. It's viewed as antipatriotic.

Especially when dissenters are called anti-American and unpatriotic.

Yes. That's really troublesome. I guess that's why I hope for daring acts of art this year. I was reading a book by Arthur Miller on politics; he wrote, "Art has always been the revenge of the human spirit upon the shortsighted." I think it'll be interesting to see what we do with this repression, this oppression, and how we bring these issues to the fore in creative, surprising ways that bypass rhetoric and pierce the heart. Again, it goes back to Faulkner. We need to be bold and brave and speak out, realizing that it is our right to question. America was founded on that premise, and upon the value of dissent. We have to wake up and get our energy back. All of us grieved and were undone by what happened in September. But now I find I am renewed, I have an awakened spirit, and I feel my soul is back from the fatigue of grief. And now, what are we going to do with this stirring of awareness in our heart?

I think that's a good question for all of us.

Michael, bless you for giving this alternative way of seeing and being in the world. I think that is its own form of courage and engagement.

JANE HIRSHFIELD

Holding the Heart Space

Photo by Jerry Bauer

Just as poet-writer Terry Tempest Williams referred to Arthur Miller's comment about the power of art as a human expression and response when she pointed to her "hope for daring acts of art" in these times, Jane Hirshfield *is a writer whose poetry and writing have always been passionate and provocative. Her book* Women in Praise of the Sacred *is a breakthrough collection of women's experience of the sacred worldwide over 43 centuries and reflects the deep spiritual experience of women, whose power is desperately needed in the world. Jane has a quiet strength, speaks softly, and has, in the conversations we have had together, expressed a deep reflection and tremendous generosity of spirit.*

MICHAEL: *I'm wondering what your insights, thoughts, and reflections are relative to the events that have unfolded since September 11?*

JANE: Like many people I find it an extraordinarily difficult transformation to have to witness. Yet, from the moment I first heard the news the morning of the eleventh, I was one of those who was not surprised. If anything I have wondered subliminally, and partly consciously, for quite a long time: why should people here in this country feel immune? There has been so much suffering for so many years now in other places, in other ways, and we're not disconnected from that. We're part of that suffering. It was inevitable for it to happen here. Why should we be spared when eight hundred thousand people are slaughtered in Rwanda, when the Israelis and Palestinians have been trying in the wrong ways to solve an insoluble problem for decades, when even in Great Britain the I.R.A. bombings became a fact of life? And so I'm not surprised to see such events come here although, of course, I'm deeply grieved.

You lost your father just after 9-11, didn't you?

Yes, I did. And the two events have been speaking to each other inside of me in almost inexplicable ways.

On the eleventh, I was teaching at an artist community in Vermont, the Vermont Studio Center. I was scheduled to give a talk that afternoon, and since I was already scheduled I proceeded to do it, but obviously I did not give the same talk. I very quickly had to find my way towards something to offer this community of people, all of whom were away from home, family, and friends, witnessing this event together. I spoke about many things. I talked about interconnection, the roots of suffering, and the need for compassion for everyone involved in this, compassion that needs to go back for years — forty years, four hundred years, forty thousand years.

But I also talked about the fact that we were a group of people in northern Vermont, experiencing an extraordinarily beautiful day, and I reminded people that just as those in New York and Washington and Pennsylvania were suffering almost on a random basis, on our behalf, so we were given this extraordinary afternoon on their behalf. Any of those people would trade places with us if they could. I reminded the people in that group, as I reminded myself, that we were not to completely become ashes ourselves. We were given this life and this moment to continue living.

A few days afterward, that thought turned itself into a short poem which became my response to the eleventh. A week after that, my father died. And this poem that I had written, thinking that it was about one set of circumstances, a very public tragedy, then became something which has carried me through my own smaller, private tragedy — if one can say that any death is small or that it's large. In such things numbers don't count. Still, the events of September 11 create a different context when someone you know dies an ordinary death right now. I thought, at least I know how my father died. At least we have the ashes. What a blessing. What a grace. And so, in these ways there's been a lot of communication back and forth within me on this subject.

I can read you the poem if you like. It's very short:

The Dead Do Not Want Us Dead

The dead do not want us dead;
such petty errors are left for the living.
Nor do they want our mourning.
No gift to them — not rage, not weeping.
Return one of them, any one of them, to the earth,
and look: such foolish skipping,
such telling of bad jokes, such feasting!
Even a cucumber, even a single anise seed: feasting.
— September 15, 2001

So, you see, the poem is basically saying that the only thing left to do is to love this earth and to love this life. That thought has been carrying me through both of these times, the personal and the universal tragedy.

How has it been for you to go back and visit New York City in the aftermath of September 11?

Well, if this doesn't sound terribly odd in some ways, it's a been privilege that I was able to go down and stand by the site of the World Trade Center and pay witness to that site. You know, it shouldn't make a difference. Proximity should not make a difference as to how one experiences things. This is one earth, one community. And yet. So we go to be near, we stand witness. I didn't go down to the Trade Center site the first time I returned to New York, when my father actually died. That week, I didn't go. But I went the next trip. By then it was six weeks later, and what I saw was white smoke drifting lazily up from the ruined buildings, which looked by then as if they had been there for ten thousand years. One of the places where I stood turned out to be the street where the trucks emerge when they're hauling debris from the site. At one point a convoy of eight large trucks came past me. My impulse was to stand bowing as they passed, but it seemed like it would have been ostentatious. So I stood still. I stood formally. I didn't think I should be bowing in the streets, but in my heart I was.

In reality, it's a funeral pyre.

Exactly. It's a funeral pyre to everyone who died there and a funeral pyre to a certain innocence. Even if I don't believe the country should have felt that innocence, weren't we lucky to live that way for so long? And there was a hugeness to it, beyond emotion, in a way.

Everybody comes down to that area and has a different reaction. One friend, who is a therapist, said, "People tend to take in things that large either through their emotional body or through their spiritual body." My reaction was that of the spiritual body. For me, the experience was the closest I've ever come to the traditional Buddhist practice of sitting meditation in the charnel grounds. I've heard of another poet who went down there — she lives in New York and has children, and this might have made a difference. But she went down there and she threw up. That's the emotional body, rejecting what we're not given permission to reject yet cannot take in.

I'm reminded of battlefields where a great many people have died in violence, and there's a morphic field of energy present. As a child I felt this because I grew up in Virginia, visiting Civil War battlefields. I felt this special energy there. I still feel this energy when I go to battlefields. So I would imagine that around Ground Zero there's a morphic field of energy since approximately 3000 human beings gave their lives there. The energy of that has to be present. So, in some sense, I think this is part of it, feeling this energy.

And yet, in another way, I would add that this energy infuses every inch of this earth. There isn't a square inch of this earth that's exempt from loss, from horror.

Impermanence doesn't come to some special community. Impermanence is everywhere. In a way, what this event is and what that site represents is a particularly visible mountain of impermanence. The First Noble Truth of Buddhism is that life is suffering. This is a universal truth. It doesn't happen more in one place than in another. I know this is a very odd response on my part, but what it has awakened in me is a great reminder of the absolute implacability and omnipresent nature of transience, impermanence, and suffering. The other response — which comes out in the poem, to some degree, and came out in what I found myself saying in Vermont on September 11 — is that if you can truly live in the knowledge of impermanence, it liberates you into compassion and into a greater love of the world rather than a hatred towards it. I hope this is inevitable. Bitterness or anger is a superficial response. The deepest response of the human heart, if it can really feel the impermanence of this life, is to learn that life is an incredible treasure that you would not take away from anyone.

It's clear to me that your spiritual practice is part of what's sustaining you in this time. Is there anything else that's sustaining you?

I'm not sure that I can separate my spiritual practice from the rest of my life.

That's a good answer. I like that. I think it's a salient point. It's all one. Everything is connected; our life is all one tapestry. We're connected to everything else and everyone else. Life is one interconnected body, as it were.

Yes. That's very close to what I felt before, during, and since the eleventh. I can't say that eating a slice of toast is separate from my spiritual practice. And I can't say that my extraordinary community of friends is separate from my spiritual practice.

There have been so many small kindnesses. You hear different reports. I was marooned in Vermont for some days after September 11. I was supposed to fly home the next day and instead I was there for almost a week until the airplanes began traveling again. People would talk to their friends and families and report back to each other at the various meal tables. One person's friends would say everybody in New York is treating each other with incredible tenderness. Another person would say everybody in New York is out getting drunk. And another person would say everybody in New York is walking around like a zombie. Clearly, the multitudes of people in New York were reacting in a multitude of ways.

But the thing I've noticed, especially as I've been continuing to travel back and forth a great deal, and so have been going through airport security a lot, is that amidst the simple inconveniences of what life looks like now — they seem so small and yet, of course, everybody's stuck dealing with them —again and again I have witnessed small acts of kindness, small acts of patience, small acts of courtesy. That, of course, is very sustaining. We could all snap at each other in irritation right now — that would be a very understandable response to this trauma to the earth, to the culture, to the community of friends, to people. Everybody knows somebody who knows somebody who was lost. And you have a choice. You have the choice to become irritable or to become kind. And it looks to me as if many more people have become quieter and more tender and kinder amidst these inconveniences.

Are you hopeful about the future?

I am neither hopeful nor unhopeful. I think the future is unknowable. Actually, I'll take that back. This may be wrong on my part, but at bottom I'm an optimist, and at bottom I hope that as a result of this terrible fire that we are walking through, some good will come. I'm hopeful that something about this event will cause the Israelis and Palestinians to work harder towards the peace process. I'm hopeful that somehow this country will stop dropping bombs and that the people of Afghanistan who have been battered for so long, from within, from without, from every direction, will find a way towards a kinder world.

You know, the root of *kindness* is *kin*. It's the sense of family. It's the sense of everyone being in it together. And I suppose I hope that if people suffer enough, eventually they will make the choice to suffer less, which means finding a kinder way to live together on this earth.

So, yes, I'm hopeful. But I'm also, of course, very dispirited at the same time.

WILLIAM McDONOUGH

On the Edge

The first time I heard Bill McDonough speak was at a "Bioneers" Conference. I was stunned by his brilliance and his capacity to think boldly and break down the walls of limitations. His articulation of design as reflective of human intention provides the freedom to address emotionally difficult issues as an observer, asking questions in new ways. Later, I journeyed to Charlottesville, Virginia, for the express purpose of having a dialogue with McDonough on his home turf, which turned out to be Monticello, the home of Thomas Jefferson. This resulted in a series called "The Monticello Dialogues," broadcast nationwide on public radio in 2002.

WILLIAM: Now that we've had time to reflect on September 11, I would like to talk about two aspects that have struck me.

One aspect is our reaction to the events. I went looking at the history of terrorism to try and find out where it's been dealt with in a way that was effective and proportional because I'm very much interested in the concept of creating proportion and balance by design. If you look at the way the Germans dealt with the terrorists in the early seventies, for example, they did something rather simple: they treated them as criminals. They essentially said, "You're a murderer, and you must be treated as if you were a murderer in our society. You're a criminal." So they didn't create martyrs — they created criminals, and they dealt with them as such.

There's no question that the people who killed all the people in New York and Washington, who destroyed these places, performed a crime. That crime should be treated as a crime. Perhaps there are police actions that must be taken to accommodate the need to apprehend the criminals. But it's unfortunate that we didn't look at this as an opportunity to talk about justice and law, instead of war. War brings up a whole different dynamic, and this was just a very heinous crime. So on a tactical level, that's what we're seeing. And there's sadness there.

The other part, which is a bit ironic and strange, is what we find if we look at this as a design issue. I come at this from a designer's perspective, and we see design as the signal of human intention. What if we put some strange dynamic to the dimension of this, and imagine for a minute that we actually intended this to occur? What would we have done as designers to cause this to occur? This is just an intellectual exercise, of course, but what would we have done? How would we have alienated people to the point that they would do such a thing? What would that be like? What would our strategy have looked like? What dynamic would we have put into our culture to encourage this to occur, if we had intended it to occur by design?

We can say, well, we never designed this to happen, we never intended this to happen, it wasn't part of our plan that this would happen. And yet, it's part of our *de facto* plan, because it's the thing that has happened because we had no other plan. Here it is. What can we learn from that? What can we do to redesign the strategy, to actually design a system that encourages this *not* to occur and creates a healthy relationship among all people? What would that look like? It won't be just reaching out and smashing things. It'll be reaching out and engaging in a way that's productive and generous.

So that's what I'm thinking through right now. What's clear to me is that if there's anything good to come from this tragedy, we need to recognize that we have some authority in and responsibility for our actions. I think of the phoenix, for example, the idea of the good rising from destruction, and of rebirth, and so on. We can recognize that some of the conditions of modern culture — modern Western culture, certainly, and Eastern culture — have precipitated these things and that they can now be looked at perhaps with a more intense focus and with a more vigorous attitude. We can come to grips with the fundamental foundations of modern culture and the way they influence our actions. We can look, for example, at the issue of oil with a different lens. We've had enough experience — we saw it in the Gulf War, we're seeing it here again — to know that this stuff gets traced back to these other issues of material flows and fairness and justice and spirit-matter connections and that we can't just look at the world as a big set of resources that have dollars attached to them. We have to begin to look at the world as a place where we have the opportunity to relate very richly and very deeply.

Perhaps we can look at our own place and imagine engaging it in a celebration of abundance. For example, the United States could look at itself and say, "How do we celebrate our country in a way that allows everyone to enjoy generations of prosperity?" That question, I think, can now come forward again with a whole new sense of urgency.

MICHAEL: *You're someone who has been mentored by Thomas Jefferson and who actually lived in one of the houses Jefferson designed at the University of Virginia. I've been thinking of Thomas Jefferson in this situation, particularly in light of the "war on terrorism." We're being told that this war is fought in defense of freedom and democracy and for our national security. The FBI continues to warn us of imminent terrorist attacks. Does anyone feel more secure because of what's happened? What are your views on security?*

If you look at the Declaration of Independence, it was fundamentally a security question. What Mr. Jefferson was asking was, "How can one create a place in the world where one is free to have life, liberty, and the pursuit of happiness, without having to be concerned about remote tyrannies?" He was trying to avoid being both judged and run by some enterprise that is distant from one's reality. He was concerned about the kind of insecurity that comes from having some remote person make decisions that affect the local condition without understanding it or respecting it. Jefferson felt that was untenable.

We really need to look at that question now rather than just looking at how we can apply brute force. Certainly, force needs to be brought to bear to resist force, but the kind of force that we can bring to bear might be the force of the imagination. It might be the force of good judgment. It might be the force of good will.

Paul Ehrlich sent around an e-mail that was actually quite dramatic in its opening. At first it seemed startling, coming from someone like Paul Ehrlich, who is a well-known ecologist and a deep thinker. He started by saying, "I think it's a great thing that we could send the bombers to Afghanistan. I think we should send them out there and open the bombay doors ..." And you're reading this thinking, I can't believe I'm reading this from Paul Ehrlich. And he continues, "...and then we should start dropping food and medicine and just overwhelm people with our good will." That's really actually our nature. Underneath, that's who we are here — we actually are like that.

So what does it mean to be honest about who we are? I think we actually have that generosity of spirit, but then it gets clouded by this sort of adolescent rage, which is understandable, certainly. I don't think anybody could argue with that. It's understandable, but in the same way that rage is understandable in a child. But do you want to maintain your home in a state of rage? When we get to the notion of actually designing our larger place, there's a place for anger; it needs to be expressed, certainly. But at the same time, we know that we can't live in a state of anger. We can move through that emotion. We might have to move through it to have it resolve itself, otherwise it could sit there and fester. But we can't live in that state.

That's why I think crime needs to be treated as crime. I think it's vicious, urgent, and serious, and it requires a response based on discipline and resolve. But it's short and firm, and then it's over. The idea of going to war over a crime and then involving everyone in something like that is, I don't know, I think Jefferson would have seen it for the scale that it is, and I think he would have been looking for a more systemic response. I don't think he would have been only looking at it superficially.

One of the people I've interviewed in this series over the last few weeks brought up the analogy of Timothy McVeigh and how we brought him to justice and he was eventually executed. We didn't execute his family, his community, the people that he hung out with. We simply employed our system of justice to deal with this criminal.

Unfortunately that's not the strategy being applied today.

What is personally sustaining you in this time?

I see so many people doing so many hopeful things, and I see so many systematic possibilities, that it's just a thrill. I'm having a really tough time right now because on the one hand, I'm feeling really sad in so many ways. On the other hand, I'm having some new revelations that are just delighting me, in terms of understanding how to engage in a beautiful place. So it's a very odd time for me.

I think that's the grief and the exhilaration of engaging both the light and the darkness.

Yes. But I also think there's a sense of urgency. I'm getting a lot of people who are responding after all these years of doing our work, people who are finally saying, "Let's get it done. Let's move now. The time has come."

We can't put it off, we can't pretend it's not there. I think the whole concept of the expedience of the event has finally dawned on people. There's the famous analogy of the lily pond — you know, if the pond is being covered with lilies, if the lilies are doubling in number every day, the day before the pond is covered over, it's only half covered. We don't see the event that's coming, and we don't understand the concept of exponential growth and that all of a sudden —

kaboom, it's there! There's this notion that we're hurtling headlong toward the cliff — at a certain point, gravity is not just a good idea, it's the law. And at a certain point, it's not going to help to hit the brakes because you've built up too much momentum, you're going to go over this cliff.

I think that people have realized that the cliff is now in front of us — we now see it. There are all these components that have driven us to this, and there's so much momentum in the system to maintain this inertia, that it's time to turn this thing around. I don't even think hitting the brakes, which is most people's immediate response, is the solution. I think we have to learn how to do one of those magnificent stunts that the Hollywood drivers know how to do, which is to turn a car around while it's running full speed. I've got to figure out how to pull the parking brake, step on the brakes, turn the wheel, and hit the accelerator all at the same time. You know, that's a real choreographic moment. I'm feeling myself caught up in that choreography, trying to figure out how this momentum will actually have to turn, because it won't be good enough to hit the brakes — it's too late to hit the brakes. We have to learn how to be stunt drivers right now, and turn this thing around.

So I'm looking at that and asking myself, "How do we just go to solar power now? How do we do that now?" That's what I'm working on. If you think about it, we need ten million megawatts in this country to run a system that we might delight in, given current — both literally and figuratively. In this case, electrical current encourages desires. I look at that and say, "Okay, how would I do it with the sun?" Wind is already at four and half cents a kilowatt hour and heading for three, so it's competitive with anything — it might eclipse gas or coal and certainly nuclear power — I mean, it blows them away literally and figuratively.

Why can't we have ten million windmills in the Saudi Arabia of wind, from Saskatchewan to Texas? Why couldn't we do that? Somebody'd say, "Well, you can't have ten million windmills. You can't do that." Well, I work in the auto industry, and they're making seventeen million cars a year. They're making seventeen million pieces of rotating equipment, highly complex, computerized pieces of rotating equipment, and we can't make ten million windmills in the next twenty years? What seems to be the problem here?

I don't see why we can't be solar-powered in twenty years. And if we start to model that, it's just the tip of the iceberg. That's just one little piece of it. And that's just a technical issue. So what we realize is that the technical problems are actually the easiest ones. I think that's where the terror really comes from — that this is not a technical question, it's a cultural question. We will solve the technical problems. And what the technical problems are going to be able to celebrate is the sharing around the world with other people, so we won't have these forms of tyranny. We can share, because we live in a world of abundance. That's a wonderful vision, and it's an exciting one to work on.

It does beg the question, then: What is the cultural question? That's the question today. It's the spirit-matter connection that's fundamental. How are we going to understand our relationship with the world and each other? That's the question.

ORIAH MOUNTAIN DREAMER

Hope in the Ordinary

Receiving the prose poem "The Invitation" one day in the mail from a friend was my initial connection with Oriah Mountain Dreamer. The words were so powerful that I immediately shared them with my partner, Justine, and we simultaneously decided to use the piece in the workshops we lead on "True Work" and "Work as a Spiritual Practice." This decision prompted me to search out Oriah to ask her permission, since we had received the poem prior to her books being published. To make a long story short, she said yes, and later, the person-to-person, word-of-mouth pass-along of "The Invitation" resulted in Oriah Mountain Dreamer publishing two books. Hers is an original voice.

MICHAEL: *The events of September 11, 2001, have created a new world and a new time for us all. What are your reflections on what has happened since September 11?*

ORIAH: It certainly opens me to my deepest longing for peace, and what that means. It's not that there was peace before September 11, but it puts right in our face the degree of violence on the planet and the choice some people are making to extend that violence. So one of my constant prayers is to be the peace I want to see in the world, and to try each day to deal with places where war rages in me, where I want to strike back, or where I can't hold the place of peace and to try and expand that in myself.

I've tried to do this when I hear someone else or when I hear myself commenting on other people's behavior around September 11, referring to others as "they." "These people hate the American way of life and decided to plow a plane into a building and kill innocent people." I try to sit with it and change it to "some of us," meaning human beings. "Some of us hate the American way of life and chose to fly a plane into a building and kill a lot of innocent people." I sit with that, with the sorrow that some of us would do this to others of us.

Then, if I can, I go a step further, and although I would hope I would never engage in an action like that, I ask, "Is there a part of me that hates the American way of life? Is there a part of me that is afraid" — because I think whenever we're using the term *hate*, we could use *fear* instead; it would be truer — "and would be willing to do anything to stop it?" I just sit with that and explore where this fear lives in me, as a way of keeping my heart open to all of the sorrow and all of the fear in the world, as a way of knowing that it is "us" in this together, that there is no "them and us." It's all of us as human beings causing suffering for each other and hopefully finding a way together toward peace with each other.

What is personally sustaining you in this new time we've entered?

I think it's what's always sustained me. One thing is the connection to that which is larger than I am, particularly when I can't go to the place of being with it all. I remember on the twelfth sitting and praying and saying, "I can't see another 'myself' in this behavior. Help me not to close my heart, not to make them something less than human."

The other thing is community, seeing people's sorrow and fear but also their tremendous willingness to be with each other in grief and in sorrow, their willingness to not close their hearts, which takes enormous courage in the face of feeling truly terrified for your life.

So it's the best and the worst of human beings, of myself, that I see at the moment in the world.

Do you still have hope for the world?

Oh, absolutely. You know, though, the other day a good friend of mine who's a Buddhist said, "I'm trying to be in the place of not even hoping." Well, I can't give up hope. Human beings have done some pretty horrible things to each other. But just this morning I was thinking about how the Berlin Wall came down and how that once had seemed impossible. We've seen the end of the Cold War and of other things that seemed to go on for so long that we were sure they couldn't be reversed.

Apartheid in South Africa.

Absolutely. Yes, that was another one. But where there are human beings willing to open their hearts, all things truly are possible.

And just recently, the IRA saying we'll put down our weapons.

That's right. The peace process in Ireland started with some Protestant and Catholic women getting together and saying, "Our children are dying. Enough is enough." That gives me tremendous hope in ordinary people remembering what really matters to them and reaching out to each other saying, "I don't want my children killing your children, or vice versa. That's not how we want our children to live," and connecting on that level. That's the beginning of a shift and a change in what we create together.

THE PEOPLE: THE 4TH BRANCH OF GOVERNMENT

D EMOCRACY — THE PEOPLE RULE. Prior to the writing of the Declaration of Independence, Committees of Correspondence flourished in the thirteen colonies. People in villages came together for town meetings, discussing the Stamp Act and various other oppressive actions on the part of King George. Their deliberations were passed from village to village throughout the colonies, while little newspapers and circulars proliferated and people were informed in ways that even with today's elaborate communication technologies, we are not. Citizens wrote letters with quill pens and sent them to others. It was an extraordinary time that eventuated in the establishment of a nation and government unlike any other that had existed on the planet.

The people made it happen: slavery was abolished; women got the vote; civil rights became the law of the land. Americans fought for these advances. We have many freedoms here that people elsewhere don't necessarily enjoy. Let us not lose sight of our blessings as we struggle to return to our first principles and to move towards realizing the ideals of this nation's founders. As the famed historian Henry Steele Commager wrote, "If our democracy is to flourish, it must have criticism; if our government is to function, it must have dissent." No less a person than Thomas Jefferson wrote to James Madison, on December 20, 1787, "The people are the only sure reliance for the preservation of our liberty." Even though he was a member of the landed upper class gentry, Jefferson did not fear the people as many of our leaders appear to do today. Our government shrouds itself in secrecy, cabinet-level officers refuse to testify to Congress, President Bush supercedes the law to withhold presidential papers, and the CIA and FBI are given increased police powers to invade the private lives of Americans in the name of national security. As Americans, we indeed hold the power in our hands. May we, in accordance with the Native American tradition, express it wisely for the benefit of our children's children unto the seventh generation hence.

Matthew Rothschild

Beyond Patriotism

Matthew Rothschild, *the editor of* The Progressive, *is the Director of the Progressive Media Project, which distributes opinion pieces to newspapers around the country and has placed more than 1900 commentaries in the last nine years, reaching millions of readers every year. As someone working in a forum where a multiplicity of diverse views is being appraised and studied, he has a unique vantage point.*

MATT: This is the diciest moment in my adult life. I'm forty-three years old, and I can't remember a time when the United States had so much power to throw around the world. Congress has given President Bush virtually unlimited authority to bomb anywhere. The legislation passed in September 2001 says that the President, on his own discretion, can bomb any individual, group, or country he thinks was connected to the horrible acts of September 11. That is just too much power to give to one person, and I think it is unconstitutional. Remember, according to Article I, Section 8, of the Constitution, Congress is the body that has the power to declare war. Bush and Rumsfeld, like some wealthy couple deciding on what fancy restaurant to go to on Saturday night, are now deciding what country to bomb. We hear in the press that they are thinking of bombing Yemen and Iraq, and maybe Somalia, maybe Indonesia, maybe the Philippines. What other country in the world has that kind of chutzpah or insouciance? No one else can imagine doing that, first of all because there would be retaliation, and secondly because they don't really have that history of empire. The United States is just like the old British Empire right now.

Then domestically there has been a chill that I haven't felt before, not even during the Reagan years, where expressions of dissent are not only being frowned upon but sometimes stifled. Suddenly the FBI and the Secret Service and the police can knock on an apartment door as they did with a young woman named A.J. Brown in Durham, North Carolina, and say, "We hear you have an anti-American poster on the wall." Or they go to an art exhibit in Texas and say, "We hear you have some anti-American art on the wall." These are evocations of the darkest days of the McCarthy period, and I think we need to take that seriously as well.

MICHAEL: *You wrote an article called "The New McCarthyism." I was in the eighth grade when McCarthy was at his peak, and I remember watching the hearings. I remember seeing that famous hearing when Joseph Welch, the attorney, got up and really faced him down. It was the beginning of the end for him, I think.*

Yes. "Have you no shame?" Well, we're not there yet, fortunately. We are not at a point where thousands of people are losing their jobs or being blacklisted or having to leave the country, though we do have these horrible round-ups of immigrants who are being detained. We don't know their names, and many of them are going to have to leave the country. Some may be prosecuted. A lot of them have been held in solitary confinement, which is outrageous — their rights are being violated. We are seeing a massive violation of civil rights and liberties in this country, like we haven't seen in a long time. And people are standing for it. I look at some polls, and the majority of Americans support this crackdown.

Do you really believe those polls?

I believe polls to this extent: I think a poll is a snapshot of a reaction to a question that is phrased in a particular way. The real question is, "How was that question phrased." But I do think that after September 11 people got terribly scared. It's understandable. In my lifetime, no event that I have witnessed on TV has been as grotesque as that. Imagine the people in those planes or the people in those buildings, and three thousand funerals, three thousand families torn asunder.

The feel of the tragedy is dramatic. Immediately afterward it immobilized my mind and, in a sense, paralyzed my politics for twenty-four hours — and it would have done so longer if I hadn't been on deadline. It seemed that to do almost anything other than empathize with those victims was somehow disrespectful. But the train was moving out of the station, the train of retaliation, of vindictiveness, and it was necessary to respond.

Martin Luther King said, "Hate multiplies hate. Vengeance multiplies vengeance. Violence multiplies violence into a descending spiral of destruction." It struck me that we are going down that descending spiral, and I worry about that. I worry about what happens if the United States attacks Iraq next. First of all, we have been attacking Iraq for years. But if the United States goes in now and tries to overthrow the government of Saddam Hussein, as unseemly a character as he is, thousands and thousands of people will die. Thousands of civilians have died in Afghanistan, and we don't hear their stories in the papers very often.

As the editor of The Progressive, *do you think we have to get past these old labels of left and right, progressive and right-wing?*

I believe in those labels, not just because of trademark purposes or marketing purposes for *The Progressive*. I think there remains a legitimacy to being identified as being on the left, or being a progressive, or even being a liberal. There are those of us who for the last hundred years or more, in the progressive tradition of the United States, believe that a) corporations have too much power over our lives, over our economy, and over our political system; b) U.S. militarism is a dangerous force; and c) we need to maximize civil rights and civil liberties. Those are basically the three wheels of the progressive tricycle, and those are still pretty sturdy. There is no reason to blur the distinction between what a progressive is and what a mainstream Joe Lieberman Democrat might be, for instance, or, for that matter, what a George W. Bush Republican is.

I get a little uneasy when people say it is time to go beyond left and right because I think there still is meaning to these labels. To me, the meaning is very important because these are the values the progressive movement in America has espoused for the last hundred years.

What about the two party system, Democrats and Republicans — or, as we might say, "Republicrats "and "Democrans"?

There you get into a murkier situation, because the Democratic Party, on many issues, is quite close to the Republican Party. In fact, on economic issues the Democrats are sounding more like Republicans now than the Republicans are. It is the Democrats who are talking about how we must retire the debt, how we can't have a budget deficit, when in fact there is nothing wrong with running a debt, there is nothing wrong with running a budget deficit within reason, and during a recession it is crucial to do both. Saying we shouldn't have these is a recipe for a deeper recession. The Democrats are just trying to pin the tail on the elephant, if you will, and it is a silly little childish game. This is just one example.

The Democrats themselves have gotten very cozy with corporations. Many are as involved in taking money from Enron as are others on the Republican side. And it goes on. I hardly see a difference in foreign policy, either. It wasn't an accident that only one person out of 535 in the U.S. Capitol voted against the U.S. war against Afghanistan — that one person was Barbara Lee of California, a Democrat. Every single other person in that building voted to give George W. Bush *carte blanche*. Now if that doesn't suggest to you that there is a blurring between the parties, I don't know what will.

It's similar with the U.S. Patriot Act — every single senator but one voted for that thing, which is a terrible infringement on our rights. Only Senator Russell Feingold, a Democrat from Wisconsin, voted against it. So on some major issues, Pentagon spending is another one, we see the Democrats and the Republicans converging.

That is why some of us got excited about the Ralph Nader/Green Party campaign. It is important to have challenges, whether they are at the presidential level or at the grass-roots level. We can't simply say that by going in once every four years and checking the Democratic box we are doing our civic duty, we are trying to make this country a better place. That just won't cut it.

You are saying that it is important to have challenges. That brings to mind the fact that at the heart of democracy lies dissent, the challenging of government decisions, and yet that is now being looked on in many quarters as being unpatriotic and un-American.

Yes. It is frightening how dissent is almost being criminalized right now. The U.S. Patriot Act says that if you are doing something unlawful and at the same time you are opposing U.S. foreign policy or the U.S. economy, you can be charged with terrorism. That means that if you jaywalk they can arrest you, and if at the time you are jaywalking you are also holding a sign that says the U.S. war against Afghanistan is illegal or the I.M.F. and the World Bank make poor countries even poorer, then they can charge you with terrorism. That's just craziness. We need to recognize it as craziness and oppose it.

The same is true of this notion of patriotism. I have two responses to this question of challenging the patriotism of those of us who have the courage to dissent. First of all, the most patriotic thing you can do is to express your disagreement with your government. That is the substance of the First Amendment, and when we are exercising that right, we are being as patriotic as the next person.

But I also have a bit of a different perspective on that, and that is to question the very power, authenticity, and importance of the concept of patriotism itself. I think patriotism can quickly metastasize into nationalism, and nationalism has been the cause of the deaths of millions and millions of people around the world in the last three centuries. We have to focus on the concept of patriotism itself and ask ourselves whether this is a legitimate concept to embrace, or whether it is something that is poisonous. I believe it is poisonous.

We can say that in the alternative media. The mainstream media can't. Why? Because they will lose audience, they'll lose advertisers, they'll lose money. Ninety-five percent of American people identify with patriotism, and I understand why. So the mainstream media can't do it. That was Bill Maher's lesson about being politically incorrect. He dared to say that the pilots flying five thousand feet above the Taliban, who have no anti-aircraft weapons to speak of, are maybe not that courageous after all. For that he was forced to apologize abjectly.

For the same reason, politicians can't question patriotism, because they will be voted out of office. But intellectuals can. The alternative media can. We can say that this notion of patriotism may be too fraught with disease, too fraught with germs, too tricky, too dicey for us to really get behind.

So I am not one of those progressives who are out flying a flag. Actually, on July 4th I fly a flag that a friend of mine made — it's a flag of the Bill of Rights.

You mentioned the alternative media, which begs the question, "What about the other media?" When we look at the major mainstream media, in particular mass media and the way they have presented events since 9-11, it seems as if there has been an alliance between the government and the media. I have watched the Pentagon briefings with Rumsfeld, and it is almost obvious that the hard questions are not being asked. There is this game that everybody is playing and no one is willing to say, "The emperor has no clothes."

It is even worse than that. I have watched some of those too, and I am disgusted because many of the reporters there are becoming Pentagon toadies. They laugh when Rumsfeld makes a joke about not caring about collateral damage — they're laughing at that? I mean, come on! The United States is killing people over there, and the reporters are laughing when the defense secretary fobs it off. At best they're stenographers, at worst they're cheerleaders, and that's not what our mainstream media should do.

Unfortunately, it's also true of *The New York Times* in its coverage of the war. I have looked day after day after day since September 11 for one columnist or for one freelance op-ed writer in *The New York Times* to say that the war against Afghanistan is immoral. I have not found a single voice there. They have not allowed a single voice on the op-ed page of *The New York Times* to oppose the U.S. war on Afghanistan. They are not allowing alternative or opposing views into the paper, and I find that outrageous.

However, in defense of The New York Times, *from time to time articles that present an alternative viewpoint do appear.*

True, but it may not be an alternative viewpoint. They present a conflicting fact.

What I try to do every day when I read *The New York Times*, which is kind of my bible, is look at it closely, kind of like it's a treasure hunt. I try to find the little piece of information in *The New York Times* that is curious or that is odd, and then take it from there.

For instance, there was something about a U.S. helicopter that went down in Afghanistan and about how the United States then had to bomb it because it had secret materials in it. That one sentence was the whole story. It was buried deep in a seventy-paragraph article; it might have been in paragraph forty-three. And I wondered, well, were there any U.S. soldiers in that helicopter? What was that secret stuff that was bombed? But you often find that sort of thing in *The New York Times*, even though it is a great paper and it reports facts from around the world that we don't always get elsewhere. But it doesn't always report the facts in the fullest or fairest context, and when you get to the opinions, the coverage is very slanted.

Recently, before they stopped the "A nation challenged" section, there was a major article leading off that section that quoted a number of people about the endangerment of civil liberties because of the military tribunals.

All right. I would draw a distinction between *The New York Times* coverage of the war and *The New York Times* coverage of the attacks on civil liberties in the United States or of the treatment of the Taliban and Al Qaeda prisoners. The treatment of the latter has been okay. The treatment of the war, I think, has been pretty stilted.

Where do we go from here? Let's say you are a pundit. Obviously, none of us knows the future, but what do you project we are looking towards here?

Before the Enron scandal I thought we were in for some real, real dark times, and primarily that's still my sentiment. But the scandal and what it may be doing to erode the power of the Bush administration gives me some hope. Still, by and large we are right now in a position of retrenchment, I think, where we certainly may see more wars by the Bush administration. I take them at their word on this. Bush and Rumsfeld have said this is just phase one, wait for phase two. I think there will be a phase two, and maybe a phase three and a phase four of this war. I think more and more innocent people will die. This is a very distressing thing that I see on the horizon.

As far as the war on civil liberties here in the United States is concerned, this attack on our precious rights may get worse before it gets better. The CIA and the FBI now have the right to spy on people here in the United States in a way they haven't done since the dark old days of the counter intelligence program of the FBI. The CIA wasn't supposed to do this in the first place, but it is now allowed to. So we are going to see more infiltration. We are going to see more surveillance, more wiretapping. All of that indicates a trend in the negative direction.

The trends pointing in the positive direction are the peace movement and the anti-globalization movement, the global justice movement. I was surprised after September 11 at how spontaneous the peace movement was around the country, or at least here in Wisconsin. I traveled the state talking at peace rallies, a half dozen or more of them. I had thought the peace movement would go to ground, but instead people rallied. Even people who hadn't been involved in protest before were involved here, even as complicated as this case was. It's the most complicated case since World War II, certainly, as to whether a war is justified. Yet there were people courageously protesting. That's a good thing. I think there will be more as the war continues in other countries because the excuse for the war will not be as immediate and as persuasive as the excuse for the war in Afghanistan was. I think the peace movement will galvanize.

The global justice movement has not died. The reason it hasn't died is because the conditions that gave rise to it have not ended. Look at Argentina. Argentina is a classic case of globalization gone bad. The people of Argentina are protesting, and students in this country are staging similar protests. They are protesting the policies of the International Monetary Fund and the World Bank, which, by the way, should be demystified. Those institutions work at the behest of the U.S. Government, the U.S. Treasury Department. It's George W. Bush and Treasury Secretary O'Neill that set the policy of the World Bank and the International Monetary Fund because the United States is the biggest funder of those institutions. Those institutions aren't fighting poverty; they are telling these countries to privatize their economy and to put a premium on paying back their banks and on opening up their economies to U.S. corporations. That's their role. We should be clear on that. It is a great thing that the I.M.F. and the World Bank are suddenly subjects of popular conversation and protest in this country. I remember being at a protest against the World Bank back in 1980 and there were twelve of us, just twelve people outside the World Bank with our signs. Now there are thousands. That is a great thing. I think that is promising.

And I also think the corruption in Washington is promising, in that it shows people how bankrupt the system is. Out of this corruption, from this awareness, I think people will draw some necessary conclusions that there needs to be some fundamental change. Campaign finance is a very first step. Maybe beyond that there will be other measures to give people more power and corporations less.

NOAM CHOMSKY

Challenging the System

Photo by Chris Allen

For more than four decades Noam Chomsky *has been a path-breaking linguist and a controversial critic of American policies and politics. Indeed, he is worshipped by many and reviled by many. It is also true that the mainstream media rarely interview him, yet his lectures draw thousands and his books are everywhere. He is an astute analyst of U.S. foreign policy and a keen observer of the mass media and continues to challenge the political and economic orthodoxies of our time. If we want to maintain democracy, it is crucial that we allow the voices of dissent and listen to them. Chomsky's voice needs to be heard as widely as possible.*

MICHAEL: *Professor Chomsky, since the events of September 11, 2001, all of us in the United States as well as the world at large have entered new territory. I'm wondering what your insights, your thoughts, your ideas are at this point in time about what's happened since the events of September 11.*

NOAM: What's happened in Afghanistan, specifically, is complicated, but one part of it is an unfolding human tragedy of dimensions that are very hard to estimate. Three months have gone by with a sharp reduction in the flow of food aid and other necessities on which many millions of people were relying for their existence. The U.N. estimated six or seven million. We know very little about what's happening to those people, but it surely isn't pretty. That's perhaps one of the most significant events since September 11.

There is also what's called a "war on terrorism" that's supposed to be a dominant element of international affairs. It's a curious war. Every day you read in the newspapers that it's based on a new partnership between Russia and the United States. One might ask just how Russia and the United States can be running a war against terrorism. Russia is a partner in this war for a reason that everybody knows. It wants to have U.S. support for its own awful terrorist activities, particularly in Chechnya. In fact, other members of the coalition are joining for similar reasons: China wants support for its repression in western China; Algeria was happy to join — it's one of the worst terrorist states in the world; Turkey was the first country to offer troops in gratitude for U.S. support in its crushing of its Kurdish population in the 1990s in some of the worst ethnic cleansing and atrocities of that period, which did indeed, as the Turkish president said, rely crucially on U.S. support — in fact, for eighty percent of their arms, increasing as the atrocities increased. It goes like that pretty much throughout the coalition.

And what about the United States? Remember that this war on terrorism is not the first one that's been declared. Twenty years ago the Reagan administration came into office announcing very loudly and clearly that the war against international terrorism would be the core of U.S. foreign policy. They condemned international terrorism in very much the rhetoric we now hear, that depraved attacks against civilization by barbarians are a plague that has to be overcome, and so on. How did they overcome it? It's not exactly a secret. They responded to it by creating the most extensive and destructive international terrorist network the world had ever seen. That led to a complete disaster in Central America, which was the main target of the international terrorist attack. It was so extreme that the U.S. was condemned by the World Court and would have been condemned by the Security Council, except that the U.S. vetoed the resolution.

Iran-Contra was a scandal — actually, in my opinion, it was a rather minor scandal that was domestic, and therefore it was blown up and it became significant. But the major issue in the Iran-Contra affair was the war against Nicaragua, which the World Court condemned as "unlawful use of force." The World Court ordered the United States to terminate the international terrorism and to pay substantial reparations. When the U.S. simply dismissed that with contempt, Nicaragua went to the Security Council, which called on all states to observe international law, naming no one but intending the message to be heard by the United States, as everyone knew. The U.S. vetoed it, went to the General Assembly where it got a near-unanimous resolution. All of this is more or less wiped out of history in the United States, but it happened. In fact, the United States responded to that by immediately escalating the war, including official orders to attack what are officially called "soft targets," meaning undefended civilian targets. And it went on from there.

That was only part of it. In El Salvador and Guatemala it was much worse. In fact, the people who were condemned by the World Court and the Security Council are the same people who are running the current war on terrorism. For example, the attack on Nicaragua was based primarily in Honduras, more or less a U.S. enclave. John Negroponte was the U.S. pro-consul there who was responsible for the bases from which the attacks took place. He's just been appointed as U.N. Ambassador to lead the war against terrorism. I mean, if Orwell were alive, he would be watching with stunned silence that all of this continues without comment.

So there are many questions to ask about the war against terrorism. Incidentally, it didn't end in the eighties. I mentioned Turkey, but that's only one case. These are consistent patterns, and they are continuing.

I just wanted to step in here to bring it back to the present, to the military tribunals that have been put forward, and also to Bush's executive order to seal the Presidential papers. These things threaten to impinge on civil liberties in the U.S.

The infringement on civil liberties in the United States is an important matter, but far more important is what this means for the whole world. It's dangerous. People outside of the United States are worried about it, and rightly so. The infringement on civil liberties in the United States is serious, but it's something we can control if we want to. Any power system, whatever it is, is going to try to exploit moments of crisis to ram through harsh and regressive measures that will enhance its power. That would probably be true of an earthquake. It's certainly true of the crisis of September 11. The Bush administration immediately reacted to it by exploiting the fear and anguish that people were feeling in order to implement a whole range of programs that they knew would otherwise elicit strong negative reactions. They took advantage of the crisis by appealing to a misplaced sense of patriotism in order to shut people up while they continued implementing their measures. These programs range from fast-track legislation to a cut in corporate taxes, to sharply increasing the militarization of space programs, to things like cutbacks on civil liberties. The more harsh and repressive elements want to exploit the atmosphere of fear and concern while at the same time trying to ensure that others will be passive and obedient. That's natural, but we don't have to accept it.

JEFF GATES

From Corporate Capitalism to Populist Capitalism

 Jeff Gates *first came to my attention through a series of bi-annual conferences held over five years (1996-2001), which had been begun by the late Willis Harman, former president of the Institute of Noetic Sciences, and Avon Mattison of Pathways to Peace. The purpose of these gatherings of no more than 30 individuals was to examine the role of business and organization in the quest for peace and sustainability on the planet. As counsel to the U.S. Senate Committee on Finance during the 1980s, he was directly involved in the federal legislation that encouraged employee stock ownership plans (ESOPs). Since* then he has written several books, including The Ownership Solution *and* Democracy at Risk. *His views of the free market and globalization are "people oriented" and provocatively different from most of what we see and hear.*

MICHAEL: *What do you have to say about this new time we've entered?*

JEFF: It's a great opportunity. There's a sense of tragedy paired with a rare sense of opportunity worldwide to redefine what we mean by national security. People are correct to call this a — potential — learning moment. My portal into this discussion is the financial domain. Financial forces are on track to provoke more such madness if we don't take this opportunity to learn. If we return to business as usual, we're ensuring an even riskier future. But you don't need to go back very far in the Western classics — Isaiah in the Bible, for example — to find a roadmap to managing risk: if you want peace, work for justice. That's pretty straightforward. In cultures of the East, it's often said that prosperity is impossible without harmony. Extreme economic divides ensure extreme disharmony. That's why both peace and prosperity require justice. And justice does not prevail in this world. In the U.S., for example, the financial wealth of the top one percent is now greater than the combined household net worth of the bottom ninety-five percent.

You take that abroad and, of course, it's even more appalling. Indeed, eighty countries are now worse off than in 1985. Three billion people are trying to make do on two dollars or less per day. If we continue the build-out of today's exclusive economic model — and keep in mind we're adding about eighty million people per year to the planet — in thirty years time we'll have, according to the president of the World Bank, five billion people making do on two dollars or less per day. We now have about two billion members of the human family who are malnourished in some fundamental fashion. If today's trends continue, by the time my 12-year-old son turns 40, we'll have 3.7 billion people on the planet suffering that indignity. That's the most profoundly poor risk management possible.

The good news is this: we know we can design our way out of that. We know both the financing techniques and the green technologies to create broad-based, environmentally sound prosperity. From a risk-management perspective, I argue that we *must* do that worldwide. So that's great news — we know how to do something that we must do anyway. Plus it's an amazing business opportunity and a phenomenal job-generator.

We hear a lot about the free market, and certainly we've heard a lot about globalization and bringing capitalism and democracy to other countries, and so forth. Are you saying that the free market can really work in a way that it hasn't worked up to now?

It absolutely can. We don't really have what I would call a generally free market — what we have is a financial market disguised as a free market. During the 1980s, I served seven years as counsel to the Senate Finance Committee. In 1980, there were $1,900 billion in the hands of U.S. money managers. Now, U.S. money managers hold more than $17,000 billion. We passed laws to require that fund managers focus on only those values that show up as financial values. So, now we've $17 trillion dollars operating on the basis of what I think of as money-on-automatic. I call it "Eureka-nomics." Fund managers shout, "Get yield." Or, "Show me the money." If a financial value shows up, they shout "Eureka" and do it again, over and over and over again, *ad infinitum*. What about economic distribution patterns? Social justice? Environmental sustainability? Fiscal foresight? Not their concern.

So what we have is a kind of a feedback mechanism in which the only values that count are financial values. That is a key reason for why the world feels so "disconnected." With the rapid growth of so-called "managed funds," the world seems ever more speeded-up and dumbed-down. Oddly enough, our situation is very much contrary to what Adam Smith, the great apostle of free enterprise and market economies, preached. He envisioned not global capital markets but local values in local communities as the force informing and animating market economies. They'd be attuned to what he called "human sympathies." He did not say, "Take all of society's operations and attune them to the whims and wishes of global financial markets" — which is what we've done.

My particular work has to do with how you handle capitalism and, in particular, the ownership element. How do you localize it? How do you optimally people-ize it, human-size it? How do you create a system that's generally community-wise? If you believe in market economies like I do, then the way to do that is to rewrite the rules that govern globalization, which is largely a finance-driven phenomenon, to ensure that when financial forces do their work worldwide, they leave in their wake a broad base of owners whose enterprises are embedded in their communities, who can adequately respond to the people who live in those communities.

We know the design for dozens of ownership-broadening mechanisms. I wrote much of the federal law encouraging one such mechanism called employee stock ownership plans (ESOPs). By offering modest tax incentives, roughly ten percent of the U.S. workforce now have a stake in the companies in which they work — some twelve thousand corporations. That can be done worldwide; it's not that difficult, particularly when rule-writing "capacity building" is all the rage in development circles. The financial technologies are well known, proven, and popular.

It's interesting that the local market economies are generally being impacted in a negative way by the spread of globalization and the spread of the free market because those global forces are coming in and the local market economies can't compete, and so they just sort of dissolve.

That's one of the most dangerous and dysfunctional aspects of the neoliberal-inspired, finance-obsessive force that drives globalization. My latest book is called *Democracy at Risk: Rescuing Main Street From Wall Street.* The galleys of that book were used by Ralph Nader to brand the Greens the party of "the new populism." I worked for seven years in the U.S. Senate with Louisiana's Russell Long, Huey's son, America's best-known populist. The populist challenge is the same one now faced by a globalizing democracy: how do we create a system that genuinely responds to the values of those whose lives it influences? That's a pretty good working definition of democracy, the idea of a system that grants people the dignity of self-determination. Until the 1770s, that idea was viewed as impractical; now we see it as indispensable.

How do we best ensure that self-determination becomes an everyday reality? One thing we *don't* do is simplistically defer all decisions to capital markets. The neoliberal "efficient markets" model is simple: "Maximize financial returns and … trust us … everything will turn out fine." Only intellectual dinosaurs adopt that kind of a mechanistic, formulistic, Newtonian model where you do A and get B. Unfortunately, they are the key advisors to the current generation of dinosaur-era legislators, both Demopub and Republicrat — neoliberals all.

What we're trying to do, of course, is segue from that mechanistic Newtonian age to a kind of living systems model. We know that there is a broad array of influences other than the maximization of financial returns that could usefully — and profitably — inform commercial decision-making. Unfortunately, neoliberals put all of the managers worldwide into a box where the only signals to which they respond are financial: regardless of whether you're managing physical assets or financial assets, you're basically managing a pile of money. And unless you can at least match your competitors in the generation of *financial* value, you will be fired. That's the self-correcting signaling system to which today's marketing operations are attuned. But an economy can be wired to respond to broader, more multidimensional metrics. It really is a design choice.

For example, huge "box" stores and mega-malls are one of the most devastating financial influences on local economies. When they generate financial value in a community, that value flows in only one direction: out. Another example is Medicare. During the 2000 political season, the talk was all about the need for prescription drugs for seniors, an issue that's certain to replay in 2004. Those seniors require assistance largely because legislators embraced laws endorsing such a concentration of income and wealth that voters mobilized to demand help. So what we'll likely do is provide a Medicare subsidy for medicines. But note the quandary if our legislators remain indifferent to the fact that Wal-Mart already owns 2,500 pharmacies — and the five heirs of founder Sam Walton already have $100 billion. In other words, that badly needed government subsidy is certain to worsen an already disastrous fiscal situation. How do these neolib nutcases plan to pay for their latest rich-get-richer scheme? With the Medicare payroll tax, imposing an additional levy on people's jobs.

The problem is that we've been indifferent to economic disparities. It has never made sense to me that private property is essential, yet policy makers treat its patterns as irrelevant. That, of course, is total nonsense. Ridiculing dangerous economic nonsense is a key focus of my work, plus figuring out how commonsense finance can be designed to evoke broad-based ownership. I figure that's the most promising way to ensure that the economic system itself smartens up, and it will do so when it's connected — through ownership rights — to those whose lives it influences. Modern-day risk management requires that we no longer grant unfettered dominance to pricing signals.

You referred to the local market economies, and I want to take us back 225 years to the founding of the United States. Certainly it was a local market economy at that time. When we go back to the vision of America, everything Jefferson was talking about, everything all these people were talking about was based on local market economies. In some sense, what I hear you saying is that we need to recover that vision because clearly, when we're talking about democracy, we're talking about individual human beings, individual citizens working together in community, not having a huge entity called the government taking care of everything or even trying to take care of everything. Rather, it goes back to the local communities.

California is a perfect example. In 1996, our legislature voted a hundred to zero to privatize the energy systems in California. Basically they said, "Don't worry about it. Trust us. This will work out." Obviously, it did not. And yet, at the same time, within California, in Sacramento itself, the capital of California, there was a locally owned utility. There hasn't been a problem there. I live in Ukiah, a town that has a locally owned utility. There's not a problem here.

It seems we know the mechanism but somehow there's this system that's preventing us from using it. That's what you're talking about, that's what you're addressing. I just wanted to bring in the connection to the original vision that launched this nation. It's a vision that somehow we need to reconnect with in order to enter the future in a new way.

Both markets and democracies are based on the notion that they are learning systems. Markets respond to consumers, democracies to constituents. That's their moral foundation as self-designed systems meant to grant people the dignity of self-determination. However, the current economic model assumes that financial value — as signaled by the pricing of both products and financial properties (stocks, bonds, etc.) — is sufficient unto itself. That's the bandwidth to which we should attune the system's operations. While that's not a bad idea, it's easily overdone. Markets make great servants but lousy masters, and even worse religions. While prices are clearly essential, to suggest that they're sufficient unto themselves should be portrayed not as economic science but as a modern-day symptom of insanity.

That becomes even more obvious when you realize how few people hold wildly disproportionate stakes. Even those well-heeled few were persuaded by the neoliberals to say, "Okay, let's look solely to financial value. Let's assume that all values are reflected in share prices, and then let's assume that maximizing that single value is a suitable proxy for private ownership." Mechanistic, deterministic, reductionist, Newtonian — both in concept and application. It's a money-on-auto-pilot system with the following mantra: maximize financial value and — don't worry — everything else will work out fine. Provided policy-makers stay out of it. The only appropriate role for elected officials is to create a level playing field for financial forces to work their ineffable wisdom on the world — unimpeded by the petty distractions of public policy.

The problem is that if you do that, you may indeed get cheaper and cheaper goods in your stores, but what typically happens is that in order to produce those goods we go abroad to produce them. So people don't have the income with which to buy the goods. As a result, we have what's called an "over-capacity recession," which is what we were going into before 9-11. That disaster has only made it much, much worse.

But let me come back to your localization issue. The challenge is this: "How do we get from where we are to an economic system that's sensitive to the concerns of people, place, and pace, that's localized and community-wise rather than simply being globalized and what I call 'dumbed down'?"

And we're not talking here just about the United States. We're talking about the entire world.

That's correct. I've advised roughly forty countries to date, and, believe me, the word "ownership" translates cross-culturally. People know what it means when something is mine or my neighbor's or when it belongs to my community. The more personal it becomes, the more real it gets. A property stake empowers people to have some influence over their lives, and over those firms that have an influence on their lives. With that property-legitimized stake, people can — by right — ensure that local commercial operations respond to a bandwidth of values broad enough to reflect the legitimate concerns of those who live locally. It's hugely encouraging to see communities, both here and abroad, resisting the economic model of globalization and its insistence that deference, even dominance, be granted exclusively to financial values. Ironically, it's those insisting on this model who are the most chronically clueless when it comes to risk management. If you take that finance-obsessive model to its logical end, it becomes, for lack of a better term, a modern-day "finance fascism."

I worked as an investment banker for several years. The firm's managing partner would walk in some mornings, greeting us with what I still think of as the Wall Street mantra: "Good morning. Money is smarter than people. Have we made any yet?" In the financial domain, he's correct. If you gear the system solely to financial value — and write laws that ensure its dominance — that mandated signaling system will generate lots of financial value. You'll have strong financial markets, at least for a while. What you won't have is strong communities, particularly so long as those financial values flow not to Main Street but to Wall Street.

So how do we restore and protect communities? How do we recover and preserve that key unit of democratic governance? For starters, we apply the same legal and financial skills that are applied to mergers and acquisitions in the developed world. Just over the past two decades, we've seen well over 200,000 of these shape-shifting transactions in the U.S. alone. The same investment bankers who merged and conglomerated all those enterprises would be delighted to collect fees for picking them back apart and imbedding some component of each operation's ownership in those communities where the operations are based. Those high-paid service-providers would be tickled pink to disperse the ownership of firms they previously concentrated. We know the ins-and-outs of the financial technologies required to repeople-ize capitalism and to imbed it in communities. That's what I write books about.

One helpful feature of finance is from the fact that it works in a totally metaphorical domain. Finance is not real, at least not in the physical sense. No one can see finance; its operations are invisible, intangible. It's become somewhat transparent to me because I've been immersed in it for so long. It's helpful to recall that all financial metaphors are related to water: cash flow, sunk costs, pooled assets, liquidity crunch, rising tide, trickle down, washed out. I've collected about 150 similar words and phrases. Even the term *leverage* has its counterpart in hydraulics. That gives me great hope that we can make the domain of dollars visible to people.

I'm working on that project now, in collaboration with cartoonists and graphic artists. The goal is to generate visually engaging materials so that people can see the larger financial flows in which they're imbedded and then can use that knowledge to better grasp what financial forces are at work in their own communities. I am confident that with that kind of understanding of interrelatedness, people will jump at the opportunity to design their way to a more caring and compassionate capitalism, one that's more reliant on local input. That's how we wed democracy to markets. That's how we restore a people-based sovereignty to democracy. Once people understand that that's a policy option, they'll insist on a design that designs them in, because they'll see that economic "science" is largely comprised of political choices reduced to rule-writing. That's my experience from working a dozen years in Washington, the rule-writing center of the known universe. Capitalism *can* be engineered for inclusion.

For systems thinkers, the financial challenge is crystal clear: we have 76 million baby boomers barreling toward retirement with votes and precious few assets. If you think those crafting our financial laws are conservatives, think again. Genuine conservatives would embrace laws that include some semblance of fiscal foresight. Instead, after two full decades of neoliberal legislating by both Demopubs and Republicrats, we face a fiscal train wreck. Yet we know we can turn this around. And we know we have no choice but to do so. What's not known is whether our *current* crop of legislators can be persuaded to reframe the problems so we get more sensible solutions. That's the mission ahead of us, and that's what I work at. I'm not a troublemaker so much as a problem-maker. I raise the awkward issue of ownership patterns.

We have about four percent of the population using forty percent of the world's resources. That's America. The world doesn't need any more Americans. Every new American is going to consume up to forty percent of the world's resources. How do we address that? Obviously, something needs to give here. What you're saying — is that the give? Is that the solution? And if so, how do we implement that? How do we start saying, "Hey, you two rich guys, you have to redistribute the wealth here."

Well, working with the son of Huey "Share Our Wealth" Long, rest assured, I continue to make certain that I never use the term "redistribute." It's one of those flash points, politically.

There are two built-in features of finance that favor those who believe in broad-based wealth: one, people die, and two, assets wear out. So over time, simply by changing an amazingly small number of laws, you can change the ownership patterns in the United States dramatically — absolutely dramatically. As I mentioned earlier, when I went to the Senate Finance Committee in 1980, a hefty $1,900 billion were held by money managers in the U.S. Now they hold $17,000 billion. That changed dramatically in just twenty years, from 1980 to 2000. We know how to finance, and we know how to change the ownership patterns created by finance. We know how to do it without government dictates or regulations. We know how to do it with the design that we build into the system itself. It's quite an indictment of the current education system that we would buy into a model that has us living in a capitalist system while requiring that we save our labor income to buy a stake in that system. We know that capitalism can be designed so that it creates capitalists at the same time that it finances capital. It's eminently doable and we know how to write the rules to do it. We've got the most financially sophisticated people on the planet living in this country.

The question is, "Can you get the Congress to say, 'Look, we don't want just full employment'?" That was a great national objective about two hundred years ago. What we'd like to have is full employment of our labor resources and full ownership of our capital resources. You can have both, and set that as your national objective — it only took us a few years to get to the moon, and this is much easier than going to the moon. This is just a matter of changing a few laws here and there, so that you don't have the dysfunctional system we have now.

For example, right now we have one individual in the United States —we share the same last name as myself— who is projected by the year 2020 to be a quadrillionaire. That is a million billion, or billion million, depending on which way you like your math. The current neoliberal response would be to say, "Well, what's the problem?" Now, as someone who's worked in policy-making and finance for three decades, I'm telling you that a model that treats ownership patterns as irrelevant is profoundly dysfunctional.

The current economic model says two things: "Maximize financial returns and trust us, everything is going to turn out fine." That's the operating principle driving the neoliberal model. The distributional principle is equally simple: "Drink your fill and thirst for more." Those are the only two principles I've been able to detect. Now that, I can tell you, is profoundly dysfunctional; I chronicle all the problems with this model in *The Ownership Solution* and *Democracy at Risk*, which is the sequel to that earlier book. We must, therefore, reframe the question. Imagine: We've got the entire U.S. Congress trying to create full employment three hundred years into an industrial revolution, with a globalized labor market and a policy environment where the largest tax that 80 percent of us pay is a tax on jobs — the Social Security payroll tax . Silly me, here I thought the idea was to tax what you want less of.

So we've got this system that actually makes no sense internally and that clearly is not working for people. Meanwhile, in the last thirty-six months the wealth of the 400 richest people in America went up by $1.4 billion each. That's an average daily increase of $1.9 million per person, $240,000 per hour, 46,202 times the minimum wage. Now there obviously is no sense in that. That's profoundly unfair, but more importantly, it's unsustainable.

So how can we do something that's sensible, commonsensical? We can go back to common sense. We can go back to what Thomas Jefferson and others say, and what Adam Smith assumed. We can design systems that have relationships that are able to respond to local concerns. With private property being essential, as I believe it is, that suggests the only possible alternative is broad-based, local-based ownership. We've got to go back to having at least a component of that, or this system has no chance to get a feedback loop in place so it can hear the concerns of the people who live locally. They have to have a feedback loop so that corporations are required to take people's concerns into account — the real concerns of real people, not just the abstract values of remote financial markets.

AMY GOODMAN

Manufacturing Consent for Peace

 Amy Goodman *is well known to many public radio listeners in the United States through her program "Democracy Now." It so happened that on September 11, 2001, she was operating out of a makeshift studio a few blocks away from the World Trade Center. In the days thereafter, she regularly spoke with various individuals who were in one way or another directly affected by the havoc wrought by the destruction of the World Trade Center. It was during this period that I caught up with her on the phone and we spoke of her experiences and her views of the times.*

MICHAEL: *Where were you when the events of September 11 unfolded?*

AMY: I was in the firehouse of Engine 31, just blocks from the World Trade Center, in the attic of this firehouse, broadcasting "Democracy Now: In Exile." I heard a "boom." We all did. I just kept reading. We were in an attic, and so there were only very small windows. We couldn't quite make out what it was, but we were in an odd situation, and not in a soundproof room — it's real-life radio — and so we thought it was just some loud noise on the street. Then someone in the building came up onto our floor, very agitated — at that moment we were broadcasting some tape — and told us a plane had hit the World Trade Center. We were very puzzled, and after talking a bit we went and turned on cable television, despite the fact that we were very close to the World Trade Center. That's when we saw the tower on fire, and the other tower as well.

Then I broke into our broadcast and just said what we were seeing. Very soon after that, as we continued with the program, the towers started to crumble. The towers started to topple over. To say the least, it was absolutely incredible to not even be able to process all that I was hearing. I was just saying it as fast as I was hearing it on television. Although on the one hand we were very close, the experience of it was watching television and hearing the producers shout to me as I repeated everything on the air.

131

And then we just stayed on for hour after hour, not even sure who was broadcasting the signal, because we felt it was our responsibility to let people know what we were hearing as it was coming out. Having covered disasters before, we knew that a lot comes out in the beginning that you know isn't true. But we just kept repeating what we were hearing. So on the one hand we had TV, but we were right there.

Downstairs, though I had no time to go downstairs, people in the firehouse were setting up phones and water for people that were just tumbling away, stumbling down the street from the site. After a while we brought people up to the studio, people who were coming from the area, who were covered in soot or some kind of ash, and they told us their stories and we broadcast them on the air to whatever community radio station in the country was still listening. At one point it dawned on me that it was possible we weren't broadcasting anywhere. We had just kept on going. I said on the air, "If anyone's hearing this broadcast, give us a call." After a while we got calls from Florida and Vermont. We got calls from Minneapolis and California, and we realized, yes, people were listening and depending on us for information. So we kept going, and I said it as I heard it and started to get the stories of the people who had been in the World Trade Center Towers.

Since that time, since September 11, what have you primarily been doing?

We've been broadcasting the voices of people all over the world right back down to Ground Zero, broadcasting the perspectives of people who are not just responding to what they hear in the U.S. media, which are very much, as Noam Chomsky says, manufacturing consent for war. That's very much the purpose the corporate media in this country serve. But we've been hearing from people who themselves have been the victims of terror, because that's what we've seen here and that's what is so deplorable, so heinous. It is people who are victims of terror. Now that has happened in this country and in my community in New York, in the many communities of New York. Terror, the killing of innocent civilians, is a horrible thing. We're having long discussions about it, including the survivors in those conversations and the people who've lost loved ones in the World Trade Center.

I see such a difference between what people on the ground are saying, people who are directly affected, and what I'm seeing in the media. In the media, they'll have the people who have lost family members talk about who those family members were, but then they go to the so-called experts to find out where we should go from here. If you ask the people who lost loved ones in the World Trade Center, you rarely hear expressions of vengeance or bloodlust or desire for revenge. I hear tremendous sorrow and sympathy. Covering different places in the world, including places where people became victims of U.S., I find the same thing everywhere: when people are victims of terror, their hearts go out to others. They don't want this kind of thing to happen again. And that's what I hear from people who are the victims of the World Trade Center attack: "Never again." We can't answer this killing of civilians with the killing of civilians somewhere else.

As someone who is among millions on the outside looking at how New York responded to these tragic events, I and, I think, many others find that New York is a model of how to respond to a terrible tragedy like this. One would hope that our government, our leadership, would see New York as a model.

I hope that's the case, but I don't see that reflected in the media, unfortunately. I wonder how clearly people can see New York. A good example is what happened in those first few days in Union Square, which has a long radical history. It's called Union Square. It became a kind of Peace and Democracy Park. They've cleaned it out right now, but thousands of people came and put up the pictures of their loved ones, of those who were lost, pictures with the person's name on them, and then a few words, like "Last seen on the 104th floor of the south tower. Please call."

And then there were so many people who just gathered for discussion and debate and vigil in the park. I think they cleaned it out because it was too much of a threat. I think they cleaned it out because that was where the honest discussions were going on about where we go from here, very reflective discussions, discussions about why people would be so angry about who committed this crime and about those people being brought to justice, but not about whole populations being wiped out as a result.

I stayed in the firehouse for three days. I never left because we were within the evacuation zone and the police and military had closed off the whole area around the firehouse that we were broadcasting from in Chinatown. At night I would walk out. Everything was closed down, and there were police checkpoints everywhere. I was afraid we'd be thrown out and not be able to broadcast, so I didn't leave.

One night it was pouring rain, and people were walking around with those pictures. I was thinking about the mothers of the people who disappeared in Argentina, and how they must have felt as they roamed the streets looking for their loved ones. And that was now happening in New York.

We're going through a different phase right now, although we're still in shock. But as we're in shock, in Washington they're mobilizing for war. So there really is not time to just live in this surreal world where we know that just down the street is an unfathomable funeral pyre, a funeral pyre of more than six thousand people who have been incinerated. And it's just down the street from us.

As the search and recovery operation continues — and we know that we won't find anyone alive — there has to be a rapid response to how those in power in this country are mobilizing billions of dollars for war when we can hardly deal with the people in the streets who are homeless and the people who have crumbling schools. We're also dealing with all of these laws that are being put into place, a kind of wish list of those in power who are getting through a series of repressive laws that are taking away our civil liberties, moving toward fast-track, and pouring money into the military. Bush could never have gotten these through before, but he is using this as an opportunity to push it all through, to shore up very blatantly repressive regimes in the world, and to get rid of any restriction on selling them arms. It's a real bonanza for the military contractors and those who would make a buck off of people's suffering.

It does seem that Colin Powell, Secretary of State, in attempting to put together a coalition, has been a balancing force in the Cabinet. What do you think?

Actually, I see it this way: what do we expect when the Secretary of State is a military general? I don't see Colin Powell as distinct from President Bush or Vice President Cheney. What we see in this country right now is a serious mobilization of all the international resources for war.

Do you have hope that there's another possibility, another alternative that might unfold?

I have tremendous hope in people who can see through this war frenzy. Right now, there a major rally in New York on Sunday, October 7, at 3:00 at Union Square, where people have been gathering from the first day of the terror attacks. Last week I was in Washington, D.C., for the first major rallies. I know there were others in San Francisco, as well as thousands of people protesting all over the world. There is a major discussion going on, a global discussion about what is happening in the world, why people perceive the U.S. the way they do, with the U.S. pulling out of the U.N. World Conference Against Racism just the week before the terror attacks happened. There are conversations about justice, about finding those who are guilty of these horrible attacks and bringing them to justice, but using the rule of law to do it. Timothy McVeigh was found, captured, indicted, and tried. I don't agree with the death penalty, but he was put to death. No one wondered aloud whether or not his sister should have been killed, or his dad. In the same way, no one suggested that his community should be wiped out.

And yet in this case, without even presenting the evidence, our government is saying that whole populations will be bombed. You're talking about some of the most defenseless people on earth. If we're talking about Afghanistan, you look at how these people have been victimized by a government that was brought to power with the support, ultimately, of the United States. It's called blowback. The U.S. supports these thugs who train in Afghanistan, provides them with military backing and funding, and then they come to power and they repress women, as we certainly know the Taliban have done. One of the products of this blowback, of this U.S. support for those undemocratic forces, is Osama bin Laden. His training was made possible by the United States and the U.S.-backed Pakistani military regime. We have to be very honest about what this country has done in other places in the world. If we want to see justice, we have to start right here at home.

I think history shows that we tend to demonize individuals. In the case of Saddam Hussein, and certainly of Hitler, perhaps with good reason. But this demonizing doesn't really address the source of the problem. We may take out Osama bin Laden, but that doesn't take out terrorism.

That's right. If we're going to look at terrorism, certainly this is a model case. Whoever did this did it in the United States, in Washington, D.C., in a Pennsylvania farm field, at the Pentagon, and in New York at the World Trade Center. But we have to be very honest about it and look at what the U.S., our own country, the number one superpower in the world, has done. Look at what happened in Vietnam with two million Vietnamese dead. Look at what happened in Chile with Nixon and Kissinger supporting the rise of Pinochet and the overthrow of the democratically elected leader, Salvador Allende — thousands of people killed there. Certainly look at the U.S.-backed military regime of Indonesia: Suharto was one of the longest-reigning dictators and had full U.S. support from Henry Kissinger and a number of presidents, from Ford right up through Clinton — and look at what the Indonesian regime did to the people of East Timor: two hundred thousand people dead.

We cannot have a double standard. We must condemn and stop terrorism wherever it happens. If it happens at the World Trade Center, the people must be brought to justice. And if it happens in East Timor, those responsible, right to the top — Henry Kissinger, for example — must be brought to justice. When we have a single standard, that's when there'll be justice in the world and perhaps terror will stop.

JACOB NEEDLEMAN

The Inner Meaning of America

My dialogue with Jacob Needleman, *Professor of Philosophy at San Francisco State University, began in the mid-1970s. Our conversation started because of* The New Religions, *a prescient book he authored which foresaw the explosion of Eastern traditions in the West — and it has continued ever since. He is a philosopher and addresses the world from that perspective, which is much needed in these times. Our conversations are always exciting because we both love ideas. Jacob is often ahead of the curve, as in the recent publication of* The American Soul: Rediscovering the Wisdom of the Founders, *which speaks directly to the need for the renewal of America's vision.*

JACOB: My first reflection on September 11 was about the shock, the stunning shock. My thoughts at that moment went in many directions. One was to the earthquake in 1989, when everyone was made quiet, everybody, as it were, stood still. With very few exceptions, it was as though people throughout the whole San Francisco Bay Area were suddenly lifted into a consciousness of themselves, were aware of themselves in a way we almost never are — aware of our very lives. It was, in a way, a spiritual moment, using the term *spiritual* in the toughest possible sense. People were open to each other, helping each other, and waiting. They had a sense of the illusions that had governed their lives, the attachments, the material things, the tenseness, the haste — it was a transforming moment, with all of the destruction of property and everything, and the fear.

I felt how similar, in a way, and yet how different September 11 was. In a way, the reaction to the earthquake was a reaction to nature, to God, if you like, to forces of nature that are so much more powerful than we are and that we tend to forget. But this event had another quality to it that was very disturbing to everybody — it was not what God had done to us, but what human beings had done to each other. That made us quiet, but not in the same way that the earthquake did. It made us look at ourselves and wonder what we are.

So that was my first reaction — the anguish, the fear that began to enter into all of us, the questioning, and, of course, the sense of hysteria that, in many ways, seems justifiable. Suddenly we were in the war mentality, where fear and lies and rumors and anger and impatience were devouring us. It becomes a question now of finding the mind in ourselves that cannot just be fundamentally quiet, but that can take into account everything, be attentive to everything, look at the whole picture — and be aware of the fact that we don't have the whole picture, yet that we may need to act without having the whole picture, in our personal lives and as a nation. This is such a rare thing that we need to develop in ourselves, an intelligence that can take everything into account. It's a question of becoming aware of how little we know, of being aware of how we're affected by all the emotions that are in the air and in the press and on the television, of how deeply that's affecting us against our will.

There's an agitation of the mind that is the source of all the sorrow and all the anguish and all the destruction that people visit upon each other. You can be just as agitated in a desire for peace as you can be in a desire for war. What would it mean to be effective in this world and still, somewhere, have a quiet mind? At the same time, the sense of what America is is very much in people's hearts and minds now — whoever they are, wherever they are. There is something happening here in America that suddenly makes these kinds of questions much more real: What do we have here? What is this country, really? We all know it's not just a place that's making a space for luxury, so that we can satisfy ridiculous desires and obsessions and consumer passions. What really are the values of America? What values did the founders have? If you look deeply, you see echoes of a great wisdom tradition in what they were wrestling with, whether they knew it or not. We haven't even scratched the surface of the real meaning of the values of America — the meaning of freedom, of independence, of the rule of law, the rule of reason, of democracy, of respect for one another, of equality, the intrinsic equality of all human beings under God.

What those of us who are in the kind of work that you and I and others are doing have to contribute is to deepen, in a revolutionary way, the inner meaning of the ideals of America, to really deepen them — by not making clichés out of "freedom of speech" and "freedom of the press." But what does it mean to have independence, freedom, freedom of conscience? If we look at those ideals in the light of the great wisdom teachings, we'll see that they are echoes of a great wisdom that perhaps doesn't exist in any other part of the world quite as cleanly as it has existed here.

CHAPTER

7

GOING DEEPER: THE SPIRITUAL DIMENSION

A DEEPENING THIRST FOR MEANING and purpose is abroad in the land. Spiritual longing pervades, mostly under the radar screen of the mass media. Americans are desperate for community. What's needed now is the recovery of our spiritual bearings, not in a doctrinal or dogmatic sense, but simply in the natural grace of living in harmony with our fellow humans and the material world. Practicing kindness. Telling the truth with compassion. Acting from integrity. Coming from love, not from fear. This path is not easy. However, it is clearly the only path worth following, if we are to survive as a species on the planet and if future generations are to have a life worth living. We are being called to be spiritual activists engaging the world as warriors. We can see this throughout all strata of society. Our institutions such as education, government, health, and social services are rife with decay and largely ineffectual. Nearly 50 percent of our government's budget is spent on the military at the expense of everything else: the homeless, the hungry, the 40 million uninsured Americans, and so on. This craziness is rooted in a basic disconnection from life's purpose.

The events of 9-11 brought home the essential questions to us all: Why am I here? What am I doing with my life? What's important? Will my children and grandchildren live in a better world? Since none of us is assured of a tomorrow, what is the best we can do today in our sphere of influence? Spirit is the source of our power; we can stand on the shoulders of those who came before us and were willing to act in the face of what appears to be overwhelming odds. As Bill Moyer points out in *Doing Democracy*, nonviolent social movements have doubled each decade since the 1960s. Hope pervades. My definition of hope is this: "Hope is believing in spite of the evidence and working actively to change the evidence."

JOANNA MACY

The Great Turning

To be alive at this time provides the opportunity for all of us to be part of a spiritual adventure. Our future as a species on the planet is at stake, which challenges us to move past old model thinking that fosters self-inter-est and greed. Ever since I met Joanna Macy many years ago, she has been on the front lines of leading the culture to new, positive possibilities. Often, we can feel overwhelmed, immobilized, and unable to deal realistically with the threats to life on Earth. This reac-tion to the world crisis may be a psychological defense mechanism that has its roots in the Cold War arms race when we were compelled to adapt within a single generation to the horrific possibility of nuclear holocaust. Joanna's work has always been to help us through the pain and confusion of our time to the place of common humanity and the solidarity we share with all life.

MICHAEL: *What is the significance of this new time we've entered since the events of September 11, 2001?*

JOANNA: I see an enormous challenge here, an epochal challenge to all of us who have been working with the new paradigm of the Earth as a living system and all the possibilities and requirements of sustainability. I see this as a turning point in our long evolutionary journey. We now must take seriously all that we have been learning and teaching in the last decades — to deepen that under-standing and act on it. At this moment, the challenge to our survival and even the survival of complex life forms on Earth, which was already in question before September 11, becomes more critical than ever because we, the one remaining superpower, have become distracted by an attack on us such as we've never expe-rienced before. Against the counsel of many, we have proceeded to turn it into an occasion for war, a war against an ill-defined and ubiquitous enemy. We are being persuaded and frightened to give up some of the very freedoms that we have fought for over generations, since the founding of our nation.

So we're losing time against the real war. I agree with what Robert Muller, the former Assistant Secretary General of the United Nations, said at the turn of the millennium: "We must declare a state of emergency of the earth and consider that the historical moment in which we're living is an outright war, a war against nature and its elements, a war also against our brother and sister beings, including the human beings, waged by an unsustainable industrial growth society."

The transition from the industrial growth society to a life-sustaining civilization is happening now. It is the great and essential adventure of our time. I call it "the great turning." Many of the people that you bring to the air in your interviews are part of that great turning: voices of resistance, of understanding, voices of ancient spiritual traditions, and contemporary science.

The shift to a life-sustaining society is going to be harder and rougher now because this war against terrorism is costing us irreplaceable time, resources, and attention. We are also losing access to information, which is crucial to our survival, because the mainstream media bow to money and become a vehicle for the party in power. So voices like your network are incredibly important at this time.

It's not when times are easy that you discover your true courage, your strength, and even your faith. It's not when political powers mirror your values and enact them in tidal flows of justice and care that you find out what you're really born to do. I think many of us living now were born to help us survive this crisis and to turn the immense power of life towards creating a beautiful, sustainable future. And every day matters now, and every chance we have to work together matters.

It's being suggested that if we challenge or question the actions of our government, or dissent in any way, that's unpatriotic. What's your view?

Some of us are falling for that, but a lot of us are not. I'm grateful for your broadcasts and for voices of dissent. I'm grateful for KPFA [one of the five Pacific radio stations in the U.S.]. I'm grateful for the Internet. The founding fathers and mothers of this country knew perfectly well that free circulation of information and opinions is absolutely necessary to vigilantly maintain our democracy.

How would you define patriotism?

I am very grateful for the core values on which this country was founded. They have allowed me to claim rights as a woman that weren't in practice at the time we wrote the Constitution. Those same values have helped us get rid of slavery and win the right to create unions, the right to have a Freedom of Information Act — which is now going down the tubes. I'm proud of the people who have given their lives for those values. I would give my life for them; maybe I'm doing that now. Speaking your mind and dissenting from what you consider undemocratic and brutal and a contravention of internationally recognized human rights, that's patriotic right down the line, I say.

Earlier, you used the term "the great turning." How can we show up and participate in what you're calling "the great turning?"

It is helpful to see that the great turning, this epochal transition to a life-sustaining civilization, is taking place in three main ways or dimensions. The activities in the first dimension are like hold actions because they slow down the damage being done by the industrial growth society. They include legal, legislative, electoral, and regulatory work as well as direct action and civil disobedience. They are necessary because they save some lives, some species, some ecosystems, and some genetic material. But that's not enough.

We need some alternative structures, and their arising in this time constitutes the second dimension of the great turning. Here we create systems change. It involves media, like the work you're doing. It involves teaching, which I do a lot, as well, of course, as food production and distribution. It is happening in permaculture, biodynamic farming, and the ways we hold land and build housing; it involves alternative forms of healing and of measuring wealth and prosperity. Still, that's not enough for the great turning, because these new institutions, new structures, new ways of behaving will shrivel and die unless they're deeply rooted in our values, in who we actually think we are, in what we are, in how we're related to each other and to the living body of earth.

The third dimension is a spiritual revolution and a perceptual and cognitive revolution as well. It is bursting forth from science and cosmology, and it is nurtured by currents within every major religion as well as by ancient indigenous wisdom traditions and women's spirituality, and Wiccan magic. What I love about this way of looking, which feeds me and so many of my colleagues now, is that it is no longer a question of whether it is more important to work on yourself or on society. Should I sit on my meditation cushion to try to get enlightened, or should I organize for healthy food? Should I go to personal growth seminars and get my head together and then go out to take part in the healing of our world? This kind of argument has been very boring. The truth is, you have to do it all now, and doing one helps you do the other. I bet most of your listeners are participating in two or three of those dimensions already.

You're probably right. What is sustaining you in this time?

Learning to take seriously what I've been so fortunate to receive from my root tradition and from Buddhist practice. I just took part in celebrations honoring the birthday of Dr. Martin Luther King and again I find myself sustained by his teachings and his example. In the last year of his life, that wonderful man insistently called people to recognize the "inescapable network of mutuality in which we're all held." That is also the core teaching of the Lord Buddha who had a different name for it: dependent co-arising. Thich Nhat Hanh calls it inter-being.

The challenge of that truth brings me courage and joy. It calls us to link arms, to not try to do anything alone. Whether it's a study group to learn what's happening or a sharing of information— do it together. When I fall into the old notion that it's up to me to find the total saving response for all people, that's a recipe for burnout and despair. So when I falter, I call to mind my brothers and sisters — for example Justine and Michael Toms and how faithful they've been to their vision over the years. We're learning to draw inspiration from each other, and energy, because we're all part of this dance of life, and it wants to go on.

I often think to myself that it always is reassuring to me to see your name and your work out there, and getting a brochure or some mention that Joanna's doing this or that always makes me feel good. Joanna's doing her work and that's good for the planet, good for me, good for all of us.

Yes.

Another thing is that in order to not be scared into remaining silent and hiding, we need to share what we know and see — we need to study together and also to witness together. The failure of the mainstream media to report the truth of what's happening has been taking root over the last three decades, particularly through the accelerated growth of corporate globalization. We may think it's all too much to understand, so I've been experimenting with ways we can learn together. The use of study circles is one of the great social inventions of the twentieth century. To help us wise up, my colleagues and I have also been experimenting with rituals for learning where we listen, on behalf of other beings as well as for ourselves, to data delivered in a ritual fashion with a drum.

All natural systems are self-organizing, and so are we and our minds — but we need the information. We mustn't bow out because we imagine we're too stupid. We've got to learn together, as much as lobby and petition and demonstrate together.

Are you hopeful about the future?

Oh, yes. And I also despair over the terrible waste of life. I don't know whether we're here, you and I, as deathbed attendants to a dying civilization or as midwives to a new one. Maybe the truth is that we are called to be both. Even in that, you know, there is hope, there is vitality.

DAVID LA CHAPELLE

Listening and Belonging

When David La Chapelle *first visited the studios of New Dimensions Radio, we weren't prepared for the gifts he brought to us and our audience. His merging of the spiritual with the ecological and his ability to reach to the core of what life is about were stunning. His book,* Navigating the Tides of Change, *published prior to 9-11, is prescient and abounds in stories about the power of the individual to catalyze creative change in the world. Here he provides a fresh perspective on what we're facing as human beings and citizens living in a democracy.*

MICHAEL: *What do the events of September 11, 2001, signify for you?*

DAVID: This particular event has asked me to pause and reflect deeper, deeper probably than any other thing I have experienced in this lifetime. That in itself I take as very potent, strong, and good medicine. God has asked me to stop much of what I've been doing at various levels, and to keep listening more and more deeply to discover what a true and authentic response might be to this situation. I have to say that the depth of the experience is pulling forth a new level of response, not so much in terms of what I'm thinking or saying, but really in how I'm being. That may be one of the great hidden gifts in this situation, which is so potent that it has fundamentally changed the structure of our lives. It is asking us to look and see if we can find a really new way to be. That's a very deep and metaphysical as well as a very practical issue, given that the currents of world events are many. I think there are some eloquent voices expressing those.

What I see in most of the people I'm talking to and also in myself is a very personal, extremely personal question, which is, "How do I act now?" And, more importantly, "How am I in this?" This has a very quieting effect on me. I find that I'm not thinking quite as much, I'm not reading quite as much, I'm taking more time to be by myself, and I'm listening more. In that, I'm feeling more connected to those around me and to myself. So if I were to have some gratitude for a very horrible situation, it would be because it's moved me personally into a deeper state of listening. I would hope that, in fact, that's actually what's going on in the world at large.

I was doing a little investigation about what martyrs are all about, because it's clear that if you interviewed those terrorists, they would probably consider themselves martyrs to a very powerful cause, a very powerful ideology. It turns out that the root of *martyr* means "to witness," and there's some sort of religious quality in that: to bear witness to one's faith. The ultimate act is to die for one's faith, and they moved with this very interesting dance with death. September 11 has also asked us to witness; it's kind of an inescapable witnessing moment. It's very hard to turn away from this event and not pay attention, not witness what's happening.

A theme emerging from this is that somehow we pick up this collective witnessing so that we don't have to take it to death in order to have an impact, so we don't have to become terrorists in a certain way. I think we become terrorists in our lives by not witnessing correctly or by not paying attention correctly, so we exert some of the same subtle forces as the damage, violence, and disarray, because we're not simply paying attention in the way that we could. Attention becomes a huge issue in these times, and a very paradoxical one at that because there's so much in the air. There's so much tension in the atmosphere. It's sometimes hard to pay attention at that level. And yet, this is the medicine that's going to help us the most through this situation — that is, to really bear witness to one another and to the situations and events in the world, so that a deeper and more humane and wise response can come through all of us.

You mentioned listening to yourself. Can you make a bridge between this event and listening? In some ways, perhaps, this terrible act happened because these nineteen people didn't feel heard or listened to. What about listening in this whole process?

There are many dimensions of listening, obviously. There's the external world where we listen to the voices around us. Then there's the ability to actually listen within. Probably at one level you could say the terrorists were listening. They were listening to some call that took them into a very horrific act. So we have to be careful about what we listen to, both in terms of the kind of information we listen to in the world and in terms of the way we can establish a true connection to a larger whole. All the spiritual traditions speak of simply listening to our own machinations and manufactured difficulties, which come out of a tremendous lack of connection. Schizophrenics and people who are feeling disconnected from life in a particular way, whether neurologically, sociologically, or psychologically, all tend to come up with their own voices as a way to fill that void. That's not the kind of listening, obviously, that we're talking about.

We're talking about the voice of wisdom, of compassion, about listening to the quality of life that reaches through us and connects beyond us. In that we can realize the best of humanity. Many of the greatest gifts that we've brought through as a human species have come because somebody somewhere listened. They were able to turn aside from the daily concerns and the usual content of their lives and to choose an act of deep listening, which inspired great inventions, great courage, great capacities.

We were talking about Thomas Jefferson earlier. There's a man who listened very deeply. He used to go for horseback rides out from Monticello for hours and hours, culling and feeling the tone of the times so that he could respond correctly. I like to think of his horseback rides as a very elegant act of listening.

That reminds me of Thomas Jefferson and the grief he felt after his wife Martha's death. He went on long rides, and his daughter would accompany him and he wouldn't say anything. His daughter left diaries about this. He did this for a couple of months, feeling his grief, going really deep into his grief. Grief never leaves in some ways; it certainly never left him.

But it brings to mind that, with the kind of actions that we see on the part of our government now, there is no time left for grieving. It's as though we've got to move, we've got to do something, and yet there's this terrible grief that I think everyone feels. What about grieving?

I certainly don't pretend to be an expert on grief. But I believe it's a difficult human emotion because it takes us irreplaceably and very incredibly past our defense systems. Grief slices into the depth of who we are. To feel grief is to feel humanity, to feel our own hearts. The great invitation of grief is for us to open out beyond our own personal contraction. If we have enough empathy to feel sorrow for somebody else — and that's how grief often comes up — then we've touched a place in our own humanness that understands we are more than just ourselves.

The grief of an event like this, the shock of an event like this, actually turns us inside out so that we can discover this. I know from numerous stories of people connecting with each other in New York, connecting on planes, connecting across all kinds of boundaries, that there's a tremendous desire to reach beyond ourselves and to discover the connection that grief asks us to discover. I think grief can truly move us only if we feel something beyond ourselves. So grief is an interesting one.

There's another image I have from the event. When a child is hurt, there's a pause after the moment of the impact or the injury or the psychological disappointment or whatever, then you feel the breath being drawn in and then you wait for the wail to emerge, where the actual response of the organism can take place.

That's a really powerful motion. I've often likened this particular time to that kind of pause. There's been a huge impact, and I think we're being asked to bring that breath in, and then what is the wail of humanity? What is that expressed grief? And in that shared expression of grief, what commonality can we find? How can it help us reunite the fissures that have helped bring this event about?

One more question. In this moment, it's almost as though this event has taken the forefront. How do we deal with the extraordinary ecological challenge that we face today on the planet? It seems that ecology has dropped back in importance. How do you make the bridge between meeting the ecology challenge and what's happened now?

I've been reflecting on the fact that one of the basic tenets of the fundamentalist Islamic position is that the infidels should not be on the holy ground of Arabia. This speaks to a powerful sense of place and the importance of sacred ground. The irony of this position is that Osama bin Laden has spent most of his life as a man without a country. I find it curious that he comes from a family that runs the largest construction firm in the kingdom and was instrumental in modernizing the cities of Medina and Mecca. This massive building program, fueled by oil money, has remade the landscape of Arabia and most likely helped contribute to the sense of alienation from one's place which Osama bin Laden has become a symbol of. It may well be that his abstract idea of protecting the sacred ground of Arabia was influenced by the destruction of that sacred land in the service of modernization. That he must resort to violence to protect a land he cannot even return to is a powerful symbol of the wrenching dislocation that occurs as humanity becomes more and more alienated from its landscape.

In the events of 9-11, there is, perhaps, a powerful message: unless we come back down to ground, as the towers did literally, and unless we come back to honoring the ground on which we act and move — from which comes a sense of respect and an understanding of ecology — we will perpetuate violence. In one sense the attacks of September 11 were an act of very unbonded human beings, who have lived without any sense of place for probably years, in service of an ideology because they don't have a relationship to the landscape and the land upon which they live. And yet they're fighting for that very land. There's a really powerful tension, a paradox in that.

I think one of the crucial messages about the fundamental solutions to the dilemmas before us is this: we need to move beyond the rhetoric of living where we are to a more real and substantial relationship to our landscape, and unless we can find a way to do that — and this challenge is huge in these times — we will spawn more violence. It's a necessary response of human beings who are not feeling bonded to the land where they live.

*That last remark is interesting because it reminds me of the sense of place and con-
nection that the founders of the United States of America had. It was a strong
connection to the land. That may be the bridge, to go back to that spawning
vision. That may be one of the bridges.*

And if we look at the Native American influence on the founding fathers, we
can see that the Native Americans had a vision. Now we need to pull forth the
true wisdom of that stream. It's the fracturing apart of tribalism that has created our current situation. A tribe really wants to belong, and those terrorist acts
are huge expressions of the desire to belong. As terrible and as traumatic and as
deadly and as ill informed as the events were, the impulse was to do something
to belong. For them it was to transcend life and go to some eternal plane, but I
think it came out of this issue of massive numbers of people on the globe being
unbonded and ill-fed, living at poverty levels, having no sense of belonging.

RABBI MICHAEL LERNER

Looking Evil in the Eye

Photo by Herbert Banner

*Outspoken and courageous in the stands he has
taken, Michael Lerner is perhaps best known
through Tikkun, of which he is founding editor. His
book* The Politics of Meaning: Restoring Hope
and Possibility in an Age of Cynicism *envisioned
new ways of practicing democracy and was
attacked by cynical mainstream media. Of course,
the criticism of media mavens has often nothing to
do with the validity or plausibility of the ideas being
criticized. Michael Lerner speaks to the importance
of cooperation and collaboration, the art of compassion, and the intimate power
of the individual multiplied a thousandfold through the synergy of shared meaning and purpose.*

MICHAEL: *On September 11, 2001, we entered a new world, and all of us are in
this experience. I'd like to hear what reflections, insights, and thoughts you have
regarding the world we now live in.*

RABBI MICHAEL LERNER: We've entered a world in which many of the previous hidden dynamics have become very explicit and clear. On the one hand, we face a world with a tremendous amount of pain in it. But this pain was largely invisible to those in the United States who were part of, and primary beneficiaries of, a world economic system that has systematically exploited and impoverished people around the world. So the events of September 11 and the terrible murder that took place on that day have led many people to say, "What was going on? How could this happen? Why would anybody be mad at us?" From that discussion a great deal of insight has opened up.

At the same time a great deal of fear has emerged. Two days after the bombing of the World Trade Center and Pentagon, President Bush and conservatives were already ready with a massive escalation of defense spending. Subsequently we've seen a massive escalation of various forms of repression. The most recent one includes plans to allow the government to arrest people who are foreigners suspected of terrorism, to try them without any public notice, and to execute them without any possibility of public appeal to the court system of the United States. We've seen extraordinary moves to eliminate the protections that we've so fought so hard to create here in the United States. That's one level.

But on another, deeper level, what has become clear is that there really is a world struggle going on between two different worldviews. We have the religion that we call "modernity," which is a religion that came out of the enlightenment and that, on the one hand, had some incredibly wonderful things about it, namely, the recognition of the importance of the individual and the democratic rights and the protection of human rights, the insistence that the public sphere should not totally dominate the private sphere and that people should have a realm of privacy that's free from public coercion. On the other hand, all of those wonderful things go hand in hand with an economic political order that has increasingly concentrated wealth and power in the hands of the few at the expense of the many, particularly in the way it has operated as a worldwide system. That worldwide system has been both an economic-political and a religious system.

On the one hand, the economic system that we've brought to the rest of the world has caused a systematic impoverishment. There are many in the mainstream media today who talk about the globalization of capital as the salvation of the world. They talk about the acceleration of free trade in the world to make sure that capital gets all over, saying that that will certainly improve the conditions of everybody everywhere.

The reality is that there is an enormous disparity between the rich and the poor. In 1960, the top twenty percent of wealth holders owned thirty times as much wealth as the bottom twenty percent of wealth holders in the world. In 1990 that had gone from 30:1 to 60:1. By 1998 it had gone from 60:1 to 78:1.

What we've seen is that as American capital and the global system of which we're a part have been more successful in accelerating trade agreements, and the globalization of capital, the poor people in the world have become poorer and the disparity between rich and poor has grown dramatically.

Along with that has come a cultural impoverishment as our religion, one that has been based on materialism and selfishness, has been carried to the Third World and to the many places where capital permeates. In the United States we see this as well, although in a less venal form. We see the triumph of the bottom line, the looking out for Number One, the sense that we should suspect all our neighbors as ourselves, that is, assume that other people are going to take advantage of us and that we constantly have to protect ourselves from the others. With this worldview has come an elevation of money and power as the highest good, so that if you ask anybody in the United States, "What do you mean by 'bottom-line consciousness'?" they'll tell you that the institutions that they work for reward those people who can maximize the amount of money and power the institutions have. That is the bottom line and that's what they get rewarded for, and if they don't do well they're going to get booted out. This bottom-line consciousness subverts any sense of solidarity or connectedness between people.

On the other hand, when that operates outside of the United States, where the democratic constraints don't exist and where the United States has not been so much the champion of democracy as it has been the champion of the free will of corporations to operate without external constraint, we find that many people around the world experience the globalization of capital as a whole new religion, one that says what really counts is money and power, looking out for Number One — take care of yourself, don't count on each other. This religion has, in fact, generated a tremendous negative reaction, and this negative reaction has taken the form of a growing fundamentalism. Right-wing religious or spiritual communities have sought to protect themselves from the ethos of the marketplace by reasserting spiritual values.

Unfortunately, just as modernity, the religion of modernity that we offer the world, has both some positive and some very negative aspects, so also the form that spirituality has taken in the world today, that is, the reassertion of various forms of spiritual fundamentalism as a way to protect oneself from the ethos of selfishness and materialism and capitalism, has tremendously destructive elements as well. On the one hand, those fundamentalist communities affirm the sanctity of the world and celebrate the spiritual dimension, which I think is an extremely important element that is absent in, and, in fact, undermined by, the religion of modernity. But on the other hand, they are deeply committed to the view that salvation, or real spiritual truth, can only be had within their particular community.

Those particular communities, whatever they are — Jewish fundamentalism or Christian fundamentalism or Islamic fundamentalism or Hindu fundamentalism, whatever the form the fundamentalism takes — always demean the outsider and see the outsider, the other, as the enemy that needs to be struggled against; sometimes, as we've seen since September 11, through force and violence. But even those communities not really committed to force and violence nevertheless do involve themselves in the demeaning of the other, in the putting down of the non-believer or the person who's not part of their salvific community.

So we have here a distorted modernity — a modernity that has some very positive elements, but also some incredibly destructive elements — a distorted struggle against the distorted reality, namely, the distorted struggle against distortions, the forms of spirituality that have emerged in large parts of the world as the protection against modernity.

All of this has become much clearer after September 11. We are now in a period when it's possible to begin to ask, "How do we relate to this?" President Bush made it very clear, from his perspective, how to relate to this, namely, you're either on one side or the other. You're either with us or you're with the terrorists. You're either with modernity or you're with fundamentalism. But what many people are beginning to talk about, and what we at *Tikkun* have begun to talk about, is the creation of a third path, a third alternative, an alternative that affirms the democratic impulse and the value of the individual and the liberation of women from oppression. This third path affirms those positive elements that have been important in modernity, but rejects the individualism, the selfishness, the materialism, the narcissism, the worst about money and power, the negation of the spiritual dimension, the assertion that the only thing that is real is what is subject to empirical verification and that the only thing to be trusted is what can be measured. This third path rejects that part of modernity. On the other hand, it affirms the fundamentalist worldview of the spiritual dimensions of human reality, but rejects the authoritarianism of that view, the reading of scriptures in literalist ways, the oppression of women, and various other forms of distortion that are part of the fundamentalist dream.

One of the words being bandied about is "evil." In fact, on November 15, 2001, President Bush made a comment from his Texas ranch about the Taliban being the "evilest" group ever on the planet. I've never heard the word "evilest" but he said, "evilest." What is evil in your terms?

In my view there are only actions that are evil, not people who are evil. Certainly, the kind of action that involves the reckless destruction of human life is an evil action. We should know about that in the United States because we murdered three million people in Vietnam and we've been involved in the violent overthrow of many governments around the world over the past fifty years. One of the things we talk about in *Tikkun* is the importance of acknowledging not only the overt, intentional acts of evil but also the systemic evil from which we as Americans benefit.

This brings us to a tremendous evil in the world. Every year some thirty million children on our planet die of various diseases related to malnutrition. This malnutrition occurs not because the United States doesn't do enough to help other people. It occurs because the United States and other Western countries have set up a world economic system that systematically impoverishes many, many people around the planet. We live on a planet today in which one out of every three people lives on less than two dollars a day, less than seven hundred dollars a year. Two billion out of the six billion people on the planet live that way. One out of every six people lives on less than one dollar a day, less than three hundred and sixty-five dollars a year.

Let's try to really get a visual picture of that, that one billion people on this planet are living at the level of three hundred and sixty-five dollars a year or less, and that this causes tremendous suffering. This suffering is, in part, a product of the economic distribution that we benefit from, but that we close our eyes to. Now, that is evil. It is massive evil. When we're talking about thirty million children, we're talking about six holocausts, five or six holocausts, the whole thing we in the Jewish world are still traumatized by. The trauma is going on for people all over this planet.

So I believe it's somewhat obscene for the President of the country that benefits most from the unfair distribution of wealth in the world to be deciding who is the "evilest," without looking at the tremendous pain and suffering and the number of deaths caused by the impoverishment of the world that our system benefits from so much. This is part of the hypocrisy we're hearing day in and day out in this country. It's amazing to me, but nevertheless true, that many people have forgotten everything they knew about the unfair distribution of wealth in the world. In audiences I'm speaking to today, people say things to me that make it clear that they don't recognize that the United States, with five percent of the world's population, consumes twenty-five percent of the world's wealth. Now, if that isn't the height of pigginess, I don't know what is.

What if we were Venusians. If somebody told us about another planet on which some group of people with five percent of the population had taken over twenty-five percent of that planet's wealth, we would immediately say, "Gee, sounds to us like something is deeply wrong there." But since we're the beneficiaries of that imbalance on this planet, we tend not to focus on it at all. We only focus on the reactions against it.

Please, don't misunderstand me here. I am not one bit legitimizing the actions of the Taliban. Their oppression of women was outrageous all along, and I was always opposed to them on those grounds as well as on many other grounds. Then what happened on September 11 was a disgusting desanctification of human life. But that desanctification of human life, while totally outrageous and unjustifiable, is part of the same disease that has spread over the entire world, and that's the desanctification of human life that's built into our own economic and political system. And that parades around the world as modernity.

So that's why I'm talking about a new third path, and that's why *Tikkun* has now called for the creation of a new spiritual-political movement. We're going to have a founding conference for this, what we are tentatively calling the Tikkun community, in New York City, January 20 and 21. People who are hearing this could find out more details by going to our website (www.tikkun.org). "Tikkun," by the way, is a Hebrew word. It means "to heal, repair, and transform the world." But the gathering is not just for Jews. It's for people from all spiritual traditions and anybody who recognizes the need for spiritual healing of our planet.

In the new time that we've entered, what is personally sustaining you?

What's sustaining me is some knowledge of the history of the aspirations of the human race. Looking over the past twenty or thirty thousand years, I still see tremendous advances in the consciousness of people. We're at a moment in history when more and more people are coming to recognize our interconnectedness, the fact that we are one with each other. Indeed, on the one hand, we're just at a higher level of struggle between ego gone out of control, and individuals and selfishness gone out of control. But on the other hand we're at a much higher level of openness to recognizing that we are part of the unity of all beings. So what sustains me, in part, is the recognition of how close we are to a moment when that consciousness is ready to burst out.

I wrote something about September 11 called "A World Out of Touch With Itself: Where the Violence Begins." It was translated into about twenty different languages and sent all around the world on e-mail. I've had thousands and thousands of people from every possible background get so excited about somebody who's articulating a spiritual-political alternative. So I'm very much sustained because, even though I see the fear as very great at this moment, I also see the willingness of many people to open up to new possibilities and to really begin to recognize in a deep way that the choice is to either continue the craziness that led to September 11 or to begin to transcend our individual agendas and to connect to each other and recognize that there's only one world here, and that we're all part of it. More and more I see people recognize that what happens in any one part of the world cannot be escaped by people in some other part of the world. They are also letting go of the fantasy about technology protecting us, the notion that we could dump our bad things in the Third World, we could dump our pollution, we could push all the poverty outside of this country to some other countries, and then we could ignore it and protect ourselves through our military and political might.

The anthrax thing has really undermined some of that because more and more people are realizing that when somebody really wants to kill you, they'll find a way. When they really want to hurt you, they can find a way — and there is no real protection. The only real protection in this new world is for us to be able to openheartedly, and with a spirit of generosity and love, recognize that every other human being deserves what we deserve, that the well-being of every other human being on the planet is fundamental to our own well-being. More and more people are ready to take that step. This excites me very much, and sustains me.

Dawna Markova

Soul Rising

We are living in times of Olympic levels of distraction and busyness / business. Most all of the Western world is caught up in doing, doing, doing. We have become entrained to do in order to share, so that maybe in some distant time we can be. From the point of view of the soul, this is all backwards. As we become quiet enough to listen to the longings of the soul, we may arrive at a deeper level of activity in our lives. We must first live the being and from this will emerge the doing. Dawna Markova is someone who personifies this in her life and work.

MICHAEL: *Where were you when the events of September 11 unfolded?*

DAWNA: I was in Sundance, Utah, leading a retreat called "Time Out." It's something we do every other month for five days to help business leaders have a place and a structure in which to think about what really matters to them. It was day two of what was to be a five-day retreat. We were tucked in this valley in the Wasatoh mountains.

154

On September 10th, I had a very strange experience. I had been meditating in my room and had a strange daydream; when I rejoined the group, I asked, "Why is everybody standing around watching television sets?"

People looked really puzzled. Mary Jane said, "What are you talking about? Nobody's standing around looking at television sets."

It was some kind of a precognition. The next day, indeed, everybody was standing around watching television sets.

The next day was September 11. What happened then?

Well, we were basically stuck there. Most of the people had come from places they could not get back to. One participant was supposed to be at a meeting in the World Trade Center that particular day. But we were a community, and as a community we began to center and breathe. People needed to make connections to the rest of the world, of course, or at least find out what connections could be made. Mostly we were in the same confusion and the same unknown as everyone else was.

Sometime after these five extraordinary days that you spent in Sundance, Utah, dealing with the experience the way you dealt with it, you went to New York City and spent ten days there. What about that?

What came very clearly to me at Sundance was the message that it was for this we had come. We were doing grief work. We were doing basic support. We were helping people find and make connections. The first step to developing faith, I think, is to realize how you're connected and to what you're connected, and then very gradually you can move through the wreckage. The question is, "How to make from the debris the greatest possible good?" That's what we have been doing.

Tell us about your experience of being in New York. What was it like for you?

The first thing I was aware of was a state of complete disorientation. I've experienced that before: when my house burned down and we lost everything; when I was told I had cancer. I understand about loss, including the total loss of one's bearings. That's what I was experiencing, and I think that's what we all are still experiencing: a loss of knowing where magnetic north is. Everything was covered with a thick gray ash. It seemed to be internal as well as external. Everything that isn't really important needs to be blown away until you get back down to the bones of what's important and what we really value. To do that, you need to be willing to be disoriented and to live in confusion. Most of us are not comfortable in confusion, and yet that's where change always starts. It's almost like trying to focus one's eyes. Moving slowly through the confusion until it opens into curiosity, so you can ask, "What can I make from this? What kind of meaning can I make from this?"

One of the other things that kept running through my mind was the image of pain carving a channel, a deep channel in my heart. I believe that the channel needs to be carved in all of us because the deeper it is, the greater our capacity to allow the river of life to run through us.

I had to keep bringing myself back to experiencing the loss, the grief, so that I could make sense of it. It was difficult. It was especially challenging to allow anyone else to give the pain meaning for me. I drew on guidance from Victor Frankl, reminding myself that determining what meaning we attach to our experience is our ultimate personal freedom. All around me in New York's ash and agony, I saw Confucius' words coming to life: "The greatest glory is not in never falling, but in rising every time we fall." Meaning is yet to come, but all over New York, all over the East Coast, the people were rising and, even more importantly perhaps, were helping one another rise.

THOMAS MOORE

New Ways of Being

Thomas Moore's Care of the Soul *was a breakthrough book and has sold millions worldwide. The man behind the book is a former monk, who trained and practiced as a psychotherapist. He lives a relatively quiet life with his family in rural New England, where he continues to write. My conversations with him over the last ten years have always been illuminating, insightful, and inspiring. I always come away knowing something more about myself. Underscoring Moore's writings is his inner probing, his wanting to go deeper, to embrace the mystery. Because of this quality, his spoken words are that much more relevant.*

MICHAEL: *What do you have to say about the trauma and the tragedy of what happened on September 11?*

THOMAS: I think that when we have a tragedy of these proportions, where we just can't conceive of what has happened, it opens us up, it pushes us, I hope, to imagine our situation in ways we never would have been able to imagine before. This can go in a direction that is purely self-protective, so that people can put on a cloak of patriotism and toughness and just keep all those difficult challenges away. Or it can move us to think of new ways of being and to make a much greater effort, an infinitely greater effort, to connect with the peoples of the world and to be constructive in creating some kind of real peace.

The term "crusade" has been used. It brings to mind the history of the relationships between various great traditions, particularly between Christians and Muslims, and what has been going on in the Middle East for a long time. What are your views towards what we're dealing with now?

As many people have been saying, there is madness in every religious tradition. There's plenty of that kind of madness, some of the fundamentalist madness, in America, and it's in the rest of the world as well. So the problem is not religion. To present it this way, as some people are doing, to say this is the result of a religious belief, is really to miss the point altogether. Religion can be used as a way of understanding what's going on or of rationalizing what one does, but that doesn't mean, in fact, that the problem is a religious one. The same could be true in Northern Ireland and other places on the globe, where the issue is really not so much religion as the very deep feelings of anxiety, a history of suspicion, and a lack of real communication among people.

What do you have to say about the grief that all of us are experiencing around this?

It's almost beyond anyone's capacity to hold — the images are so powerful, they just sort of white-out your mind. A friend of mine talks about this kind of thing as a sort of Titanic madness. By that he means an irrationality that goes beyond the capacity to understand at all, or even to hold in your mind. That's very difficult, and I think it's tempting to reach out for easy solutions, to want to fight back immediately, or to blame somebody. These are the typical ways of defending against those feelings. What we need is some time to let these outrageous feelings have a chance to settle down, to coalesce, and to form some sort of picture that we can live with. I don't know any other solution. I think the longer we can hold them without acting, the better.

Do you think there's a strength or weakness in grief?

It depends on how you use grief. Grief can be a strengthening process, and I think most of the time it is. It's a way of being initiated, of making a passage in life, of moving into a new way of seeing things, even if it's only a slight difference and not terribly noticeable. I think it's very important that we hold this grief and that we express it to each other honestly and, again, do not try to find an easy way out of it, and that we eventually let that move us to a new way of being.

What is sustaining you in these moments?

Not much. I feel a lot of anxiety for my family and for our future, the future of our country and of our world. The only thing that sustains it for me is the people around me, each of them offering just the slightest insight or word of comfort or understanding. What I find is that there's a lot of repetition of ideas now about what we should do, and what we should think and feel. But within all of that, I do hear some new ideas now and then, and I think that's very helpful. I'm glad that the nation is talking to each other. I'm proud of the fact that several very fine psychotherapists have gone on television and radio and have made some good observations. We need people who are used to dealing with tragedy and grief to speak to us and say, "This is what I have learned." I'm very proud of that.

Personally, being able to pray sustains me. I can rely on my Catholic prayers, which are of great importance to me, and on my friends who can gather and can find means of expression. For example, my Jewish friends in celebrating the Holy Days or my Catholic friends celebrating a service, a Mass, and other friends in other traditions are all doing similar things. All of that helps. We certainly are pushed to rely on a world and a source of life that is far beyond us.

SOGYAL RINPOCHE

Prayer and Practice

Sogyal Rinpoche's The Tibetan Book of Living and Dying *was first published in 1992 and has been translated into 27 languages, including Chinese! The book has introduced millions to the extraordinary spiritual tradition inherent within Tibetan Buddhism. Having first met Sogyal Rinpoche in 1980, I've been able to observe his ever-widening circle of influence and the ascent of Buddhism in the West, particularly in Europe and the United States. Because I have had the opportunity to interview him numerous times, I knew he would have some insights to share about the events and the aftermath of 9-11.*

SOGYAL: I was shocked and saddened by the tragic events on September 11. Our hearts go out to the families of the victims, as well as to all their friends and colleagues. The world right now is in a highly volatile state, with people everywhere gripped by fear, apprehension and uncertainty. So this is a crucially important time for spiritual practice, whatever our practice may be, and for us to practice and pray as strongly and as wholeheartedly as we can. As we do so, we need to think of all those who have had their lives taken from them, and all those who are suffering, shocked and traumatized by this terrible act of violence.

First and foremost, we should do a very strong practice of "refuge" for them all. As strongly as possible, invoke whoever for you is the embodiment of wisdom, compassion and holiness, the source of spiritual inspiration and the object of your faith. It could be Buddha, God, Christ, or Allah. Then pray that refuge may be given to all those who have died in this tragedy. Think of them, and think of their families and loved ones too. Bring them all, every one, within the embrace of the refuge. Please include all of us as well because, you see, we all need the blessing and the protection this practice will bring.

Pray and practice with as much strength and fervor as you can. Because you never know: your practice and your prayer may be very powerful. It could make all the difference. First of all, it might contribute towards averting a disaster altogether. Or else if one erupts, it could prevent it from becoming as terrible as it might otherwise have been, and keep it from spiraling into something worse. Practice and pray strongly for yourself and for the world.

Sometimes a situation like this can make us go through a real change in our lives. Because our day-to-day existence can often leave us slightly complacent, until one day something wakes us up. Suddenly we realize that life is precious, and that the life we have may not be too bad. The only thing is that we constantly forget to appreciate it. What makes it even more precious is that it is impermanent. When you know you are going to die, and it is merely a matter of time, then you feel and appreciate each and every moment. You appreciate those who are close to you as well, and understand how important it is to show them your love.

Now we know there is no choice: we have to use our time wisely. Remember that whatever we do, say, or think has consequences. So make a resolution to live in a responsible way, respecting the law of cause and effect in our actions. Don't fall back into those old habits, tendencies, and patterns that dominate or obscure our lives. Live true to your nature, for that is what is really good for you, good for others and, of course, of tremendous benefit for everyone.

This is time for wisdom, for courage. On the one hand we need to pray strongly for all those who have died, and on the other, we also need to pray for the world and what lies ahead. Think of all the leaders of the world. Pray that they may have wisdom, discernment, courage and foresight. Pray that whatever may happen next does not cause innocent casualties and unnecessary suffering; that in the future it will not spiral into new areas of conflict, that it will not aggravate the conflicts that already exist in the world. Pray strongly that all the harm be transformed into good.

For the time being this tragedy seems to have brought many countries together. If this were to be used well, it might change the world. There is an opportunity here. Pray strongly that this will happen. May all countries be united, and may the world find the stability it craves. May these terrible events awaken us to the deeper causes and grievances that may have provoked them. Pray as strongly as you can that, whatever the causes, they may be remedied, healed, and removed through the blessing and love of the Buddhas, or God, Christ, or Allah. Let us have the courage to look unwaveringly at the causes of the hatred and despair behind this violence, whatever they may be, and really address them. Because at the root of it all lie hatred and despair. If you make compassion and altruism your motivation, invoke the Buddhas, or God, Christ, or Allah as strongly as you can, feel their presence and then direct it — your practice will have enormous power.

Pray that something good may grow out of this tragedy. Above all, that it may lead to peace and harmony, thereby giving meaning to the loss of so many lives. Pray that the death of all these innocent people was not in vain. May it bring the world together, and not just incite anger, which will help no one, least of all those who have died. Let us hope that that our decision-makers will be wise, prescient and precise. Pray strongly that we do not give in to the temptation to think only of the short term, but pray that we will think in the long term. For this is how history will judge us.

You might ask, "What about the feelings of anger?" Yes, there is anger. And it is inevitable. But at the same time, the anger was the cause of this atrocity in the first place. If we feel anger, but leave it at the level of revenge and retribution, we become no better than the terrorists. We need to rise above it to transform the anger and realize that behind such actions, finally, is ignorance — a kind of madness. As Jesus said, "Forgive them, for they know not what they do." The perpetrators of these horrors cannot truly know what they are doing. They feel they have won some kind of victory; all they have done is to have created immeasurable suffering in the long-term for themselves, as well as for the world.

Think about this. Because if we can realize this fact, and if we can see the greater picture, then we can see how the cycle of violence continues, or how it can be broken. As Buddha said, "Anger is not destroyed by anger. But by love alone. This is the ancient and eternal law."

The reason we can still feel anger is because we are still alive. Think of all those poor people who have died. Focus on them now. Reflect on what is truly going to help them. Your getting angry is not going to help them. Taking revenge is not going to help them, either. What is going to help them is our love, our practice, our good actions, or noble aspirations, and the spirit of compassion in our prayers and actions. These are what will help alleviate suffering and its causes.

What is *extremely* important is to let this time be an opportunity for spiritual renewal all over the world. Could this be an opportunity as well, for the world to be united as never before, and for our leaders to take wiser and more enlightened action? Could this tragedy be turned into a commitment by all countries to renounce violence and resolve their conflicts peacefully? Changes like these would give meaning to the loss of all those lives, you see. If there is only more violence and death, they will have been meaningless. I think it is important for the sake of all those who have died to ensure that their deaths bring some good to the world.

ANDREW HARVEY

The Power of Spirit

Enthusiasm, joy, and commitment are the three quali-ties I most recall from my meetings with Andrew Harvey *over the years. I have always been impressed with his scholarship and his ability to articulate difficult spiritual subjects with ease, grace, and clarity. He was born and raised in India and educated at Oxford University, where he was the youngest fellow in the his-tory of All Souls College at the age of 21. His lifelong spiritual quest gives him a singular view of what we face in these times.*

ANDREW: When 9-11 happened, two images came very fiercely and strongly into my mind. The first image, as I watched that airplane go again and again and again into the side of the building, was the image of the spear ramming through Christ's chest, ramming into his heart and splitting his heart open. The second image that came to me very clearly, as I watched the towers collapse again and again, was of a woman breaking waters to give birth.

Those two images have been acting very deeply into my imagination, to say to me that this time what we have entered is a time of unprecedented danger, horror, and difficulty as well as an unprecedented opportunity for transforma-tion. They have both come together. The Divine has given us the most dramatic possible time in order to force us to transform ourselves before it is too late and we take the whole of nature with us in a bloodbath of unimagin-able proportions.

The events of 9-11 offer everyone who contemplates them the experience of the spear driving through our heart to shatter it open and make us aware of all of the injustice, all the cruelty, pain, and suffering that is going on everywhere in this world in which nature is being destroyed and two billion people live on less than a dollar a day, a world in which war after war after war is being fought in the name of religious fundamentalism, a world in which the media is by and large pouring an avalanche of trash into people's minds.

I also see that this is a time of birth. If we can allow our hearts to be split open, if we can allow ourselves really to face where we are, what a time we're in, and what an enormous effort we are going to have to make if we are going to turn this around, then we will also be in a time of birth. Just as this is a time of tremendous disaster, so it is also a time in which, if we really consider what we could mobilize to deal with the current tragedies, we can see that there could be enormous transformation.

For example, all the mystical traditions with all of their sacred texts and all of their technologies are now poured at the feet of anybody who wants to use them and understand them. At the same time we have all kinds of highly developed sciences, external sciences that can help us really understand the world and in many ways change it to our will. If only we could mobilize all the sciences and power that we've dedicated to destruction in the service of divine love. Then, the world as we know it could be transfigured.

What I see very clearly both in my own life and in the lives of everybody else is that we are in what I would call "the end times." I don't think this is going to be a short conflict. I think this is going to go on and on. It is going to become bloodier and bloodier. Anything at all could happen. The Middle East could blow up at any moment. Pakistan and India could have a war at any moment. We must see that people really understand the dangers of this time and really, *really*, do something about them.

For my part it's been a time in which I felt tremendously galvanized. I've known for a long time that disaster is coming. I've written about it, I've tried to warn people about it in my work. I've cried about it, I've prayed about it. I thought it would be an environmental disaster. But I see now that the thinking and feeling of the Mother are much more terrifying. Two matricidal societies, that of McWorld and Jihad, are going to be fighting each other, perhaps even to the death. What now matters is that we really see what has to be changed on our side. We can't change Islam as it is. We have to change ourselves.

What is obsessing me is that so few people are really taking this opportunity to look at the dangers of our culture in all the different ways and really to transform them. But I believe that as the situation darkens — and it will darken — more and more people will be driven to the kinds of deep spiritual mystical work that I love, and they will be driven into the arms of what I call "mystical activism." I believe the future will only be a future if we combine the passion and knowledge and stamina and strength of mysticism with a path of radical, political, economic action in the world to transform all institutions quickly so that they can reflect the love and justice of God and not the greed, possessiveness and domination of human beings.

MICHAEL: *As someone who has written several books about Rumi, don't you find it interesting that in America Rumi sells more books than any other poet while at the same time he is the most famous poet in Afghanistan?*

Absolutely. Rumi is a key to both societies. And yet neither society is hearing him. Islam is clearly not hearing Rumi's all-embracing understanding and tolerance of all paths, and we are not hearing Rumi's challenge to us to shatter our hearts open, become infused and possessed by divine love, and act out of that divine love in all the arenas of the world. So he might be our favorite poet and the Afghans' favorite poet, but it doesn't seem to me that we are using his poetry in the right way as an incentive to transfigure ourselves and really become servants of love and transformation.

To continue with the spiritual connection: you have written about the dark goddess and I know you have a connection with Our Lady of Guadalupe. How do you see the relevance of the Dark Mother in these times?

I think this whole crisis is in a sense being organized by the Dark Mother to try and finally wake us up. I think September 11 was a catastrophe that she gave as a kind of terrible grace to humanity, to try and wake humanity up to the extent of the danger. This means, of course, trying to wake America up to the extent of the danger of continuing an exploitative foreign policy, a policy that includes raping and degrading the environment and treating other nations and other cultures with real disdain and real ignorance. This has to be transformed in us if we are going to survive. And the Dark Mother works by the grace of catastrophe to try to wake people up. But she also, if you turn to her, gives you the strength and inspiration and the passion to really be effective within catastrophe, and to see the secret meaning of her grace, and to act upon it.

So I have been, these last months, turning to the Dark Mother all the time. I wrote a prayer on September 11 that went something like this:

Oh Dark Mother, Dark One,
Do anything to wake us up,
And then give us what we need
To help bear our illumination.

That has been a prayer that has only grown more and more timely in the months since.

One has to have a lot of courage to say a prayer like that because when you ask for anything, then you are probably going to get it.

The only kind of prayer that I think is really helpful at this moment is what I call "dangerous prayer." Dangerous prayer occurs when you pray to be endangered by transformation, endangered by grace, endangered by the living flame of the Divine Presence, so that instead of just playing with God and rattling one's crystals and changing one's name into a Sanskrit name, one actually does commit oneself, like a Teresa of Avila, a Rumi, or a Saint Francis, to the burning fire of transformation, so at last you will become truly useful in a horrible time.

Another dangerous prayer that I've been using a lot and recommend to everybody is Saint Francis's prayer "Oh Lord make me an instrument of Thy peace." I don't think any of us wants to become an instrument of His peace by our own will. I think we have to be dragged there. But there comes a moment in anybody's path when they become really serious about the need to serve and when they see just how dangerous things are. They begin tremblingly and with humility to say the words "Oh Lord, make me an instrument of Thy peace," and they really wish to be endangered by them into a new kind of being.

Why is it, from your perspective, that we often utter words of peace, but then our actions are quite different?

I think we are totally split as a human race, and people are split within themselves between the part that wants power and the part that wants love. The part that wants love is the divine part; it is connected to the Divine Love and the Divine Consciousness. But that love really demands a great deal. It demands that we give the whole of ourselves to it and allow the whole of ourselves to be transformed into it. That demand is very annoying and very savage to the part that really wants power, that wants money, sex, success, that wants to be a big shot. That part yields its empire very gracelessly.

For a long time the spiritual world has been in a kind of bland coma, not really showing people the nature of evil, not helping them to understand their own shadow. Now, everybody who has a brain and a heart can see that unless large numbers of the human race really prepare to go through a real transformation that costs not less than everything, then the everything that is our world is going to be destroyed. We've been brought to a moment where it is not only our visions of politics, economics, and the media that are going to have to be transformed — it is our visions of what the spiritual life really is. The true spiritual life is now revealing itself. It is not just people cultivating a mystical inwardness, sitting on their futons, reciting their rosaries or praying to Tara or whatever. The spiritual life is revealing itself as the most urgent, imaginable necessity, a life in which we are inspired from within by God to do outer action on every level, a life in which we really do risk our own lives to stand up for justice and peace in a terrible world.

In fact, what this time is asking all of us is to become truly authentic and truly serious and truly impassioned and truly, sacredly active with whatever gifts and resources we have in the core of a burning world to try and transform it before it's too late.

Let us hypothesize for a moment. If you were invited to the White House and asked to advise President George W. Bush as to what he should do at this point, what would you say to him?

I would say, don't try to smuggle through your appalling ecological agenda under the umbrella of a world war. For God's sake, don't drill in the Arctic Refuge. Realize that we must preserve our sacred relationship to the earth. I would say to him, don't plunge this economy into becoming totally a war economy. We must defend ourselves, obviously, but equally importantly we must really make very, very generous gestures towards those people who now hate us. We must try and show them that our hearts are really open to them. That we really do want to learn about the sacred truths of Islam. That we want to honor the real nobility of Islam and its ways of being. That we are not going to just go on being smug, arrogant, selfish, and self-absorbed.

I would say to him that a real statesman at this moment would not be somebody who simply keeps banging the table, saying we are going to get Osama bin Laden, but someone who, as well as leading the country in a time of war, would also be preparing in very deep, profound, and spiritual ways for the making of a worldwide peace. And I would say to him that this would, in fact, have to mean a total revolution of the heart. He would have to really see the danger of all of his economic policies and of being in bed with corporations. He would have to face the scientific evidence of environmental degradation and the tremendous danger that it poses. In other words, he would have to abandon almost all of the positions that he has held up until now. And it would take a very brave man to do so.

But that is what we need in power now. We need someone who is brave enough to tell the American people that theirs is not a sacred way of life, as Bush keeps saying, but actually a way of life that, in its selfishness and materialism, endangers a great deal of the world. I would also tell him that it is very important not just to be negative, not just to rail, and not just to dissect the forces that have created this situation, but to appeal to something that very few politicians have appealed to recently, which is the sacred enterprise of an authentic, living democracy in this culture.

The reason why I stay in America and teach in America, for all of America's corruption, faults, and self-absorption, is that I believe America is the place in which the new humanity can be born for one very simple reason: because democracy is an essential condition of that great birth, and democracy despite everything is still alive as a vision and as an idea. So I would beg President Bush to make this a living democracy by ensuring finance, health, education, and environmental reform and by opening up all the institutions to people of all colors and all persuasions and galvanizing the soul of this country. It is not going to be galvanized by drilling in the Arctic Refuge or talking of a materialist way of life as a sacred one, but by honoring the soul of the democratic vision out of which this country was created.

I don't think I'd last very long in this particular interview with the President. But I would get a lot in.

You've articulated quite a lot. Earlier, you mentioned the connection between taking whatever spiritual practice we have and using it as energy to change the world for the better, to change it actively in our daily life. Do you have some insights that you could share as to ways to do that?

First of all let me talk about practice. I think it is very important to realize that we need two kinds of practice. We need cool practices and we need hot practices. The danger has been that in these times people have chosen mostly the cool practices, the practices that chill you out, that introduce you to Divine Being, that introduce you to the calm and spaciousness of your authentic nature. The cool practices would include imageless meditation, walking meditation, and breathing. These are very important in a hysterical time. But they are not the only ones.

We also need hot, warm, passionate heart meditations that help us stay alive in burning compassion to others. These would include the great heart practices of the Tibetans, practices like Tonglen — breathing in and out the pain of the world and breathing towards the world feelings of peace — and other practices that keep you endlessly, vibrantly, passionately alive. It has never been more important to be inspiringly compassionate.

Having said that, I think that people can go out and serve in five fundamental ways. First, they can serve the Divine itself by honoring it in prayer and adoration. This is essential because from that service to the Divine come all the others kinds of power.

Next, they can serve themselves in the deepest way by keeping their lives clear and simple and pure so that the Divine can use their lives as an instrument. This means eating properly, seeing that you sleep properly, seeing that you do not let the trashy and violent images of this time depress you.

The third form of service is to look at all the beings who are around you in your life — your friends and lovers and of course the animals in your household — as Divine Beings whom you are here to treat with divine elegance, divine compassion, divine honoring, divine support. You must do that with all of your energy.

The fourth way is to look at your community and to look at what needs to be done in your community. There is always something that you can do. For example in Las Vegas, where I live, there rages at this moment a huge controversy about Yucca Mountain and whether or not the government should dispose of nuclear waste there. I have been active in fighting against it because I realize that it could be overwhelmingly dangerous. Someone else I know has decided that her form of protest is to go every day and clean the local bus stop, which is usually covered with obscene messages and vile remarks and racist epithets. This is her form of service. You must find something that you can do that makes the community life better.

The fifth kind of service, which everybody now must do, is a service to the world in general. This means being informed about what is going on. I am shattered when I travel around and find out how ignorant so-called seekers are about the political and economic dimensions of this crisis.

So each of us needs to keep informed, to really listen to everything that is going on, to keep using your power as a citizen to write to your congressperson, to senators, and to the President. And if possible, start using your resources to support whichever institutions and societies are doing true radical work. Support the Sierra Club in its fight to preserve the environment. Support Amnesty International in its fight to keep political action as sane and generous as possible. Support any society that is trying to bring some peace. And if you can, also join one of these great societies and do something real yourself.

There is so much we can do in all of the different aspects of our lives. If you keep in mind those five kinds of service, service to God, service to oneself, service to one's family, service to one's community, and the service to the world as a citizen of the world, you won't have a lot of time left to despair and look at your hands. You'll be exercising your right as a citizen of love, to protest, to work for justice, to love and honor others.

We are citizens in American democracy. We are the fourth branch of government. We are the Government.

That's right. There again, this is something that I think all spiritual teachers in America should be reminding people of. We are not impotent. We are not powerless. The government keeps doing things that deeply disturb many of us. I believe this is the time in which thousands and thousands of people will need to take to the streets as they did in the sixties to start exercising our right of democratic protest. We must not let this war badger us into accepting all kinds of things in the government that go against everything that we believe about democracy. It is very important that spiritual teachers galvanize people not merely to their mystical depths, but also to their responsibilities as guardians of a democratic vision that is destined to birth the new humanity, if only it has time and if only it can be realized.

May I ask *you* one question? In talking to all of us and being yourself someone of deep vision and deep love of the world, do you feel there is a consensus amongst the spiritual teachers now as to what is going on and as to how to respond to it? Are you struck by a consensus?

I don't know that I would say there is a consensus among the spiritual teachers because I haven't spoken to that many of them since 9-11, but I would say there certainly is a large communion, a large consensus about alternatives to the current direction of the U.S. government. That seems to be almost universal. I have been seeing that not only through the work that we've been doing here, but as I've been using the Internet since 9-11. Just the amount of energy out there, outside of what we are hearing in the mass media and from our government leadership, clearly shows that huge numbers of people, millions of people believe differently. They are seeing the world differently from what is being presented to us.

That is very encouraging. How will we get those people into positions of power and into inspired action to make a difference? If we don't, the governing classes, who are clearly blind, will go on controlling everything and in the end, which of course is potentially not far away, will destroy everything.

We have to do the best we can in the present moment and trust that there is Divine guidance underneath it all. All we can do is what we do today.

I agree. If you see the problem too overwhelmingly, despair can get you and then the dark has won.

Yes, then nothing happens. People become paralyzed.

I don't know if you have read the new United Nations World Survey. The United Nations tries to be very optimistic and up, and onward and upward. But what they are actually telling us about poverty and the environment and about how little is actually being done is devastating.

One of things that came out of the U.N. that struck me was the fact that it would take twenty billion dollars a year to provide food, health care, and education to those who don't have it around the world. This is roughly ten percent of one of the contracts that was just signed in late 2001 to build two hundred billion dollars worth of fighter planes for the U.S. Air Force. We have a few priorities mixed up here. We have to work on it.

Can I ask you one more question? You've been such a mover and shaker in your spiritual work for so long now. Do you feel the last twenty years have prepared people for this event, or do you feel that we are all at sea in it?

I think that this is what we have all been working on, preparing for what we did-n't know, what was going to come. But it is like the Hopi prophecy that said this is the eleventh hour, now it's the twelfth hour, and, guess what, we are who we've been waiting for. It is time for us to assume the responsibility for being who we've been waiting for. So everyone is stepping it up.

That is exactly what it is. It is really raising up the heat on everything.

It has all been preparation for this time.

That is exactly what I believe. And I believe if enough people do step up to that plate and do allow themselves to be driven forward, amazing things can happen. It is astonishing how Divine Grace does work.

Absolutely. All we have to do is look at history and see that often down through what we know about history, a few people have made an amazing difference in the world. So it is quite possible to make a huge transformation. Look at Gandhi and Martin Luther King Jr.
I believe that, too. I also think that things such as "the hundredth monkey" and the whole morphogenetic field idea are very encouraging. If we press forward sincerely and passionately, then all kinds of people will become inspired. It does-n't take millions of enlightened beings. We need a few people to see the path through, and millions will be inspired.

I think it is going to happen.

So do I, despite and beyond everything. I don't know how, but I do believe.

It is good to believe.

It's essential. What would've all these years of faith and prayer meant if you did-n't believe in the power of grace to transfigure?

MANY VOICES / MANY VIEWS

America is made up of all the nations of the world. We are a receptacle for all the cultures of the planet, giving us the blessings of diversity and multiculturalism. Other than Native Americans, whose roots are here, each of us can trace our ancestry back to other countries, other lands. Especially in these reactionary times, when our government and some citizens want to pull up the drawbridge and close the door to immigrants, it is paramount that we recognize we are a nation of immigrants. In California in the 2000 census, Whites made up less than 50% of the total population. In California we are all minorities — and this is clearly the future for all of America. We have much to learn from one another and as we open ourselves to other cultures and traditions, we become more enabled to accept differences as positive and worthwhile, adding substance to our own life in the process. Most Americans are insulated from the world beyond our borders. Some have suggested that 9-11 represented the loss of America's innocence. Outside of the United States, people realize that we are all interconnected. That's the good news. They already know. We still have to learn.

The Lessons of History

During the late 1970s when New Dimensions Radio was getting started in Northern California, prior to becoming a national and then global series, we received a publication entitled Akwesasne Notes in the mail. It was filled with useful information, difficult or impossible to find anywhere else. This was my first encounter with the work of John Mohawk, who served as editor of Akwesasne Notes. Since then, John has become a popular lecturer in Native American studies. In Utopian Legacies, he traces the history of Western civilization and of what he calls "revitalization movements," which have shaped Western culture. He has opened a dialogue that may, indeed, be one of the most important conversations on the future of the planet.

MICHAEL: *Can you tell us about your insights, thoughts, and perspectives on the new world we've entered since the events of September 11?*

JOHN: Let me preface my remarks by saying that in some ways it's a continuation of an already existing world. What I think happened on the eleventh was that people were forced to face a reality about things that were going on in the world — and it was a very dramatic event. One imagines that centuries from now people will still remember that event.

What we're facing here isn't merely the fact that there are people in the world who have grievances against the United States. It's true that the United States has enemies, and if we go to other countries we'll find a lot of people there that have an opinion of the United States that's different from the way a lot of the people here see themselves. There's quite a lot of criticism of the United States when you travel abroad. In some places that criticism increases in intensity. Probably nowhere is it so widely spread as it is in the Islamic countries.

But I don't think that's exactly what we're looking at in terms of the September 11 event. I think that event was the result of a very specific movement of militants, of a group around Osama bin Laden and the leadership of Al Qaeda who enacted a very dramatic thing. We need to understand it in terms of a historical pattern. We've seen patterns like that before, and this was a very dramatic example of what can happen when people who perceive themselves as living in a state of oppression come up with a plan about how to free themselves or how to solve the problem of their oppression. Quite often they come up with very dramatic, but not very realistic plans. And sometimes they give themselves permission to do really horrific things in the name of a cause that they believe in very intensely.

So I think it would be useful to look at that as something that was distinct and separate both from the politics that people express when they look at the history of U.S. foreign policy and from the way people in the world currently view the United States.

Can you go forward or deeper with that? What are the differences as you see them?

I think the people around Osama bin Laden represent something that we could call a "regressive revitalization movement." They became convinced that they were going to be able to challenge the United States, that they were going to be able to put together military forces that could defeat American military forces. A couple of events had heartened them a lot. The bombing that happened in Africa was, in their minds, a great victory over the Americans. They thought the Americans couldn't fight in that kind of street fighting. They had bombed a few places, and it looked to them as though the Americans were not capable of responding. So they convinced themselves that they were going to be able to wage a successful kind of war against the United States, and they became extremely enthusiastic about that perception.

I believe that when those people facilitated the airplane bombings of the Pentagon and the buildings in New York, it was essentially not an invasion of the United States. They were daring the United States to come to Afghanistan because they thought the same thing would happen to us that happened to the Soviet Union there. Their primary objective was to cause the United States to attack them, and they thought that they would then fight the United States to some kind of a draw or that there would be a war going on for a long time. They imagined that, in the course of that war, they would be able to mobilize these street forces, radicalize them enough to either coerce the governments in those parts of the world to take radically anti-American stands or overthrow those governments. In their wildest dreams they were hoping to establish either a giant Islamic state or a series of Islamic states.

We see these things happening occasionally because what's peculiar about revitalization movements is that they create people who are willing to commit extraordinary crimes or acts of violence, acts of ethnocide, genocide. They're willing to do that because they believe they understand a way of resolving all their problems. And they're regressive in that they believe violence, and the utter eradication of the enemy from their world, is the way to resolve their problems.

So contrary to some of the rhetoric that was espoused early on in the war, I don't think that the thing was an attack on Western civilization or designed to destroy the United States. I don't think that was the objective. I think the objective was to stimulate change in the Islamic world, to build the foundation for Islamic states, and to drive Western influence out of those states.

What do you think the situation is now?

First of all, this attack was made possible by the propaganda of grievance that was founded, to a considerable degree, on actual history. When the people who have these grievances are listing what their problems are and telling why they say the things they do about the world as they find it, they have a pretty good list of grievances, and those grievances are founded in history. They're not imagined grievances. The solutions are imagined, but not the grievances. So we are alerted to the fact that when people perceive themselves to be oppressed and when they can identify their oppressors — in this case these Islamic radicals identify the West as the source of their oppression — this can mushroom and grow into a movement. Some of these movements can be very dangerous to us. It's in our own interest to first understand what creates those movements, what can disempower them, and to take steps to address that.

I was struck by how many people in the press, when asked about the idea that the history of American foreign policy might have contributed to the events of September 11, said, "Oh, we don't care about that. I don't want to hear that we were responsible for whatever happened on September 11." I took that to mean that they didn't believe there was anything that could have made those attacks excusable. Of course, on some sort of moral ground I agree with that. There's no excuse for murdering lots of innocent people. But that's also beside the point. The point is that situations are created in the world that give rise to conditions in which such acts of violence take place, and when they do, we should try to understand what it is that gives rise to that and what we need to do to see to it that that isn't empowered.

I don't think that you could say that people like Osama bin Laden could be reformed. I don't even object to the idea that those people have to be punished. But, in fact, punishing or killing them doesn't speak to the main issue, which is that conditions have arisen in a part of the world which make it possible for suicide bombers to exist, and those suicide bomber conditions haven't been addressed.

I don't believe you can frighten a suicide bomber. The usual idea about deterrence and the law is that somebody does something wrong, and the law makes certain that the punishment for that is so powerful that the next person will not be willing to subject themselves to that punishment. That works if you're trying to keep accountants from stealing money or bank robbers from robbing banks. But it doesn't work as well if the people you're talking about are willing to die for their cause. In that case the idea of a deterrent — even killing a whole bunch of people who did the wrong thing — doesn't really guarantee that there won't be more people who will volunteer to die for the same cause.

Instead of creating deterrents, you need to address the cause. It isn't that hard to do. The United States is certainly capable of doing it. The United States could take steps to make the world safer for Americans and for everybody else by making the idea of bombing Americans unpopular in the world. But so far we haven't really had much of a discourse on that. I won't say there hasn't been any; there has been some. But there hasn't been much conversation about that. Even people who are suicide bombers, people who are so motivated by their cause that they're willing to die for it, even such people can be disempowered. Steps can be taken to lift the level of stress on that culture, so that they don't produce suicide bombers, or at least they don't produce them in great numbers.

I can't say that we can make the world absolutely safe because, as we've seen, one of the realities of the time we're living in is that talented people who are motivated now have materials of mass destruction available to them. Somebody like Timothy McVeigh, acting with very little money and very little organizational support, was able to pull off a major bombing. That's the reality of our time. Materials are cheap, and the information about how to do that kind of thing is widespread. There are going to be people who will do something like that.

But now we're looking at a world in which a very large population of young male adults is being radicalized and energized to the idea that the only solution to Western hegemony involves violence. Whether they have an Osama bin Laden to organize it or they organize it in much smaller cells and do it in a different way, this is going to continue for the foreseeable future until steps are taken to address the foundation, the core of what it is that motivates them.

Do you see an alternative to continuing the war on terrorism? Is there another way to do it?

First, I don't think anything would have stopped the United States from attacking Al Qaeda and Afghanistan. That was something they were so highly motivated to do that it was impractical to think anybody could have intervened with a plan other than that, and prevailed.

But after they have done that, what are they going to do about all of the conditions that exist in that part of the world that can create people like those who did what was done? I hear the argument that it was well-educated middle-class people from Saudi Arabia, from Egypt, who were flying the airplanes. But while that's true and needs to be addressed, it's also true that it's the street masses that provide the energy that make those people the martyrs, that give them the foundation, the backing that they need in order to do that kind of thing.

Look at a place like Pakistan. Pakistan has hundreds of schools that are basically propaganda centers for a very radicalized form of Islam. Those schools are filled with little boys who are there because their parents can't feed them. So the reason that you have students in those kinds of schools is that there's poverty and hunger in that part of the world. When Pakistan turned to the United States, they said, "For us to address this we would have to provide a public education alternative to these schools and we don't have any money to do it." The reality is this: not only does the education have to be there, but there also needs to be a way of addressing the issue of hunger in that area. The same is true for the even poorer areas of Afghanistan.

If we can't address the issue of hunger in a part of the world where there's also rage and if we can't find ways to subsidize an education alternative to the school systems that are creating people who are willing to die to attack Western interests, if we can't have enough enlightened self-interest to do that, we're really not going to come up with a plan other than bombing everybody we can. And I think one thing that we can agree on is this: We can't bomb them all. Not only that but, I'll make a bet, it's cheaper to feed them than it is to bomb them.

I think that's for sure. Are you hopeful about the future?

The immediate future — I think this problem can be solved. I don't think this is that hard of a problem to solve.

Once upon a time the United States did something that made them heroes in the eyes of the world. Right after World War II they initiated the Marshall Plan. The Marshall Plan was in place to provide dollars to rebuild the industrialized countries that were bombed to the ground in World War II. Of course, you can go back and you can look at it cynically and say it was motivated by the desire to counter the rising energy that was emitted by communism and the communist block. But there were a lot of people who simply understood that Europe had come apart because after World War I they'd put the responsibility for reparations on Germany. They'd humiliated Germany and actually bankrupted her. The Depression was pretty much triggered by the bankruptcies of German banks. Those bankruptcies happened because they couldn't pay the war reparations.

People tried to rethink that after World War II, and what they came up with was that they would help to rebuild the industrial countries in Western Europe and make them self-sufficient, to rebuild those societies so there would be trading partners, other people who were productive. And they came through. Instead of giving them loans, they gave them grants. It worked. They took what had been the most horrific event in the history of humankind — World War II — and they came out of it with a plan to build on the foundations of human dignity and local self-sufficiency. They made it possible for France to build a new France, not an American France — and on and on. The idea behind that model, the enlightened self-interest of that model, could change things in the Middle East, in Afghanistan, in Pakistan, in all of central Asia. It could change things.

The problem is that American culture has been changing in a way that hasn't shown a lot of enlightened self-interest lately. That needs to change. Maybe it will change. Ask me if I'm optimistic, and I'll tell you I think it's a fifty-fifty thing. It could go that way, but it could also not.

Is there anything else you'd like to share?

Just a thought. The thing that has really been wrong with American foreign policy in the Third World for more than half a century now is that it hasn't treated people fairly. It has been constructed in such a way that our worst version of our self-interest has been imposed on other people. Those other people are fiercely resentful of it. We can't change that, we can't go back and un-kill the people we've assassinated, and we can't turn over and undo things that happened fifty years ago. But the United States could take a track that tries its best to treat everybody in the world fairly. I know there would be an argument about what that means, but I tell you what: so far, that thought has not driven our foreign policy. If we want to live in a world where Americans aren't in danger — and I think they are in danger if we don't do this — we would be wise to consider it. Not only that, but I don't think we'd lose anything by doing it.

I suppose it's naïve to suggest that we would really like to be trading partners with countries that have honest government, that we would really like to be friends with people all over the world and do good works everywhere. The fact that we sometimes decide that our national interests require us to do things that seem to be unfair, things that are not a win-win for either side — that we sometimes take that track suggests that we don't learn the lessons of history at all. I would even go so far as to say that if somebody did a historical analysis, even in terms of dollar figures, of whether it was worth it to do all the nasty, dirty tricks that have made us the most unpopular country in the world, we would find that we didn't even make any money doing it.

AS'AD ABUKHALIL

Taking Responsibility

An American citizen of Arab descent, As'ad AbuKhalil is an associate professor of Political Science at California State University, Stanislaus, and a research fellow at the Center for Middle Eastern Studies at the University of California at Berkeley. I spoke with him because of his recent book Bin Laden, Islam, and America's New "War on Terrorism." His views as an Arab American are poignant and incisive. In particular, he points to the reality that other people's views of America, and especially of our government, are often very different from our own. It is not atypical that George W. Bush, prior to being selected President, had rarely traveled anywhere outside the U.S. borders except to England.

MICHAEL: *As someone who has written a book about Osama bin Laden and the Taliban, tell us how you see the "war on terroism."*

AS'AD: This is an unjustified attack against the people of Afghanistan, who've suffered over the years from the policies and actions of the United States, especially because of the Cold War with the Soviet Union and our support of the Mujaheddin in the Afghan war. It's very important to note that when the President of the United States says that you're either with us or against us, he's setting up a false dichotomy that most people in the Middle East will reject out of hand. Their choice, which is in fact more moral than either of his two choices, is this: most people in the Middle East can very easily condemn the attack of September 11 without in any way endorsing the record of American foreign policy and, in particular, their actions in the Middle East. People in the Middle East can see that the acts of September 11 are crimes against humanity, but the United States is also guilty of crimes against humanity. People of the Middle East see that bin Laden is a very dangerous person. Is he the most dangerous person in the world? Certainly not. The President of the United States is the most dangerous person in the world. He has the ability to inflict the most harm and damage worldwide.

In addition, when we look at that situation we ask ourselves, "Is what happened on September 11 unique?" As horrific as it is, there are equally horrific acts and crimes that should be equally condemned, for which the United States is directly responsible. What about the 1998 bombing of the medicine factory in the Sudan which produced half of all the pharmaceutics needed by the people and children of Sudan? That has resulted in the deaths of thousands of people, mostly children, in that country. What about the sanctions against Iraq, which, according to the School of Public Health at Harvard University, are resulting in the deaths of at least five thousand children every month? All these factors are well known by people in that region.

If the United States government can repeat the mantra that they are not against Islam or Arabs, why were the bombs dropped over people's heads in Afghanistan? They say they are not against Islam and yet there is a rise in the climate of anti-Arabism, anti-Islamism in this country. Also, although they say they are not against Islam, every time they have a list of terrorist groups and networks, every single group has an Arabic or Islamic name. It makes people wonder, and they justifiably suspect that there are motives that certainly are inconsistent with the declarations of tolerance that come from the U.S. government.

In addition to this, when they started bombing Afghanistan as part of their fight against terrorism, many people in the Middle East asked, "Will they be bombing northern Ireland? Or will they be bombing the Basque region? Or Corsica?

What would you do in this situation?

I believe that a fight against terrorism has to fight terrorism committed by any group and any state, whether it is bin Laden or the United States. A fight against terrorism should require an international effort that does not make distinctions based on the nationality, religion, or ethnicity of the victims. Neither should it favor, disfavor, or make distinctions based on the identity of the tormentors, whether they are Muslim, Jewish, Christian, American, Middle Eastern, or otherwise. Also, the United States government is the last government that should lead a moral fight against terrorism, given the guilt that it carries based on its actions throughout the world.

We heard stories of other professors like yourself and other academics who have been advised not to speak out against the campaign. Have you experienced any of that yourself?

Not directly, although the climate, of course, is instilling fear and panic among many of my compatriots, colleagues, and friends, that's for sure. We have to remember what the White House spokesperson said. He said that people in these times should "watch what they say and watch what they do." I'll tell you, and I'm very determined about this, as an Arab living in this country I resolve to never watch what I say and to never watch what I do.

Are you an American citizen?

I am an American citizen of Arab descent. I am one of those people that according to polls, forty-nine percent of the American public wish to have carry a special I.D. card with me at all times. Of course I never would do that, even if it became law.

I think it's important to point out that there were people of eighty nations in the World Trade Center. So in many ways this is not just an American event, it's a world event.

Absolutely. And the response should be a world response. Also, we should ask questions of the United States. We should ask, "Who created the Taliban? Who created Osama bin Laden?" We in the Middle East know what most Americans do not know. Bin Laden and the Taliban are much more the product of American covert foreign policies than they are of Islam or the Middle East. We have to ask those questions. The Taliban would not have been able, ever, to rise to power without the covert, indirect support of the United States and a tacit agreement between the United States government and the Pakistani Intelligence Service.

Isn't it true that the Pakistani government actually has been one of the major supporters of the Taliban government?

Of course. It's also true that the ideology of bin Laden is indistinguishable from the ideology of the corrupt royal family in Saudi Arabia, which is one of the best friends of the United States government. So all this invocation of human rights and democracy doesn't sell except in Iowa and Oklahoma. It doesn't sell in the Middle East. People know the truth.

I think at a time like this it is incumbent on the citizens to be skeptical of their government, to ask questions of their government. The climate of conformity that prevails in the United States is chilling; it will allow the government not only to fight the brown people over there, the people with those funny turbans in the

Middle East whose plight most Americans really do not care about, but also to trample on the civil and constitutional rights of American citizens living right here.

Perhaps it's a time for all Americans to return to the values and ideas that created this nation, certainly those that are embodied in the Bill of Rights.

Well, not that the record of the history of this nation has been perfect in any way, but it's always a struggle. The United States has never been able to achieve the extension of constitutional or civil rights to all people in this society without a struggle by the citizens themselves. It is time for all of us to join in that struggle, because if it's the Arabs today it will be some other group tomorrow, just like the Japanese Americans suffered in the Second World War.

I think Abraham Lincoln said it best when he talked about "government of, by, and for the people." The people are the sovereign force here. The fourth branch of government is the people. We're only hearing from three right now — we want to hear from the fourth, don't we?

Women and Afghanistan

RAWA, the Revolutionary Association of the Women of Afghanistan, was established in 1977, just prior to the Soviet invasion, as an independent political/social organization of Afghan women fighting for human rights and social justice in Afghanistan. Since its inception, RAWA has become known the world over. My colleague and producer, Christina Fleming, talked with Pakistan-based Tahmeena Faryal, a spokesperson for RAWA. (For security reasons, Tahmeena Faryal's face cannot be shown).

CHRISTINA: *I've often wondered, watching the news and reading news reports about Afghanistan, what the women's conversations are like, in circles, as they cook or as they go through their day. Do you have any idea what women are talking about as all this is going on?*

TAHMEENA: In the situation that the people of Afghanistan have been living in for so many years, almost none of the conversations — regardless of whether they're conversations among men, women, or even children — can be separated from what is going on in the country because no aspect of life can be separated from what has been going on for so many years. It has totally affected the lives of people, changing their lives in so many ways. It's a country that does not have an economic, political, or social infrastructure. That makes fighting for a piece of bread and living for another day the primary concern of the majority of the population. Obviously, their conversations are usually about their situation and how or what they can do to make the situation a little bit better for themselves.

But there are also talks about resistance, especially in women's circles. They share their stories of the resistance that they've shown towards the Taliban or other fundamentalists, or they try to find out how they could resist in more effective ways. For example, under the Taliban there were thousands of classes run by women as individuals. It was definitely resistance by women, which would be considered a very simple and basic act in the United States.

How is the situation in Afghanistan personally affecting you?

I have been in Pakistan for quite a long time, so I'm not one of the RAWA members who are based in Afghanistan, but I've been there many times on visits. But we do have many members who are based in Afghanistan. What has been going on in Afghanistan, especially since 1992, is, in short, a real hell for women. Half of the population there is totally paralyzed: the women have no right to get an education, no right to work, no right to choose their dress. They have to be accompanied by close male relatives. In the capital Kabul and in other cities, there are thousands of widows. As a citizen of that country, I have, of course, been affected by this situation. When I was a child, the Soviet invasion forced me and my family to leave Afghanistan. As a woman who studied in RAWA schools, I couldn't be indifferent towards the oppression against women in my country. I couldn't be silent; I couldn't remain uninvolved. And I am glad to be part of a resistance movement that is struggling for changes in the lives of women and for a democratic society.

I can't imagine being a woman who was educated, had been able to work, and then all of a sudden someone said you have no right to do any of that anymore. What are these women's lives like, in their homes, in their daily affairs?

Unfortunately, most of the women who used to work as professionals today find that begging or prostitution are the only options that enable them to live or feed their children, and most of them suffer mentally and psychologically. According to a study by Physicians for Human Rights, ninety percent of Afghan women suffer emotionally, especially in the major cities where they used to be very active in society. We believe that if tomorrow there were peace and stability in Afghanistan, it would not take very long to rebuild the country, but it definitely will take us a very long time to rebuild people, especially women. Each and every family in Afghanistan, and in particular the women in the family, have been in one way or another affected — not only under the Taliban, but prior to the Taliban when we had this other fundamentalist government under the Northern Alliance.

Do you have a sense of what women are saying about America's actions in Afghanistan right now?

I think the people of Afghanistan are now very much aware of the fact that different countries, including the United States, played a very negative role in

Afghanistan during the Cold War when Afghanistan was at war with the Soviets. This included creating, supporting, and nurturing the fundamentalists, including the Taliban and the Northern Alliance before them. Each and every Afghan knows well that if they had not been created and supported by the different countries — especially Pakistan, Iran, Saudi Arabia, and the United States — they would not have been able to seize power in 1992 and continue. They absolutely don't have any support among the people of Afghanistan. Each and every Afghan knows this. Regarding the current situation, people believe that just as these fundamentalists were created by the other countries, they should be rooted out by them because it's not something that people in Afghanistan would be able to do. However, we believe and people in Afghanistan believe that the bombing campaign was not the way to do it, because hundreds of civilians have been killed as a result of the bombing and thousands of them have migrated to Pakistan and other neighboring countries.

RAWA is the Revolutionary Association of the Women of Afghanistan. What does RAWA do?

RAWA has for years been struggling for a democratic government. We believe that only a democratic government could heal the wounds of the people and that only in a democratic society can women's participation in society be a meaningful one. Democratic government is not possible where one or another fundamentalist group is in power, whether it's the Taliban or the Northern Alliance. So RAWA feels strongly that the United Nations should intervene by sending its military peacekeeping force to Afghanistan. Especially the neighboring countries that still support the Northern Alliance and the Taliban should cut that support. Finally, the way should be paved for a democratic process in Afghanistan, where the people of Afghanistan themselves can decide about their leadership and future — in a democratic process. As the representative of half of the population of Afghanistan, RAWA wants to be part of that. RAWA is also engaged in many humanitarian projects in the fields of education, heath care, and income generation.

What is your greatest hope for your country and the women of your country?

We want to see our country free. We want to see the women in our country free. But, once again, we believe that neither the freedom of our country nor the liberation and freedom of women is possible until there is a democratic government in Afghanistan. So RAWA has been struggling for years for a society that can guarantee women's equal participation with men in political, economic, and social fields, a society in which women in Afghanistan have the right to choose their dress, have the right to an education, and have the right to play a meaningful role in all the different aspects of society. Obviously, people in general should have stability, peace, and security, and human rights should be guaranteed. People should have freedom of speech, freedom of press, and freedom to form different political parties. We believe, therefore, that democracy is vital for such a society. It is absolutely vital for Afghan people as much as it is for people in the rest of the world.

What are some ways other countries can aid and help Afghan women?

After September 11, a lot of attention was drawn to Afghanistan and especially the plight of women in Afghanistan. We see more and more support from people and solidarity with us, especially from women from all over the world. We hope that they continue with their support and sympathy. They should not forget the suffering of their Afghan sisters, even if tomorrow Afghanistan is not in the news anymore. It should not be a forgotten country any longer. We definitely need the help of the international community. Afghanistan has been at war for more than two decades, and it cannot be rebuilt without international support for our country and its people. In particular, women in other countries should support organizations such as RAWA, which is the only visible and organized voice of resistance for women in Afghanistan. This voice must not be stopped. Through their financial support, through their political and moral support, they can enable us to continue our struggle.

Do you get a sense that, as the government shifts in Afghanistan, women will be playing a greater role in the leadership of the country?

Again, it depends on what the future government will be like. If the country is ruled, once again, by the Northern Alliance, we don't see any such hope, neither for the women in Afghanistan nor for the general population. We really don't see any difference between the Taliban and the groups that are involved in the Northern Alliance.

One of the forgotten aspects of the Afghan catastrophe is the role of Rabbani-Masoud & Co (the Northern Alliance, also called Jehadis) in looting and destroying the country, in bringing death and destitution after the fall of the Soviet puppet regime. More importantly, hundreds of girls, women, and even young boys were raped, and a great number of girls committed suicide lest they be assaulted by the barbaric Jehadi henchmen. Most of the the measures to deprive, suppress, and insult women were taken when these Jehadi murderers were in power, until in 1996 their brethren-in-creed, the Taliban, replaced them.

According to Amnesty International, Human Rights Watch, and other human rights groups, during their bloody rule over 50,000 innocent people were killed in Kabul only.

So if such a force is again given the opportunity to rule Afghanistan, Afghan women may not be in a better situation to regain their rights.

What is personally sustaining you during this time?

It's a very difficult time, a sensitive and critical moment in the history of our country. On the one hand, people have suffered for more than two decades, and they have suffered under different regimes: the Soviet puppets, the fundamentalist regimes of the Northern Alliance and then the Taliban. On the other hand, people believe that this might be the beginning of a new era where stability, peace and security, and their rights can be guaranteed. Given this situation, I can also have these feelings.

After so many years of bloodshed and tragedy in Afghanistan, perhaps the international community has realized at this point that they should not rely any longer on the fundamentalists, that the people of Afghanistan need a stable and peaceful government. If there is not stability in Afghanistan, there cannot be stability in the world. That has been proven after September 11. I think anyone who has a little bit of awareness and consciousness about the situation in Afghanistan, especially any Afghan, cannot just stay silent and remain uninvolved. Just seeing and watching our people and our country, our wars and blood and ruins and destruction, you want to do something to help them.

And then there are also the many other RAWA members who have always been an inspiration.

How can people get involved in RAWA?

People can visit our website. It is www.rawa.org. There is a section on the website that suggests many ways people can help and be involved. When we say we need people's involvement, we don't necessarily mean they have to become RAWA members. They can help us as supporters — we already have thousands of supporters all over the world. People can also donate money and support one of our projects. This has really been the most meaningful and practical way, at this point, to help. We also list a bank account on the website so people can send money. And there are also other ways that they can support us politically and morally.

The North American Way

Carlos Mota *entered my life through my active participation in Peacebulding 21 (PB21) a semi-annual gathering of various business and social leaders, educators, management consultants, and others, which began in 1996 and ended in 2001. PB21 was conceived by the late Willis Harman, president of the Institute of Noetic Sciences, and Avon Mattison, founder of Pathways to Peace. During this time I traveled to Mexico twice, once with the Peacebuilding 21 group and once to gather material for a radio documentary on the Monarch Butterfly. Both times, Carlos was immensely helpful and supportive. He and his two Mexican colleagues Felipe Herzenborn and Esteban Monteczuma, who were part of PB21, have become our friends and taught all of us who hailed from "north of the border" the value and meaning of the word American. Both Mexico and Canada are part of North America, and people from the U.S. are often guilty of not including our Canadian and Mexican continental partners in our view of "America." The perspectives of our Mexican colleagues, who live on the southern tip of North America, are much needed. Carlos Mota's voice is one whose resonance and global vision exemplify what we can learn as Americanos del Norte.*

MICHAEL: *Where were you on September 11?*

CARLOS: I was at home getting ready to go to work and watching a local newscast with the volume turned down on the TV and I saw a fire in one of the twin towers. When I turned the volume up, they still didn't know what had happened, but apparently a plane had crashed into the tower. I remembered a time when I lived here in the States, when there was an airplane about to hit one of the twin towers by mistake because a pilot from Argentinean Airlines didn't speak English very well. So I assumed it was something like an accident. But then I realized it was not. So it was early in the morning in Mexico, and I was getting ready when this happened.

What were your thoughts when you did realize that it was obviously a terrorist attack on the buildings?

When I first saw the second plane, live, I was really in shock because I lived in the States for a few years and I just couldn't believe what my eyes were seeing. When the first tower collapsed I couldn't talk. I couldn't think. I was just thinking about the people who were dying in that instant, in front of my eyes. For some reason I started to think about the consequences of that, not only to the families of the victims but the consequences around the world because I believed at the time that this was just the beginning of something that could be terrible for humankind.

Since that time the American government has launched the "war on terrorism." What do you think of all this as a Mexican national observing what's happening? How do you see this?

The way I see it is that this is not a U.S. problem. This is a world problem. I believe that what we are witnessing is humankind acting against humankind. I believe that it's very tough to admit it but we are hurting ourselves as a human race. So my feeling is that war will only increase retaliation, and that we really need, for the first time in many years, as a whole, as humans, to step up to a higher level of consciousness and to try to reflect on why this happened. What is the root cause that is creating this problem? It's as if a human being would produce a cancer that would damage and threaten his own life. I try to look at it with me involved. I don't see this as a foreign problem or a problem between two nations. I think none of us could think that we are ourselves external to this situation. We are all part of it. We are all affected.

To unleash such a war is perhaps the first instinctive reaction of a country. However, I believe that the effect, the immediate and medium-term effect, will be very tough because this kind of war is not directed against a country. I really am very sad that many Afghan people have died, because none of the terrorists was from Afghanistan. I understand it was a base for the Al Qaeda group. However, I think that we are acting foolishly. We're using old-fashioned actions that we know, for sure, will not be the solution to this situation.

So I have mixed feelings because I regret terribly what happened in New York, and yet I don't think we are taking the right measures. I'm really worried because, as a foreigner, I don't see in the U.S. government any bit of space for reflection in terms of asking the right questions, such as, "In what way have we as a nation contributed somewhat to this situation that is now emerging?"

So I believe we really need a time to reflect and to go to a deeper level than just reacting instinctively to this terrible act.

One of the things that's happened at the same time as the bombing in Afghanistan was the meeting of the World Trade Organization in Qatar, and there are those who say that economic globalization is part of the problem, not the solution. What is your view?

I would say it's part of the problem, yes. And I'm really worried because with China with its huge population coming in as a member, the growth rate of this globalizing activity will increase substantially. The problem, I think, is not globalization per se, but the fact that globalization is mainly financial. Our economic system has been working only for the few, not for the many. And if globalization is a way to accelerate capitalism, as it is right now, I believe we're going to face substantial problems in the future. If we do not change course, if we do not envision a way to create a more just, a more equitable capitalism, then this is just the beginning of a really difficult era.

However, if we use this opportunity, if we ask the right questions and devote our talent, creativity, and experience to influencing our economic system so that it is more fair for more of the people, if we ask the right questions and focus on how to alleviate all the misery and poverty of millions and millions of people, I think we have a chance. But I'm really worried. With China becoming a member of the World Trade Organization I would expect to see immediate consequences that will increase the velocity of this globalization. We really need to reflect on that and make the adjustments that are needed around the world.

Why are you particularly concerned about China? Is it because of the population or for financial reasons or what?

I'm concerned because its population will start demanding more goods, and producing those goods will be hurting nature as it has done in the past. So what I would expect is an increase in the consumption of energy — oil and gas — and in the production of pollutants on the Earth. I see a new wave of the consequences of a system that is neither careful nor in harmony with nature and with human beings. The size of China really scares me, because all of a sudden we are going to start seeing an increase not only in the demand, but also in the effects of that demand around the world. I would say that pollution and financial volatility will increase because of the new wave created by China joining the World Trade Organization.

Are you hopeful about the future even though you may also be worried?

I am hopeful. However, there is a big "if." I am hopeful if we take this chance in human history, if we stand up and create the conditions in which people can talk, reflect, and act consciously. This is a wake-up call for humankind. I believe we have everything that is needed to make a change in history, to identify new ways, new pathways for a better life for the many. I'm hopeful because we have everything that is needed. However, we need to act and we need to act fast. Maybe we haven't asked in every corner of this world. The most important thing to me is to network, to connect to each other, to have a way that our ideas, our comments, our possibilities are exchanged and shared so that we can identify and make the right decisions at all levels, including the political and governmental levels, the companies, the business world, the social and educational spheres. This is going to be a very tough time, but I'm hopeful because we don't need anything other than what we already have: our consciousness, our intelligence, and our spirituality. The key action we need to take is to connect to each other, to be able to share ideas and to share our hopes. That will create the possibilities of moving ahead, of making the next step in this evolution of humankind.

Ronald Takaki

Multicultural America

What does it mean to be an American? In these times it is an appropriate question to ask, as we meet the challenges of the 21st century. The world is made up of many minorities. Americans are a minority as well. We live in a global society in which the United States has an important role to play. Being American in a changing world is a topic that Ron Takaki's *life has been about, since he was born as a Japanese American in Hawaii at the outset of World War II. An internationally recognized scholar, he is the author of several books addressing multiculturalism. As a historian, he speaks with a breadth and depth of knowledge and personal experience that is important and relevant.*

RON: I hope we won't let history repeat itself. There have been two days of infamy. The first, of course, was December 7, 1941. The second was September 11, 2001. Both events stirred immense patriotism across America. Before December 7, 70 percent of the American people polled said that they did not want to get into World War II, which had been underway in Europe as well as in Asia. They wanted to just isolate their nation from the rest of the world. But on December 7 everything suddenly changed. All of a sudden there was this attack and then there was a declaration of war, and the American people rallied around the President and rallied in defense of this nation. And the good war was fought, but the good war contained contradictions. It was also a war that stirred racism in this country. Americans remembered Pearl Harbor by attacking Japanese Americans, assaulting them in the streets, spitting on them, vandalizing their homes and businesses.

After September 11, again we have this explosion of patriotism across the land, and accompanying this patriotism has been a rise in hate crimes, this time directed against Arab Americans and Muslim Americans. In the aftermath of Pearl Harbor, Japanese Americans were also persecuted by their own government. A hundred and twenty thousand Japanese Americans, two thirds of them citizens by birth, were placed in concentration camps. This was indefinite detention, if you will. Since September 11, again our government has been racially profiling Arab Americans and Muslim Americans.

Still, our government is violating the constitutional rights of individual Arab Americans by detaining them. I know they're doing it because they have suspicions, but still, if they do have suspicions then I think they ought to present their case in court and make arrests rather than detaining persons. The Constitution clearly states that no person will be denied the right to life, liberty, and property without due process. That's a constitutional right. I hope history will not repeat itself in the aftermath of September 11.

MICHAEL: *Since you used the term* patriotism, *let me ask you something. There was an outpouring of patriotism after Pearl Harbor, and it's happening now. As patriotism is a very personal experience, how would you define it for yourself?*

After Pearl Harbor there were leaders who displayed and acted on patriotism. One of them is a hero of mine. We all know about the internment of Japanese Americans on the West Coast, but most of us do not know that Japanese Americans in Hawaii were not interned, and yet there were 150,000 of us, including myself, living in Hawaii. But I was not interned and my family was not interned. Now, why is it that Japanese Americans in Hawaii were not interned when Hawaii was the site where military action had, in fact, occurred?

Well, at that time we had a military governor, General Delos Emmons, who publicly stated that Japanese Americans were loyal Americans and that they didn't need to worry about being incarcerated in concentration camps — and he did used the term *concentration camps*. He said, "This is America and we have to do things the American way." In other words, he was saying that patriotism means we recognize that all Americans are Americans and that we have a Constitution and that we must respect the Constitution, which guarantees all of us the right to due process of the law. That's what patriotism means to me.

But what I see surfacing today in this country is a patriotism that disregards our founding principles of equality and the right to life and liberty. We have a patriotism that is xenophobic. It's a patriotism that is reflecting what I call "the master narrative of American history." It's the familiar but mistaken story that this country was settled by European immigrants and that Americans are white. This is a patriotism that goes against the grain of our founding principle of equality and the vision of America as a multiracial, multicultural democracy. So we have two kinds of patriotism, I think, existing side by side in our country at this very moment.

CHAPTER

9

VISIONS OF THE FUTURE

WELCOME TO THE FUTURE. We have arrived. Every minute is counting now. No longer can we point to the 21st century ahead of us. With 9-11, we are in it big time. The actions we take during this pivotal time will set the track for the decades to come. Is the track to be a "war on terrorism" that has no hope of ending or can we rise to the occasion and choose another way? Clearly, a field of possibilities awaits us. It is fenceless, without limits, other than those we choose to place upon ourselves. It requires courage to enter the unknown. Let us recall the Marshall Plan of the late 1940s when America arose to help the war-devastated nations of Europe on the road to recovery. Out of the ashes of World War II, hope was brought to millions in the tangible form of food, medical supplies, money, and direct aid at many levels. Today, of all the industrialized nations, America gives the least percentage of its wealth to the rest of the world, and we are the richest and most powerful nation in the world. In the past much of America's aid went to secure the often dictatorial regimes in power and little reached the people. Examples like El Salvador, Chile, Zaire, and Indonesia come to mind. A new paradigm is in order — and "we the people" can allow it to happen.

The Power of Circle Technology

From the first time I met Vicki Robin, it was clear that this woman was a committed social activist. She was a colleague of the late Joe Dominguez when he was presenting seminars on creating financial independence. The seminars evolved into the now classic book, Your Money or Your Life, *originally published in 1992. Since that time and Joe's untimely death in 1997, Vicki has continued to write and lecture about ways to simplify life. More recently, she has launched "Conversation Cafés" to expand the dialogue. She was also a member of the delegation that traveled to Dharamsala, India, at the invitation of H.H. the Dali Lama to explore how to express spiritual truth to the secular world.*

VICKI: My instinct in the last three weeks has been entirely what you might call the feminine response to stress, which is "tend and befriend." The male response to stress is "fight or flight." I think we're seeing the fight-or-flight options played out in a stark black-and-white debate where either we're going to go to war or we have to swallow the fact that we've been global bullies and therefore deserved the hit and have to wage war on our own consciousness here at home and be peaceniks and not kill anybody. There it is: "fight or flight." I can feel it physically, the polarization that's happening between those two approaches. And my whole urge has been this female thing of tending to human pain.

The day the twin towers came down, I wrote within hours an e-mail to something like four hundred people, saying, "Watch what we make this mean, because the meanings we assign to this in this moment will govern how we respond." I was concerned about the kind of thing that would soon transpire: the sense of retaliation and revenge would be strong, and there would be an insistence on kicking back. I was also concerned about the people in this broad transformational change movement in the United States getting painted with the brush of the internal terrorists, about somehow the gap between these strange people elsewhere who hate us and these people inside the country who have been facing criticism being too narrow in people's minds. So out of that, the first thing I did was to send out an e-mail talking about love. Within a day I was sending out more e-mails about the question, "How can we frame this to help us understand, to slow down the process of reaction so that we can choose our response?"

Then I realized that everybody had an opinion. Everybody had ideas. Everybody had a statement. I thought, "No, no, I'm not going to be one more talking head." And I shut down. Since then I have worked on creating a very simple technology. It's a very simple circle technology that all of us know about: it involves sitting in a circle and passing a talking stick around. The idea is to go around in a circle twice without any feedback and to just allow people to say what's on their minds and in their hearts, and then to open the conversation in a spirit of dialogue. I've been conducting what I call "conversation cafés" in public spaces. I'd done a small experiment over the summer getting the kinks worked out, so I knew how to do it. And I'm finding that, first of all, this process reframes the situation from one of war or even of law to a situation of learning, where we admit that none of us knows how to respond in this twenty-first century reality and that we need to learn. We need to turn to one another in the process of gathering not only the information but the stories and the feelings, the full-bodied knowledge — or wisdom — that needs to emerge here.

In particular I've been sensitized to the need to sit in circle with people who do not agree with me. It's not easy: usually, I'm surrounded by people who agree with me. So I've been trying to create these conversation cafés in public spaces and to draw in people who see things in another way, because that cracks me open. It allows me to move from opinion to wisdom.

That's where I've been putting my energy and response. I think that the longer we can hold this tension, this global tension, this global paradox of not knowing what to do, the more wisdom can flow into our collective space.

JEAN HOUSTON

A Passion for Peace

Jean Houston *is a visionary and a philosopher, a lover of wisdom, as the Greek root of the word signifies. She is a friend, colleague, and mentor. I have learned much in our conversations over the years. Her tireless treks around the planet on behalf of important causes have become legendary. Jean is an antidote to the doomsayers and cynics who preach that humanity is on a downward spiral to destruction. For that reason alone, she's worth listening to — her vision is well informed and comes from a scholar's perspective. Jean says, "It's time to wake up and learn to cook on more burners" because we have "come to the edge of our tolerance and it's time to jump."*

JEAN: "We are all New Yorkers." That is the gist of the message I've received from the thousands of e-mails, the countless phone calls, faxes, and communications from people writing or calling me from over thirty countries; this outpouring of love, of service, even of life itself is the miracle of humanity surpassing itself. All over this country and throughout the world, people are affirming their unity with us and, even more, their unity as a whole people. I actually believe that this tragedy is bringing us together in shadow and in light, for richer and for poorer, in sickness and in health, for as long as we all shall live. The desecration that occurred is also the announcement of a potential global union, a potential global marriage.

I have often spoken of how technology and the Internet gave us the world mind taking a walk with itself. But in light of the events of September 11, we now must speak of the world heart, the world stomach, the world spirit. America is no longer insulated from the peoples of other nations. We are present at the birth of an opportunity that exceeds our imagination. The poet and playwright Christopher Fry wrote, "Thank God our time is now, when wrong comes up to meet us everywhere, never to leave us, to retake the longest stride of soul man ever took." I believe that all oppression rises in our time, all shadows, all terrors.

The unique factors of human history emerge to compound our folly, to confuse our desire. We yearn for meaning, yet we deal with trivia. We are swept in currents over which we have no control. Government has become too big for the small problems of life and too small in spirit for the large problems. The tyranny that threatens to destroy us is not just terrorism. It's the tyranny of the unjust demands we have made of nature and the tyranny of some nations being kept in economic slavery by other nations.

We are the ones who have the most profound task in human history, the task of deciding whether we grow or whether we die. This will involve helping cultures and organizations to move from dominance by one economic culture or group to circular investedness, to sharing, to partnership, not just in economics but in culture, in feeling, in aesthetics, in belief. It will involve putting economics back as a satellite to the soul of culture rather than, as the case is now, the soul of culture being a satellite to economics. It will involve deep listening, past the arias and the habits of cruelty of crushed and humiliated people. It will involve a stride of soul that will challenge the very canons of our human condition. It will require that we become evolutionary partners for each other.

This is a huge test we find ourselves in. We have newly emerged from a century of war and holocaust. Our hopes for the new century, the new millennium, for a new way of being between nations and people, between the earth and ourselves, between spirit and matter — those hopes still live. If anything, they've become more powerful, more necessary. For America it will mean a deep shift in our attitudes towards other cultures around the world, to service and support and away from exploitation and dominance. Yes, the perpetrators have to be found and dealt with through therapeutic law and international justice. They are not a nation, but a cancer, and a cancer is rarely removed through a cycle of violence. Rather, as in holistic medicine, a cancer is subdued by the strengthening of the immune system, by the envisioning of the pattern of health and, yes, by the removal of the cancer wherever it can be excised. I think the metaphor is apt. Our health and security are built on friendship. What if we were to use some of the billions of dollars we now spend on weapons of destruction, which we manufacture ourselves and sell globally, to feed the hungry, to house the homeless, to make all those efforts that can result in the healing of the wounds of nations?

Real security demands real friendship, global marriage. One correspondent of mine brilliantly addressed these issues when she said the problem is not just terrorism, but generations of not having had an identity. The question is, "What made human beings incapable of feeling love, compassion, or empathy toward themselves or anyone else, and thereby made them destroyers of their own species? What happened that human beings could become so psychologically, emotionally, and spiritually distorted that they could believe that Islam, one of the most spiritual paths in the world, could encourage murder and suicide to gain heavenly reward?" These are not Muslims, she wrote, these are marginalized fanatics who have made a travesty of their faith.

The challenge is to discover how we can join together to create a world in which such pathology will no longer be nurtured or necessary. Many of us feel impotent before the enormity of the prospect. Some I know have experienced meltdown, some have had visions or dreams. Many have had the portals of their mind blown open to deeper realities, potent reflections. Tragedy has drawn us together, sent us deeper and given us the option of preparing for life rather than death.

I've been considering some of the things we may wish to do in the days and weeks to come that will give expression to our feelings and our need to act. What I'm offering is drawn primarily from my own reflections but also from that of others.

First, in these spirit-quaking times, align with your own spiritual resources. Take time to meditate, to pray, to reflect in solitude and in nature. Allow yourself daily sacred time and space to be re-sourced. Consider living daily life as a spiritual exercise. Watch your finer intuitions and ideas and share them with others. Commune with your spiritual allies, archetypal friends, quantum partners. In the place of spiritual connection, feel the flow of strength and compassion and intelligence. Become creative in your actions. Prepare scenarios of optimal healing and begin wherever you can to put them in place for events as well as people. Practice miracle management.

Second, give yourself vacations from television; so much of it is infomercials for war. However, the local New York City stations were filled with human stories of compassion and courage. But do listen occasionally to talk shows and call in with your own opinions and ideas for making a better world. Write that letter to the editor. Write or call your congressman or local government official.

Third, gather in groups and, if possible, in ongoing teaching-learning communities of wisdom and empowerment. But let everyone speak and do not deny anyone the authenticity of their feelings, even if they diverge widely from your own.

Fourth, talk to the kids, your own or other people's children. Let them express their feelings, let them tell you what is on their minds. Give them a grasp of the larger issues at hand. Tell them about mercy and compassionate action. If possible, engage them in service-oriented activities. Let them see the larger story.

Fifth, show up at town meetings or other places where people meet to pray and talk and engage each other. Sign petitions, if you're willing, and join in other activities that are sending a big message. Have vision circles to put forth images of what the world can be. Envision the possible society together. "Get thee to a mosque." Give support and compassion to Arab friends and colleagues and people of Middle Eastern origin you just happen to meet. Stamp out hatred and fear surrounding these people wherever you can. Let them tell their stories, their hopes and dreams. In fact, try to learn as much as you can about the Middle East, the political situation there, as well as the teachings of Islam.

Sixth, give up your own holding patterns and your old self. This is the time to become, or at least to enact, the possible human. Let your senses take pleasure in the glory of this world, let your heart celebrate the incredible gift of life, and share this with others. I live in a double-domed house. It was the last design that my old friend Buckminster Fuller completed before he died. I asked my house what words it would give you, and it responded with Bucky's own. They came out of a time of tremendous personal crisis in his life. He wrote, "So I vowed to keep myself alive, but only if I would never use me again just for me. Each one of us is born of two, and we really belong to each other. I vowed to do my own thinking instead of trying to accommodate everyone else's opinion, credos, and theories. I vowed to apply my own inventory of experiences to the solving of problems that affect everyone aboard planet Earth."

And this is what I try to do.

DAVID WHYTE

The Dangerous Truth

"Poetry opens people's thought, removes limits, and allows them to conceive, often for the first time, new and unexpected answers to old problems." These are the words of David Whyte, poet, writer, and organizational consultant, whose perspective I have enjoyed since meeting and interviewing him at an International Conference on Transpersonal Psychology in Killarney, Ireland, in 1994. He brings the much-needed voice of the poet to the problems we face in the world. It is this voice that enlivens the imagination and stirs the song of our souls. The human quest for freedom is rooted in the cultivation of the simple, more natural aspects of our existence. If 9-11 was anything, it was a wake-up call for all of us to remember that part of ourselves.

MICHAEL: *You travel around the world as a poet, writer, and author of some very successful books, and you're invited to speak everywhere. So I'm wondering what you've been seeing since the events of September 11, 2001, and what your perspective is?*

DAVID: My experience has been one of a coming-to-ground, in a sense. The image of those towers falling was literally an image of coming to ground. And I think there has actually been an inner template that has been equivalent to it. I feel like the abstracts of our world. There was the abstract of the dot-com boom and the total and absolute obsession with the financial industries that has all disappeared, and the obsession with abstract work has disappeared too. It seemed as if we were headed towards a world where the only people who got any respect were the people who were using their mouse button to make money in an instant. Suddenly, we have images of ordinary people in ordinary work, particularly in public service, whether it is fire fighters, policemen, or flight attendants, who are suddenly seen in a new light. And so out of the terrible tragedy has come a sense that we are actually on a more solid ground. Now, I think that is happening on an individual level. On the political level, I feel as if we have actually lost a sense of ground, or at least the ground that we are standing on is one that has been manufactured by a certain political class for their own ends, and we're all being bullied into standing in that ground along with them. But we don't necessarily agree.

I can't think of anyone better qualified to speak about the metaphor and the symbolism of the terrorist attacks on the World Trade Center and the Pentagon, probing underneath and looking at the deeper significance of those events from the perspective of a poet. How do you see it?

Well, this poet and the poets in general are always attempting to find the dangerous truth, you know, and the dangerous truth is the one that we find very difficult to face up to. I think it was an absolute tragedy and a sorrow, the loss of so many people in such a concentrated place. And yet, what it did was enfranchise us into an experience that most nations in the world and most people have on a daily basis the sense of absolute vulnerability. I do remember I was in Oxford the day it happened, in England. And Oxford is probably the epicenter of social coldness as well.

And yet, in those days, right after the fall of the towers and the attack on the Pentagon, there was an incredible reaching out, an indiscriminate, intimate reaching out towards Americans, in the streets, in the small hotel where I was marooned along with many others. And it was actually an unfolding of individual Americans into the world community, and I thought there was a tremendous opening and possibility at that time, which has since somewhat closed because of what I'd say has been the over-robust military response to what occurred. Now, I do believe that there does have to be a military response. I do believe that there has to be a vigilance and a seeking out of the revenge motives that have come into being, the wish to attack — not only America but other Western countries too. But I also believe that there should be an even more vigilant investigation of the sources from which this frustration and this kind of bitterness and hatred have come. I feel that the absolute obsession with taking revenge is covering over the opening that occurred at that time, and the possibility for America to be welcomed back into the world community in a psychological sense. In a political sense, America is a member of the world community, but over the last few years since the end of the Cold War, it has actually created a kind of aristocracy of one, in which the rest of the world is somewhat fearful of the direction that our country, the United States, is taking. Now, I'm English and Irish, but I also say "our" because I've been here long enough — 20 years now — that it is my country too. But I don't think it has been well represented. I don't think that many of the great qualities that are in this country escape beyond the border. We seem to export the worst qualities of the country to the rest of the world and the good qualities seem to nestle within its borders and you actually have to come to the country to see them. But America abroad has disenfranchised itself from the international conversation.

Now, on one level, I actually think this might be a good thing. The reason we have George Bush in power at the moment may be to bring the American century to an end. I actually thought that when Bush pulled out of the Kyoto Treaty, he was actually enfranchising the rest of the world into the conversation and into taking a leadership. I think there is going to be a lacuna, a kind of gap, a void for a few years before the other nations step in to take leadership. But there has to be a gap there before they will. But I do think that George Bush has brought the American century to an end. And that is, in the greater scheme of things, a good thing. He has pulled out of international treaties over landmines and chemical weapons. He has pulled out of the Kyoto international treaty on the ozone layer, and yet, the world is still working with Kyoto. It is still working to rid the world of mines, so there is another leadership coming to the fore. Rather than to the United States, people are beginning to look elsewhere for leadership, and I think that actually may be a healthy thing. And so out of a lot of isolationism, perhaps we'll see a coming to maturity of leadership in the rest of the world. I hope so, at least.

I think that's a really positive and good hope to have, and I know for myself that as I have traveled abroad, it seems that people overseas seem to differentiate between the U.S. government and U.S. citizens. There are so many people every-where, outside of our borders, who really love Americans but have a different view of the government. What would you say?

Well, I would say that there was a tremendous love of Americans in the few weeks after September 11, and it came to the fore and all the best qualities of America were seen because they were just like everyone else. They weren't a dif-ferent species, where every wrong had to be avenged to the nth degree. But since that time I have actually felt, as I have gone abroad, that there is starting to creep in a more personal animosity towards individuals abroad. It was there during the Vietnam War, but we haven't seen it for 30 years, and there are just little indi-cations of that. I do think the rest of the world is getting weary of the United States and its seeming wish to make the world in its own image. People, espe-cially in Europe, tend to think that North America has a greatly inflated image of itself. It's constantly saying that it is the home of freedom, as if there are no other parliamentary systems of government or no other democracies in the rest of the world. It's constantly saying that this is the place where people can actu-ally have a sense of safety — when, you know, it has one of the highest crime rates in the world. It's constantly saying that they have the best health care in the world when 39 million people don't have health insurance. I'm not saying that it isn't a wonderful place here. What I'm saying is, what would you think of a person that you knew who was constantly telling you that they were the best person in the world? You'd have to worry about them for a start.

And you might want to check them in for counseling, because there is some-thing not right in the basic psychic foundation of a country which is constantly having to tell itself that it is the best in the world. This is a wonderful place to live, full of wonderful people, full of diverse geographies, with diverse literatures, superb music, incredible creativity, both artistic and technological, and it does-n't need to tell the rest of the world that it's the only place to be. The Swiss don't want to be American. Most British and Irish don't want to be American. The French definitely don't want to be American. We've got to stop acting as if all the rest of the world wants to be us. They don't. But they want America to be itself, in conversation with the rest of the world, because America has so much to offer. But in conversation, not rammed down people's throat, which is what they are beginning to think is the general dynamic at the moment.

And not unrealistically so. Going back to your good news in the midst of what appears as very dark times, I've noticed that the rest of the world seems to have the idea that this is, indeed, one world and that we are all interconnected and that

what is done in Australia affects what is done in Cambodia and every other coun-
try and every other place, and that what we do here affects everyone else,
everywhere else — but we haven't gotten that message yet. So the good news is
that the rest of the world has it and that, with a simple attitude shift, we'll get it
and catch up.

I'd say so. I think America is in shock at the moment. Because of the wounding
that occurred in September, America is not itself at the moment. We talk about
the "axis of evil" in the world, and there may well be an axis of evil in Iraq and
Iran and Korea. There are suddenly a lot of awful things occurring there that we
should rightly fear. But there is also a potential axis of evil in this country —
namely between Ashcroft and Rumsfield — and that axis has to do with the subversion of the Constitution and the subversion of robust political conversation,
for example the incarceration of hundreds of people who have not been able to
actually have their voices heard with regards to their basic rights to a lawyer and
to legal help. So I think we are actually in danger of taking the first baby steps
towards a police state. You can see it in airports. You land at Seattle Airport,
from London, as I do and you have a soldier in a military uniform literally
standing over you, ordering you this way and that. Now, there is nothing wrong
with having security and having soldiers there, but you don't want them ordering civilians about. You don't get on a plane to go to a country in order to have
this first impression that you are entering a kind of fortress which is deathly
afraid of the least thing occurring. We have to learn to live within uncertainty. I
lived in Britain for most of my growing-up years, with terrorist bombs going off
all over Britain and civilians losing their lives and the only way it actually came
to an end was when a dialogue began between the nationalist forces in Belfast
and the Protestant voices. All of the revenge killings in the world did nothing to
actually heal what was an essentially hidden dynamic, hidden from the normal
light of political discourse, and certainly hidden from the normal light of the
media discourse.

Since those events, since September 11, what has been personally sustaining you?

I think what has sustained me is that in my work, whether it has been with the
general public or whether it's been with middle top managers or top managers
in organizations or people on the line even, the bedrock of meaning is very close
to the surface and people are impatient with frippery and with things that do
not speak to a greater context. And I think that's a very, very healthy sign. And
people do want the larger metaphor. They do want the greater picture and they
want to know, I suppose in a kind of religious sense, where their immortal souls
stand in the midst of all this difficulty, they want to know how the particular

threshold of history that they are standing at, with everyone else. I wish that America could understand that every threshold is a revelation that includes lots of vulnerability. And that the task is not to cover over that vulnerability and don a new set of armor but to actually inhabit it and create a robustness in the midst of the knowledge that you too are mortal like everyone else. There is a sense of trying to flatten or destroy anything that, in the least way, breaks through our parameters. Again, I'm working with a kind of an inner metaphor here, and I do believe that there is a place for a military response with regard to this kind of attack. But I do believe that the military response has swamped any sense in people's hearts or minds that it has actually been rethought or re-invented or re-imagined. It's the same despair you see in Palestine and Israel right now, the cycle of revenge getting tighter and tighter and tighter. You can kill as many people as you want in those caves in Afghanistan and there are 20 to take each of those people's places. And especially if America comes to represent a kind of world oppression under the name of free enterprise and democracy, then I don't think that's a very fruitful way to go. There are hundreds of millions of Arabs and Muslims in the world who are deeply distrustful of the United States, whether or not they are extremists or terrorists. My feeling is that hundreds of millions of people can't be entirely wrong. There must be something that they have that we've got to listen to about our role in the suppression of Palestinian hopes and freedom and about our approach to Islam itself. And if we can look at those things without being self-indulgent, without saying everything is wrong about America, and still keep all our great virtues in sight, then that is a sign of maturity. You can look at your vulnerabilities, your weaknesses, and not feel as if the world is coming to an end or that you are being too anti-American. But that's what's happening right now — it is a very frightening McCarthyite dynamic in the country at the moment. If you try to put your head above the parapet and speak against these issues, you are somehow undermining the soldiers in Afghanistan or you are undermining this great crusade, as President Bush incorrectly called it. This is something we have to address. We all have to put our head above the parapet and speak out.

I would say as an American and not just as a host in this interview, the heart and soul of democracy, as I understand it, is dissent, and this country was created out of dissent. And out of dialogue, out of challenging authority. The colonials in the American colonies challenged the authority of King George III. That's where we started. We have to recover those first principles.

Exactly. With some kind of understanding created in the world that we're not just about our own agenda. And, at the moment, it seems the feeling is, "Well, as long as it goes our way, then we stand behind whatever treaties are there." So we want no tariffs and free trade — until it comes to steel. Then the rest of the world says, "Well, what happened to that free trade you were so enthusiastic about just 24 hours ago?" America replies, "Oh, well, in this case, we need to be treated differently." So as I said, we're creating an aristocracy of one, which is making the rest of the world feel as if they are in a kind of international serfdom. George W. Bush has his work cut out to reverse that tide because the tide is actually turning against the United States, whether it's in the developed world or the undeveloped world, whether it's in the Muslim world or in the non-Muslim world. I just hope to God he wakes up, realizes the force of that tide and what it can lead to, and joins in a real international dialogue before it's too late.

CLAYBORNE CARSON

Martin Luther King Jr. Speaks

In the tradition of revolutionary activists who sought peace through nonviolence, like Jesus and Gandhi, Martin Luther King Jr. became a force at a time when voices were needed to address the injustices, the poverty, the inequities and the violence in the world, a time not unlike our own. As he said, "... use any means of legitimate nonviolent protest necessary to move our nation and our government on a new course of social, economic, and political reform." King also spoke from the heart to the heart. His words are as relevant today as when he spoke them: "I have a dream ..." Let us all dream of a world at peace. Slaves were freed. Women got the vote. Apartheid in South Africa is gone. The Berlin Wall fell, and communism collapsed in central and eastern Europe as well as in the Soviet Union. Anything is possible!

MICHAEL: *As the autobiographer of Dr. Martin Luther King Jr. and the editor of his papers, you are in a very unusual and distinct position to comment on what he might say if were alive today. What would he be saying at this point in time about what's going in the United States and what's going on in the world?*

CLAYBORNE: I think first of all he was quite concerned about international issues during his lifetime. As you may know, he traveled to the Middle East in the late fifties and was quite aware of the conflict that was going on there at that time. It was shortly after another war in the Middle East. He understood how destructive that conflict was on both sides. So I think that he would see the current conflict in that long-term perspective. He was always concerned about the emergence of what at that time was being called the "Third World." The emergence of newly independent nations, nations that were moving out from the shadow of colonialism or European domination. He was determined that that change take place in the context of nonviolence. I think that over the last fifty years, what is striking is the degree to which that has occurred. Most of the nations that gained their independence did so nonviolently. Or primarily through nonviolence. It's the exceptions that have drawn attention. Much has been achieved through nonviolence. So I think first of all he would see things in that longer-term context.

He was always consistent that the message of nonviolence needs to go to the powerful as well as the powerless. One of the ways in which his message has been misinterpreted is that the tactic of nonviolence is usually brought forward simply as a response to the violence of the oppressed. He always understood that things depend on how the oppressor responds to the oppressed. Whether we have a nonviolent solution to a problem is not simply in the hands of people struggling for their freedom but also in the hands of those who react to them.

I think that in this conflict he would be directing his message of nonviolence towards those who have power as well as those who don't have a great deal of power, all the while emphasizing that the primary advantage of his approach would be that it doesn't lead to a cycle of violence. In many of the analyses of the conflict in Afghanistan, people have pointed to the way in which violence in the past has played into that current conflict. How, in our effort to get rid of the Russians in Afghanistan, we created some of the conditions that made possible the current conflict. How our effort to reverse the Iraqi invasion earlier in the last decade also generated the resentments that led to some of what happened in September 2001.

What Dr. King would be concerned about is that in our effort to use violence in this conflict, we may be sowing the seeds for future violence. So I would see him reminding us of all of those possibilities.

One of the things Martin Luther King Jr. mentioned in his autobiography, just to extend what you were saying, is that he would speak to people in power and speak to people without power. In the context of the Vietnam War era around 1967, King said, "There isn't a single official of our country that can go anywhere in the world without being stoned and eggs being thrown at him. It is because we have taken on to ourselves a kind of arrogance of power. We've ignored the mandates of justice and morality ..." Reading those words, I realized that the same thing could be said today.

Well, perhaps not quite as much. I think there is a great deal of sympathy for the United States because after all we were attacked in September. But even with that sympathy there is an underlying message from many places in the world, including from people who are allies of the United States, that we display a certain arrogance, a certain sense that we're good and the other side is evil and that therefore practically any means are okay. That when we're attacked and when we're the victims of terrorism, we don't have to worry about the means. What King often said was that an eye for an eye eventually leaves everyone blind. This is one of those situations where it is difficult to ask for restraint when someone has been injured. But often that is what those in power ask from those who are powerless when they've been injured. Don't react in violence. After Martin Luther King's assassination, those in power in this country advised African-Americans not to respond in anger, not to respond with retaliation. And I think that is the correct message. But it should apply to everyone. We need to exercise restraint. Not simply because the other side deserves it. I don't think that is the argument. We need to exercise restraint because eventually we have to live in the same world with those we're struggling against. Demonizing them, attempting to destroy them, King pointed out, doesn't work. It leaves behind a trail of bitterness and resentment that eventually comes back to haunt you.

Let me say something about American patriotism. We're hearing about patriotism these days and I'm going to the sermon that Martin Luther King Jr. gave at Ebenezer Church in November 1967. The one about a cause or idea so precious you will die for it. He said, "I say to you this morning that if you've never found something so dear and so precious to you that you will die for It, then you aren't fit to live." Then he goes on and says, "Don't ever think that you are by yourself. Go on to jail if necessary, but you never go alone. Take a stand for that which is right. The world may misunderstand you and criticize you, but you never go alone. For somewhere I read that one with God is a majority." I see Dr. King speaking to the deep spiritual side. I would like you to speak to that.

One thing that passage points out is how difficult it is to speak up at certain times. Later, in the Vietnam conflict, it was fairly easy to be in the opposition, so someone like Martin Luther King wasn't totally isolated and ridiculed. But early in that conflict it was very difficult to speak out. And sometimes we forget that in the current context. We see professors in universities being suspended because they make what are deemed unpatriotic remarks. We've seen that kind of a tendency in previous conflicts, and what King was pointing out is that it's in those periods when it is difficult to speak out that one must speak one's conscience no matter what the cost. And if you lose that courage because of fear, and in his case he was talking about the fear of death, then you are already dead in some sense because your spirit, your conscience, is dead. Personally, I'm not so much worried by the people who either express support for what's going on in the world with respect to the conflict in Afghanistan, for example, or oppose it. What worries me are those who just remain silent because they fear that by speaking out they will draw negative attention, criticism, perhaps some kind of retribution against them. When everyone in the arena is standing up and being patriotic, it is very difficult to be the one person who doesn't join the crowd. I think one of the reasons we should honor King is that he stood up for that tradition of standing up when everyone else is opposing you. Or in some cases sitting down when everyone else is standing up. He saw his religious and ethical and moral duty to take a stand no matter what the cost.

The next-to-last chapter in the Autobiography of Dr. Martin Luther King Jr., which you edited, opens with a quote from Dr. King: "We have moved into an era where we are called upon to raise certain basic questions about the whole society. We are still called upon to give aid to the beggar who finds himself in misery and agony on life's highway. But one day we must ask the question of whether an edifice which produces beggars must not be restructured and refurbished. That is where we are now." This, of course, was 1967. Would he say something similar today or not?

Oh, definitely. Part of what I think makes his death especially tragic is that we've lost one of the consistent voices against economic injustice. That was something that was his concern throughout his lifetime. At the time of his death the nation was far more committed to dealing with that problem than it is now. At the time of his death it was the national policy of the United States to eliminate poverty. Now that is not even on the political agenda of the nation. There is the myth that we fought a war on poverty and we lost when, in fact, we fought a minor skirmish against poverty and gave up. I think the historical lie that an enormous commitment was made to a fight against poverty and that it failed is certainly something that he would argue against if he were around today. He would point out that the total spending on anti-poverty programs never exceeded one percent of the federal budget and that was at its height. So this mantra I sometimes hear in conservative circles that we spent three trillion dollars or two trillion dollars fighting poverty and that it failed is certainly a distortion of history. Which brings us back to the fact that we have not addressed the issue of the gulf between the rich and the poor. As a result, the gulf has become wider and wider and continues to become wider and wider not only in the United States but around the world. That to me is a recipe for disaster. It would really help to have King as a strong voice reminding us of the moral issue involved in this widening of the gulf between the rich and the poor, reminding us that this problem is not simply the result of some people not doing well, but of the unfairness of the process, of the unfairness of the economic system. We need to have that voice — we really miss it in this nation.

Epilogue

THE UNITED STATES OF AMERICA, as I as well as many others perceive it, is out of touch with its original vision. But I also know that out of death, resurrection is possible — it is my hope and prayer, that this nation be reborn with its "first principles" once again the guiding force.

When Jefferson wrote that all men have the inalienable right to "life, liberty, and the pursuit of Happiness," by the right to "life" he meant the individual right to have food, clothing, a home, and work; by the right to "liberty" he meant the right to think and speak freely as well as to hold religious convictions of any persuasion without fear of persecution; by the right to "the pursuit of happiness" he meant every citizen's right to find meaning and purpose, and thereby a deep and abiding joy. All these rights were to be "inalienable," that is to say they "cannot be taken away." The Declaration of Independence is a spiritual document meant for all people everywhere, not just for Americans.

America has lost the connection to its founding roots. It is floundering in a rising sea of chaos caused in part by corpocracy, and increasingly creates the cancerous growth of an endless stream of irrelevant product choices and mindless distractions while engulfing and devouring individual liberties. Our government is being controlled by corporate interests through lobbying, Political Action Committees, and heavy campaign contributions. Federal agencies, whose responsibilities are to serve the public, often act to benefit the companies they are supposed to oversee. Former government officials find executive positions with defense contractors or become lobbyists, reaping great financial wealth, because of their taxpayer-subsidized previous employment. This, in a much abbreviated version, is America's corpocracy.

With five percent of the world's population, we are consuming upwards of 40% of the world's resources because of our addiction to consumerism. This penchant for economic growth is supported by the sacrifice of the eco-system, including the ozone layer; the rape of natural resources; the obliteration of indigenous cultures; the monopolization of products and services in the name of the "free market," which ironically requires exorbitant capital to enter into and engage with; the control of the communications media by a few behemoth corporations; the absence of ethics in the applications of capitalist principles where "the bottom line" and quarterly dividends outweigh human values; and the on-going purchase of political largesse by corporate interests at the expense of the people's "life, liberty, and the pursuit of Happiness." In short, we Americans are aboard a rudderless ship led by a crazed captain (the corpocracy), whose sole guiding principle is economic expediency without regard to the implications for future generations. It is a rampant tyranny of the future. It calls to mind Jefferson's eloquent statement, "I have sworn upon the altar of God, eternal hostility against every form of tyranny over the mind of man."

I recognize in myself the need to speak out and to reveal the fact that the emperor has no clothes, that the foxes are in the hen house, and that the whole enterprise is a house of cards, begging for a recovery of meaning and purpose, a return to the spiritual underpinnings of American democratic ideals as set forth in 1776 in the Declaration of Independence and later in the Constitution and the Bill of Rights. It is time to move beyond blame and judgment, all the while not ignoring the dangerous erosion of civil liberties and personal freedoms that has occurred during the past quarter century and continues unabated. Compassion and kindness are the actions required to overcome the lack of consciousness that has allowed this erosion to occur. At the same time, the age of leaders is over — each of us must now avail him- or herself of the leader within. Working together from the deepest center of our hearts and intelligence, we can transform the present malaise and perhaps, in the end, realize the true attainment of a government and a nation created of, by, and for the people.

These are perilous times. The tragic events of 9-11 have given us an opportunity to recover our bearings, to revisit the founding principles of this nation, which were inspired by the Native peoples of this land. It is time to recover those principles and to create a world that works for all. President Lincoln expressed these guiding principles very eloquently at the dedication of the Gettysburg national cemetery: "That we here highly resolve that these dead shall not have died in vain — that this nation, under God, shall have a new birth of freedom — and that government of the people, by the people, for the people, shall not perish from this earth."

Since its inception as a nation, America has served as a beacon of freedom and democracy to oppressed people throughout the world, inspiring a steady stream of immigrants to come to its shores. So, in the last analysis, the present reality turns us back on ourselves to what each of us as an individual can do to make a difference in our life. As I change, the world changes. At the same time as I work on myself, I must do everything I can to effect a difference in my sphere of influence. We're all interrelated in mysterious ways. Whatever inner wisdom I may discover needs to manifest through my external actions. The times require an activist spirituality that engages the challenges we face in the world.

Besides the communication and broadcast work I do, here's how I am addressing the deteriorating American dream and the challenges of the post-9-11 world.

Specifically, I
- stay politically active in my local community in a variety of different ways — for example, I helped start the local community radio station in Mendocino County, served on the county-wide Self-Esteem and Personal Responsibility Commission, and have supported creative activities for young people;
- stay abreast of legislative activities affecting my community, state, and nation and write, where appropriate, to my local, state, and federal legislators regularly (personal letters are demonstrably more effective than e-mails or faxes);
- speak out, in both personal and public situations, wherever and whenever appropriate, hopefully without being a bore;
- scan and read various publications such as *The New York Times*, *The Nation*, *The Wall Street Journal*, *In These Times*, *Business Week*, *Z Magazine*, *Fortune Small Business*, *The Progressive*, *Bottom Line/Business*, *The Washington Spectator*, *FAST Company*, *Business Ethics*, *The Christian Science Monitor*, *Utne Reader*, *Yes!*, and *The Sun*;
- financially contribute to various organizations working to positively affect America and the planet;
- vote in every election;
- write letters to the editors of various publications on behalf of important issues;
- critique the blatantly negative stories as well as praise the media when they report a positive story;
- receive relevant daily Internet news briefs such as *The New York Times* headlines and editorials (www.nytimes.org), global stories from UNWire (www.unfoundation.org), ecology-related updates from *Grist Magazine* (www.gristmagazine.com), socially relevant communications from the Benton Foundation (www.benton.org), progressive news from www.CommonDreams.org, and Move On, a site that facilitates countering the influence of monied interests and partisan extremes (www.moveon.org);
- pray.

About the Contributors

SHARIF ABDULLAH is a leading proponent of and catalyst for inclusive social, cultural, and spiritual transformation. He has facilitated empowerment and leadership sessions for local, national, and international public and private organizations. Abdullah is the Founding Director of Commonway Institute, which is designed to build inclusivity, understanding, and civic engagement between diverse groups. He is the author of *The Power of One: Authentic Leadership in Turbulent Times* (New Society Publishers, 1995) and *Creating a World that Works for All* (Berrett-Koehler, 1999).
His website is www.commonway.org.

AS'AD ABUKHALIL was born in Lebanon and received his BA and MA in Political Science from the American University of Beirut and his PhD in Comparative Politics from Georgetown University. His articles on Middle East politics and society have appeared in English, German, Spanish, and Arabic. AbuKhalil is the author of *Bin Laden, Islam, and America's New "War on Terrorism"* (Seven Stories Press, 2002).

FRANCIS BOYLE is Professor of International Law at the University of Illinois College of Law. He was educated at the University of Chicago and Harvard Law School. Duke University Press and Athena Press have published his work on issues of international law. He served as consultant for the U.N. Committee on the Exercise of the Inalienable Rights of the Palestinian people and served two terms on the Board of Directors of Amnesty International.

In 1985, Coretta Scott King invited **CLAYBORNE CARSON** to direct a long-term project to edit and publish the papers of Dr. Martin Luther King Jr. Under Carson's direction, the King Papers Project has produced four volumes of a projected fourteen-volume comprehensive edition of King's speeches, sermons, correspondence, publications, and unpublished writings. Carson's scholarly publications have focused on African-American protest movements and political thought of the period after WWII. His writings have appeared in leading historical journals and popular periodicals. He is the editor of *The Autobiography of Martin Luther King, Jr.* (Warner Books, 1998), *A Knock at Midnight:*

Inspiration from the Great Sermons of Martin Luther King, Jr. (Warner Books 1998), and *A Call To Conscience: The Landmark Speeches of Dr. Martin Luther King, Jr.* (Warner Books, 2001). For more information on the King Papers Project, go to www.stanford.edu/group/king.

NOAM CHOMSKY is a major figure in twentieth-century linguistics. Since 1955, he has taught at the Massachusetts Institute of Technology, where he became a full professor at the age of 32. He has received honorary degrees from the universities of London, Delhi, Chicago, Maine, Massachusetts, and Pennsylvania as well as from Swarthmore College, Bard College, and Loyola University of Chicago. In addition to his work as a linguist, Chomsky has written many books on contemporary issues. Recently, he published *9/11* (Seven Stories Press, 2001) and co-authored *Manufacturing Consent: The Political Economy of the Mass Media* (Pantheon Books, 2002). His political talks have been heard, typically by standing-room-only audiences, all over the country and the globe.

HARLAN CLEVELAND, political scientist and public executive, is President Emeritus of the World Academy of Art and Science. He has served as a U.N. relief administrator in Italy and China, a Marshall Plan executive, a magazine editor and publisher, a U.S. Ambassador to NATO, and Assistant Secretary of State. He is the recipient of the U.S. Medal of Freedom and the author of a dozen books on executive leadership and international affairs, among them *Birthday of a New World: The Future of International Governance* (Aspen, 1992) and *Nobody in Charge: Leadership in the Knowledge Environment* (Jossey-Bass, 2002); Cleveland co-authored *The Global Commons: Policy for the Planet* (University Press of America, 1990).

ANNA CODY, a program coordinator with the Center for Economic and Social Rights, is an Australian lawyer who has worked in Australia, El Salvador, the USA, Mexico, and Honduras. Throughout her work she has focused on human rights law, specifically on women's human rights, Indigenous Peoples' rights, and human rights issues in mining. Cody has practiced as a lawyer and litigated individual and public interest cases as well as advocating in U.N. and domestic forums. She has a Masters in Law from Harvard University and has taught law and legal concepts in universities and community settings.
The Center for Economic and Social Rights' website is www.cesr.org.

KEVIN DANAHER is a co-founder of Global Exchange, the noted human rights organization based in San Francisco. He has a PhD from the University of California and has written or edited eight books dealing with U.S. foreign policy and the global economy, the most recent being *Corporations Are Gonna*

Get Your Mama: Globalization and the Downsizing of the American Dream (Common Courage Press, 1997), *Globalize This!: The Battle Against the World Trade Organization and Corporate Rule* (Community Archives Publications, 2000), *Democratizing the Global Economy: The Battle Against the World Bank and the International Monetary Fund* (Common Courage Press, 2001), and *Ten Reasons to Abolish the IMF and World Bank* (Seven Stories Press, 2002). Global Exchange's website is www.globalexchange.org.

ORIAH MOUNTAIN DREAMER is a teacher and writer. She gives speeches and leads workshops, ceremonies, and retreats throughout the United States and Canada. She is the author of *The Invitation* (HarperSanFrancisco, 1999) and *The Dance: Moving to the Rhythms of Your True Self* (HarperSanFrancisco, 2001). Her website is www.oriahmountaindreamer.com.

TAHMEENA FARYAL is a Pakistan-based member of RAWA. When she was a child, the Soviet invasion forced her and her family to flee Afghanistan for a Pakistani refugee camp. She was educated in RAWA schools in Pakistan and as a result became committed to working for human rights and women's rights. She has taught children in refugee camps, has distributed food, medical supplies, and other humanitarian aid to refugees, and has taken part in RAWA demonstrations and functions to protest the inhumane situation in Afghanistan and to support women's rights. As a member of RAWA's Foreign Committee, she has also traveled internationally to raise awareness of the plight of Afghan women and RAWA's work. RAWA's website is www.rawa.org.

ROBERT FULLER is a physicist and the former president of Oberlin College. During the 1980s, Fuller made dozens of trips to the Soviet Union, carrying out projects to lessen mutual stereotyping by the two Cold War antagonists. His writings have appeared in *Utne Reader, Harvard Magazine, Whole Earth Review,* and *In Context.* He is the author of the e-book *Breaking Ranks: In Pursuit of Individual Dignity* (www.breakingranks.net, 2001). His website is www.breakingranks.net.

JEFF GATES is the president of The Shared Capitalism Institute and has been a specialist in "ownership engineering" since 1973. He served as counsel to the U.S. Senate Committee, where, with others, he crafted federal pension law and the legislation encouraging employee stock ownership plans. He has since worked in more than 30 countries on various ownership engineering projects. He is a lawyer, investment banker, political advisor, and consultant to government, corporate, and union leaders. Gates is the author of *The Ownership Solution: Toward a Shared Capitalism for the 21st Century* (Addison-Wesley,

1998) and *Democracy at Risk: Rescuing Main Street from Wall Street* (Perseus Press, 2001). The Shared Capitalism Institute's website is www.sharedcapitalism.org.

AMY GOODMAN is radio host of the public radio program "Democracy Now." She is the 1998 recipient of the George Polk Award for the radio documentary "Drilling and Killing: Chevron and Nigeria's Military Dictatorship." Her documentaries have been honored by The National Federation of Community Broadcasters and the Overseas Press Club. Goodman has reported from Israel and the occupied territories, Cuba, Mexico, and Haiti and was the first journalist ever to interview the jailed U.S. citizen Lori Berenson, who is serving a life sentence in Peru. In addition to hosting her daily radio shows, Goodman speaks about media activism on university campuses as well as to human rights, church, and community groups. She also runs workshops on grassroots coverage at community radio stations throughout the country. The website for "Democracy Now" is www.democracynow.org.

The author of more than twenty books, **SUSAN GRIFFIN** has won dozens of awards for her work as a poet, writer, essayist, playwright, filmmaker, and eco-feminist. Her book *A Chorus of Stones: The Private Life of War* (Doubleday 1992) was a finalist for the Pulitzer Prize and the National Book Critics Award. She is a frequent contributor to *Ms Magazine*, *The New York Times Book Review*, and numerous other publications. She is the author of the classic *Women and Nature: The Roaring Inside Her* (Sierra Club Books, 2000), *The Book of Courtesans: A Catalogue of Their Virtues* (Broadway Books, 2001), and many others titles. Her website is www.susangriffin.com.

BEAU GROSSCUP is Professor of International Relations at California State University in Chico. He writes for the layperson as well as the academic and works as a consultant for the CIA, the FBI, and the U.S. Armed Forces. Grosscup is the author of *The Newest Explosions of Terrorism: Latest Sites of Terrorism in the 90s and Beyond* (New Horizon, 1998).

BISHOP THOMAS GUMBLETON is the Auxiliary Bishop of the Archdiocese of Detroit and the Founding President of Pax Christi. His dedication to peace has taken him all over the world, including Columbia, Hiroshima, Iraq, and Vietnam. He participates in actions of civil disobedience and has done fasts and prayer vigils. Holding many honorary degrees, he has appeared on television and radio and has written and published numerous articles, reports, and book reviews as well as recorded audio cassettes. Bishop Gumbleton has received many awards, including the University of Notre Dame Peacemaker Award and the Humanitarian Service Award in 2001.

FATHER G. SIMON HARAK, S.J., entered the Society of Jesus (an order of Catholic priests) in 1970 and has served as a missionary in Jamaica and the Philippines. He has a BA from Fairfield University, an M.Div. from the Jesuit School of Theology at Berkeley, an MA from the University of Notre Dame, and a PhD in ethics from Notre Dame. A member of various professional organizations in theology and ethics as well as of the American Arab Anti-Discrimination Committee, he is currently organizing the "Mirror of Truth" tour, addressing the issues of Weapons of Mass Destruction and Terror. Father Harak is Adjunct Professor of Ethics at Fordham University, the author of *Virtuous Passions: The Formation of Christian Character* (Paulist, 1993), and the editor of *Nonviolence for the Third Millennium: Its Legacy and Its Future* (Mercer University Press, 2000). He is associated with www.vitw.org.

ANDREW HARVEY was born and raised in India and educated in England. At the age of 21, he became the youngest scholar ever to be awarded a fellowship to All Soul's College at Oxford University. Harvey became disillusioned with academic life and traveled the globe to study world religions. He served as co-editor for the best-selling *Tibetan Book of Living and Dying* (HarperSanFrancisco, 1992) and is the author of *The Direct Path* (Broadway Books, 2000) and *Sun at Midnight* (Tarcher, 2002). He has edited and/or authored over 30 other titles. Harvey's website is www.andrewharvey.net.

Formerly a highly successful entrepreneur, **PAUL HAWKEN** has been called the "poet laureate of American capitalism." He founded several natural foods companies in the late 1960s and early 1970s. He went on to co-found Smith & Hawken, the retail and catalog company, Metacode, a content management software company, and Groxis, a software company providing enterprises and individuals information navigation, visualization, and organization capabilities. Hawken is the co-author of *Natural Capitalism: Creating the Next Industrial Revolution* (Little Brown, 1999) and the author of *The Next Economy* (Holt, Rinehart 1983), *Growing a Business* (Simon & Schuster, 1987), and *The Ecology of Commerce: A Declaration of Sustainability* (HarperBusiness, 1994).

MARK HERTSGAARD is an independent journalist, author, and activist whose work has appeared in *The New Yorker, Vanity Fair, Harper's, Time, Newsweek, The New York Times, The Washington Post, The Los Angeles Times, Rolling Stone, Esquire, The Village Voice, Mother Jones,* and many other publications. He is the political observer for National Public Radio's weekly program "Living On Earth" and has appeared on many national radio and television shows, including "Fresh Air," "The Today Show," "Nightline," "New Dimensions," "Larry King Live," and "The Bill Moyers Report." He speaks frequently before activist, community, political, and educational groups in the United States and abroad. Hertsgaard is a member of the Society of Environmental Journalists and the Author's Guild. Among other books, he has published *Earth Odyssey: Around the World in Search of our Environmental Future* (Broadway Books, 1999) and *The Eagle's Shadow: Why America Fascinates and Infuriates the World* (Farrar, Straus & Giroux, 2002).

To find out more about Hertsgaard's work, visit www.globalgreendeal.org.

JANE HIRSHFIELD is a poet, translator, editor, and writer. She is the author of five books of poetry, most recently *Given Sugar, Given Salt* (HarperCollins, 2001); she also published a book of essays called *Nine Gates: Entering the Mind of Poetry* (HarperCollins, 1997) and edited *Women in Praise of the Sacred: 43 Centuries of Spiritual Poetry by Women* (HarperCollins, 1994). Hirshfield has received fellowships from the Guggenheim and Rockefeller Foundations as well as the Poetry Center Book Award and numerous other honors. Her poetry has appeared in *The New Yorker, The Atlantic, The Nation, The New Republic,* and many literary periodicals. She has taught at the University of California at Berkeley and at the University of San Francisco and was featured in the two 1999 Bill Moyers PBS poetry specials "Fooling With Words" and "Sounds of Poetry."

JEAN HOUSTON is a scholar and researcher in human capacities. For the past 30 years, she has co-directed, with her husband, Robert Masters, the Foundation for Mind Research. Houston has worked with numerous corporations, including Xerox, General Electric, and Rodale Press. She has been a consultant to the U.N., UNICEF, and other international agencies. A past president of the Association for Humanistic Psychology, Houston has taught philosophy, psychology, and religion at various colleges across the country. She is the author of many books, including *A Passion for the Possible: A Guide to Realizing Your True Potential* (HarperSanFrancisco, 1998) and *Jump Time: Shaping Your Future in a World of Radical Change* (Putnam, 2000).

Her website is www.jeanhouston.org.

A writer and a political activist, **ROBERT JENSEN** is an associate professor of journalism at the University of Texas at Austin. He teaches graduate and undergraduate courses in media law, ethics, and politics. In addition to teaching and doing research, Jensen writes for both alternative and mainstream media. He is also involved in a number of groups working against the U.S. military and economic domination of the rest of the world. Jensen is the author of *Writing Dissent: Taking Radical Ideas from the Margins to the Mainstream* (Peter Lang, 2001) and co-author of *Freeing the First Amendment: Critical Perspectives on*

Freedom of Expression (New York University Press, 1995).
For more information on his work, go to www.nowarcollective.com.

DAVID LA CHAPELLE is a resident of Juneau, Alaska, and literally grew up on a glacier. Trained in a variety of somatic therapies and yoga psychology, La Chapelle received eight years of clinical supervision under both a medial doctor and a Lakota Medicine Man. He has been in private and group practice since 1980 and co-founded Wellspring Partners in Health, a successful medical/holistic clinic in Boulder, Colorado. For several years, he was a core presenter at the annual conferences of the Association for Humanistic Psychology. La Chapelle has led over 150 Wilderness Quests, integrating psychology and group process. He is the author of *Navigating the Tides of Change: Stories from Science, the Sacred, and a Wise Planet* (New Society Publishers, 2001). His website is www.tidesofchange.org.

RABBI MICHAEL LERNER studied at the Jewish Theological Seminary in New York City and was mentored by Abraham Joshua Heschel. He received a PhD in philosophy at the University of California at Berkeley in 1972 and a PhD in clinical psychology at the Wright Institute in 1977. In 1979, he became principal investigator for a National Institutes of Mental Health study. Having launched Tikkun, a magazine offering a Jewish critique of politics, culture, and society, in 1986, he still serves as its editor. Rabbi Lerner is the author of many books, including *Jewish Renewal: A Path to Healing and Transformation* (Harper Perennial, 1995), *The Politics of Meaning: Restoring Hope and Possibility in an Age of Cynicism* (Addison-Wesley, 1996), and *Spirit Matters: Global Healing and the Wisdom of the Soul* (Walsch Books/Hampton Roads Publishing, 2000). Tikkun's website is www.tikkun.org.

JOANNA MACY, PhD, is an eco-philosopher and a scholar of systems theory and Buddhism. She is the leading voice in the movements for peace, justice, and the environment. Over the past twenty years, thousands of people around the world have participated in Macy's workshops and trainings. She is known worldwide for her work focusing on the interdependence between spiritual breakthrough and social actions. She serves as adjunct professor to two graduate schools in the San Francisco Bay Area and is the author of, among other titles, *World as Lover, World as Self* (Parallax Press, 1991) and *Widening Circles: A Memoir* (New Society Publishers, 2000); Macy co-authored *Thinking Like a Mountain: Towards a Council of All Beings* (New Society Publishers, 1998). Her website is www.joannamacy.net.

DAWNA MARKOVA is a former senior affiliate of the Organizational Learning Center at MIT and is now a consultant member of the Society for Organizational Learning. She is a board member of the Visions of a Better World Foundation. Markova has established learning communities across the country, founded the Institute of Human Ecology and Professional Thinking Partners and served as a faculty member at the Union Institute as well as the Lesley and Antioch graduate schools. She has authored many books, including *The Open Mind: Discovering the Six Patterns of Natural Intelligence* (Conari Press, 1996) and *I Will Not Live an Unlived Life: Reclaiming Purpose and Passion* (Conari Press, 2000).

Professional Thinking Partners' website is www.ptpinc.org.

WILLIAM MCDONOUGH is an internationally renowned designer and one of the primary proponents and shapers of what he and his partners call "The Next Industrial Revolution." Time recognized him as a "Hero for the Planet" in 1999. He is the former dean of the School of Architecture at the University of Virginia. McDonough is the founding principal of William McDonough and Partners, Architecture and Community Design, an internationally recognized design firm practicing ecologically, socially, and economically intelligent architecture and planning in the U.S. and abroad. His clients include companies such as Ford Motor Company, Herman Miller, Gap Inc., and IBM. McDonough is the co-author of *Cradle to Cradle: Remaking the Way We Make Things* (North Point Press, 2002). In 1998, he received the Presidential Award for Sustainable Development, the nation's highest environmental honor, which was presented to him by former President Clinton at the White House.

McDonough's website is www.mcdonough.com.

JOHN MOHAWK, PhD, is a Turtle Clan Seneca from the Cattaraugus Reservation (Iroquois). He was formerly the editor of *Akwesasne Notes*, once the largest Indian publication in the U.S. He is an Assistant Professor of American Studies at the State University of New York at Buffalo and lectures widely on topics in Native American studies, including sovereignty, community, and economic development. Mohawk is the author of *Utopian Legacies: A History of Conquest and Oppression in the Western World* (Clear Light Publishing, 1999).

THOMAS MOORE is a writer and lecturer. He was a monk in a Catholic religious order for twelve years and has degrees in theology, musicology, and philosophy. A former professor of religion and psychology, he is the author of many books, including the best-selling *Care of the Soul* (HarperCollins, 1992), *The Re-Enchantment of Everyday Life* (HarperCollins, 1997), and *Original Self: Living with Paradox and Originality* (HarperCollins, 2000).

CARLOS MOTA has an MBA from Stanford and is co-founder and director of HMS Consultores, S.C. He specializes in organizational transformation in a variety of fields, such as strategic and scenario planning, dialogue, knowledge, and systems thinking. He has worked in Mexico, the United States, Canada, Latin America, and Southeast Asia. Mota is professor of Scenario-based Strategic Planning at Universidad Iberoamericana in Mexico City.

JACOB NEEDLEMAN is Professor of Philosophy at San Francisco State University and the author of many books. In addition to teaching and writing, he serves as a consultant in the fields of psychology, education, medical ethics, philanthropy, and business and has been featured on Bill Moyers' acclaimed PBS series "A World of Ideas." His books include *The New Religions* (Doubleday, 1970), *Money and the Meaning of Life* (Doubleday, 1991) and *The American Soul: Rediscovering the Wisdom of the Founders* (Doubleday, 2001).

SOGYAL RINPOCHE was born in Tibet and raised by one of the most revered spiritual masters of this century: Jamyang Khyentse Chokyi Lodro. He travels and lectures throughout the world and is the founder and spiritual director of Rigpa, an international network of Buddhist groups and centers. He is the author of *The Tibetan Book of Living and Dying* (HarperSanFrancisco, 1992). Rigpa's website is www.rigpa.org.

VICKI ROBIN is president and co-founder of the Seattle-based New Road Map Foundation, an all-volunteer, nonprofit, educational and charitable foundation teaching people tools for shifting to low-consumption, high-fulfillment lifestyles. Vicki is also a founding board member of the Center for the New American Dream, a national organization with the goal of changing the pattern and overall quantity of consumption in the United States — without sacrificing the quality of life. Vicki has lectured widely and appeared on hundreds of radio and television shows, including "New Dimensions," "Good Morning America," and National Public Radio's "Weekend Edition" and "Morning Edition"; she has also been featured in *People, The Wall Street Journal, Newsweek, Utne Reader, and The New York Times.* She is the co-author of *Your Money or Your Life: Transforming Your Relationship with Money and Achieving Financial Independence* (Viking Penguin, 1992).
The New Road Map Foundation's website is www.newroadmap.org.

ANITA RODDICK is the founder of The Body Shop. She has dedicated most of her working life to finding new ways of doing business and has, during the past decade, continued to explore ways for organizations, large and small, to take the lead in making the world a better place. She is the author of *Business As*

Unusual (Thorsons, 2000) and *Take it Personally* (Conari Press, 2001). Her website is www.anitaroddick.com.

MATTHEW ROTHSCHILD, formerly editor of *Multinational Monitor*, a magazine founded by Ralph Nader, now serves as editor of *The Progressive*, a voice for peace and social justice in the United States and abroad. He is also the Director of the Progressive Media Project, which distributes opinion pieces to newspapers around the country. Rothschild has appeared on "Nightline" and C-SPAN's "Washington Journal."
The Progressive's website is www.progressive.org.

NORMAN SOLOMON is a nationally syndicated columnist on media and politics and the founder of the Institute for Public Accuracy. He speaks out about the seductive power of the media and the way they shape our understanding of the world and our response to critical world events. He is the author of *The Habits of Highly Deceptive Media* (Common Courage Press, 1999) and co-author of *Through the Media Looking Glass* (Common Courage Press, 1995). The Institute for Public Accuracy's website is www.accuracy.org.

RONALD TAKAKI is one of the foremost nationally recognized scholars of multicultural studies. He holds a PhD in American History from the University of California at Berkeley, where he has been a professor of Ethnic Studies for over two decades. The Berkeley faculty has honored Professor Takaki with a Distinguished Teaching Award, and Cornell University appointed him to be the prestigious Messenger Lecturer for 1993. Takaki is the author of *A Different Mirror: A History of Multicultural America* (Little Brown, 1993) and *Double Victory: A Multicultural History of America in WWII* (Little Brown, 2000).

MICHAEL TOMS is the founding President of New Dimensions Foundation and the co-founder of New Dimensions Radio and the New Dimensions World Broadcasting Network. He serves as the Executive Producer and principal host of the award-winning, internationally syndicated "New Dimensions" public radio series. For seven years, he was the Senior Acquisitions Editor at HarperSanFrancisco. Toms is Board Chairman Emeritus of the California Institute of Integral Studies and serves on the Board of Advisors of the Alliance for Transforming the Lives of Children as well as on the Board of Directors of the Process Work Center of Portland, Oregon. A former editor of *The Inner Edge*, a newsletter for enlightened business practice, he is the author of *At the Leading Edge* (Larson, 1992) and the co-author of *True Work: Doing What You Love and Loving What You Do* (Bell Tower/Crown, 1998) His website is www.newdimensions.org.

LYNNE TWIST is the president of the Turning Tide Coalition, a gathering of like-minded global organizations committed to inspiring a worldwide conversation about global sustainability, and co-founder of The Pachamama Alliance. She is a trustee of the Fetzer Institute and an advocate and spokesperson for the end of hunger, the preservation of the world's rainforests, and the emergence of women in cultures throughout the world. Twist contributed to *The Soul of Business* (Hay House, 1997) and *Money, Money, Money: The Search for Wealth and the Pursuit of Happiness* (Hay House, 1998). She is the author of the upcoming *The Soul of Money* (Norton, 2003).
Her website is www.fundraisingfromtheheart.com.

DAVID WHYTE grew up among the hills and valleys of Yorkshire, England. The author of five books of poetry, he is one of the few poets to take his perspectives on creativity into the field of organizational development, where he has worked with many American and international companies. He holds a degree in Marine Zoology, has worked as a naturalist guide, and has led anthropological and natural history expeditions. Whyte is the author of, among other titles, *The Heart Aroused: Poetry and the Preservation of the Soul in Corporate America* (Currency/Doubleday, 1994) and *Crossing the Unknown Sea: Work as a Pilgrimage of Identity* (Riverhead, 2001). His website is www.davidwhyte.com.

TERRY TEMPEST WILLIAMS was born in 1955 and grew up within sight of the Great Salt Lake. Her writing reflects her intimate relationship with the natural world. Williams is the recipient of a Lannan Literary Fellowship and a Guggenheim Fellowship, and *Newsweek* identified her as someone likely to make "a considerable impact on the political, economic, and environmental issues facing the Western states in this decade." She was also recognized by *Utne Reader* as a "visionary," one of the Utne 100 "who could change your life." She is the author of several books, including *Refuge: An Unnatural History of Family and Place* (Vintage Books, 1992), *Leap* (Pantheon, 2000), and *Red: Passion and Patience in the Desert* (Pantheon, 2001). Her website is www.coyoteclan.com.

MARIANNE WILLIAMSON is one of the most recognized names in contemporary spiritual literature and philosophy. She is the founder of the Global Renaissance Alliance, an organization dedicated to all citizens and their reclamation of their place in the democratic political process. She has inspired millions with her bestsellers, which include *A Return to Love: Reflections on the Principles of 'A Course In Miracles'* (HarperCollins, 1992), *Illuminata: Thoughts, Prayers, and Rites of Passage* (Random House, 1994), and *The Healing of America* (Simon & Schuster, 1997). Her website is www.marianne.com.

HOWARD ZINN grew up in the immigrant slums of Brooklyn, where he worked in the shipyards in his late teens. During World War II, he saw combat duty as an air force bombardier; later, he received his doctorate in history from Columbia University and was postdoctoral Fellow in East Asian Studies at Harvard University. A Professor Emeritus of Political Science at Boston University, he is the author of, among other titles, the classic *A People's History of the United States: 1942 to Present* (HarperCollins, 1980), *You Can't Be Neutral on a Moving Train: A Personal History of Our Times* (Beacon, 1995), and *Howard Zinn on War* (Seven Stories Press, 2000); he also contributed to *Responses to 9/11* (Seven Stories Press, 2001).

NEW DIMENSIONS FOUNDATION

*"...the free exchange of ideas and information is of fundamental
relevance for transforming culture and freeing it of
destructive misinformation, so that creativity can be liberated."*

— from *Science, Order and Creativity* by David Bohm and F. David Peat

CREATED IN 1973 to address the dramatic cultural shifts and changing human values in our society, New Dimensions has become an international forum for some of the most innovative ideas expressed on the planet. Its principal and best-known activity is New Dimensions Radio, an independent producer of radio dialogues and other programming. New Dimensions has been nationally syndicated since 1980, reaching millions of listeners in the U.S. and around the planet. New Dimensions is heard weekly on approximately 300 (mostly public radio) stations via National Public Radio satellite, and in 134 countries over shortwave radio and the U.S. Armed Forces Radio Network as well as throughout Australia and the South Pacific over the Australian Broadcasting Corporation's Radio National. New Dimensions programming is also heard 24/7 on the Internet at www.newdimensions.org.

Many of this century's leading thinkers and social innovators have spoken through New Dimensions. The programming supports a diversity of views from many traditions and cultures. Now is a time for transformative learning and for staying open to all possibilities. We must constantly be willing to review and revise what we are creating. New Dimensions fosters the goals of living a more healthy life of mind, body, and spirit while deepening our connections to self, family, community, environment, the natural world and the planet.

NEW DIMENSIONS FOUNDATION
A nonprofit tax-exempt educational organization
P.O. Box 569 • Ukiah, CA 95482 • (707) 468-5215
Website: www.newdimensions.org
E-mail: info@newdimensions.org

If you have enjoyed *A Time for Choices,* you might also enjoy other

BOOKS TO BUILD A NEW SOCIETY

Our books provide positive solutions for people who want to
make a difference. We specialize in:

Progressive Leadership • Resistance and Community
Environment and Justice • Conscientious Commerce
Natural Building & Appropriate Technology • New Forestry
Educational and Parenting Resources • Nonviolence
Sustainable Living • Ecological Design and Planning

For a full list of NSP's titles, please call **1-800-567-6772** *or check out our web site at:*
www.newsociety.com

NEW SOCIETY PUBLISHERS